Company Reports and Accounts:
Their Significance and Uses

Company Reports and Accounts:
Their Significance and Uses

John Blake MA(Oxon), FCA
Lecturer in Financial Accounting
Loughborough University of Technology

Pitman Publishing

Pitman Publishing
128 Long Acre, London WC2E 9AN

A Division of Longman Group UK Limited

First published in Great Britain 1987
Reprinted 1989, 1990, 1992

© John D. Blake 1987

British Library Cataloguing in Publication Data
Blake, John, 1950 -
  Company Reports and Accounts: their significance
  and uses.
  1.Financial statements
  I.Title
  657'.33   HF5681.B2

ISBN 0 273 02697 6

Printed and bound in Great Britain

Contents

Acknowledgements

The author wishes to thank the Chartered Association of Certified Accountants and the Institute of Bankers for permission to quote from their examination papers. The author also wishes to express his appreciation of the hard work put into typing this book by Miss Judith Briers.

Finally he expresses his thanks to Marks and Spencer plc for permission to reproduce their accounts in Appendix C.

1 Introduction to published company accounts

Objectives

The title of this book is *Company Reports and Accounts: Their Significance and Uses*, and the basic objective of this chapter is to explain the nature of this subject matter. Specifically we consider:

(a) The nature of 'accounting'.
(b) The range of users, and types of uses, of published accounts.

The nature of 'accounting'

There is no single, universally accepted, definition of what constitutes the domain of accounting. Broadly speaking, accounting is concerned with:

(a) The collection of data on how an enterprise has conducted its activities and employed its resources.
(b) The analysis and communication of information for decision-making purposes.
(c) Control over the use of the resources of the enterprise.

Accounting has to call on a wide range of disciplines to accomplish these objectives, including:

(a) *Economics*. An understanding of economics is essential to the accountant, both to understand the nature of the economic data being analysed and to appreciate the needs of decision makers.
(b) *Behavioural science*. In order to design an information system that will promote the objectives of the enterprise, it is important to understand how individuals and groups are likely to respond to information presented to them.
(c) *Law*. The accountant needs to understand the legal position on a range of trans-actions entered into by the business. For example, we will only be able to explain how to account for a company's tax position in Chapter 7 below by discussing tax law in some detail.
(d) *Data processing*. The accountant's data collection role requires a thorough grasp of data processing systems, which may be manual, mechanized, or electronic.
(e) *Quantitative analysis*. For the purposes of data collection and analysis, a wide range of quantitative techniques can be applied.
(f) *Other management disciplines*. In order to understand what is happening within the enterprise, the accountant needs a basic grasp of other management disciplines, such as personnel and marketing.

In the UK there is an entrenched, well organized and powerful group of six major professional accounting bodies which between them have some 150 000 members and over 100 000 registered trainees. Roles traditionally covered in the UK by professional accountants include:

(a)   Preparation of the published accounts.
(b)   Auditing, both internal and external.
(c)   Cost and management accounting.
(d)   Financial planning.
(e)   Preparing and auditing trust accounts.
(f)   Taxation advice, both in negotiating with the tax authorities and in advising how to plan for tax avoidance.
(g)   Conducting company receiverships and liquidations.
(h)   'Investigation' work, particularly relating to Stock Exchange requirements for preparation of a company prospectus.
(j)   This wide range of roles often leads to the accountant becoming involved in a senior management position.

This wide range of functions need not necessarily be performed by accountants, and in practice this very broad role for the accountant is found mainly in the English-speaking world. By contrast to the 150 000 qualified accountants in the UK, there are only some 4000 in West Germany—unkind commentators have suggested that this may help explain the relative economic performance of the two countries! The definition of the work of the accountant depends on whether the accountant 'expands' into overlapping disciplines, as with UK accountants who as tax advisers fulfil what is mainly a legal role, or by contrast whether the overlapping disciplines dominate the accounting function. Thus those involved in the management accounting function in other European countries known personally to the author include economists, behavioural scientists, an engineer, and a specialist in quantitative techniques.

We have identified as one of the roles of the accountant the preparation of published company accounts. Company law requires the presentation to all shareholders of accounts in each year, and the detailed requirements as to form and content are discussed in Chapter 3 and Appendix B below. These accounts have to be filed with the Registrar of Companies and made available to any member of the public who enquires. 'Small' and 'medium' sized companies are allowed to file 'abridged' accounts, excluding some of the disclosure requirements of the Companies Act 1985. Since these accounts are publicly available, there is a wide range of potential users.

The users of published accounts

Anyone who has any form of interest in the activities of an enterprise is a potential user of the published accounts. Major potential user groups include:

(a)   *Shareholders*. The published accounts of a company give shareholders an account of how the directors have handled the resources entrusted to them; the directors are accounting for their 'stewardship'. Company law puts a special emphasis on the requirement for directors to disclose all aspects of their relations with the company, such as directors' remuneration, loans to directors, directors' shareholdings, and directors' business dealings with the company.

The accounts may also have an influence on individual investment decisions, both for existing and potential shareholders.

(b)   *Lenders.* Those who lend money to the company may well look to the accounts for guidance on the prospects of repayment terms being met promptly and in full. Thus they will be interested in assessing trading prospects, to decide whether cash flow from operations will be sufficient to cover repayments, and also in the prospective realizable value of assets in case the company suffers financial difficulties.

(c)   *Employees and trade unions.* This group may use published accounts to assess job security and prospects, and also to assess the company's ability to finance pay increases. In some cases the significance of the profit figures reported in the published accounts may be a significant point for debate in pay negotiations.

(d)   *Trade contacts.* Both suppliers and customers may have an interest in the published accounts. Suppliers may well want to analyze a customer's financial position when deciding on what level of trade credit to extend, and may also use published accounts to assess the prospect for future sales to a major customer. Similarly a customer may analyze the accounts of a supplier to assess their financial strength and, consequently, their reliability as a source of supply. Such checks are particularly common when placing contracts for major construction projects, because of the time span of such commitments and the severe inconvenience arising from failure to complete work.

(e)   *Competitors.* A company might analyze the accounts of other companies in the same line of business, both to identify opportunities to improve their own management practices and to assess the strength of competitors. This is a major reason for many companies deliberately restricting the amount of detail they disclose in the published accounts. A controlled, mutually beneficial, exchange of information between companies in the same industry can be achieved by means of an 'inter-firm comparison' exercise, conducted by an independent expert on a confidential basis as discussed in detail in Chapter 11.

(f)   *Government.* Governments commonly use published accounts for a range of regulatory purposes, such as assessing tax liabilities or applying price controls. Governments also use them as a source of information on various aspects of the national economic position.

(g)   *Non-executive directors.* The management of a business will not normally need to use the published accounts themselves, having access to the internal financial records of the business on a day-to-day basis. Non-executive directors, however, are likely to find the published accounts a useful summary of the position of the business.

(h)   *Regulatory bodies.* In the UK there is a wide range of non-governmental regulatory bodies, such as the Independent Broadcasting Authority. Such bodies are likely to find the published accounts of the companies they regulate a useful source of information.

(j)   *Researchers.* Published accounts are a useful source of data for both academic and commercial researchers.

(k)   *General public.* Various aspects of company performance may be regarded as being of public interest. Politicians and lobbyists will frequently quote published accounts to support an argument.

(l)   *Journalists.* Published accounts are frequently quoted by the press, both in the finance columns addressed to the investor community and in relation to other public interest matters.

(m)   *Investment advisers.* Stockbrokers and investment analysts will look closely at published accounts in order to formulate informed advice for investors.

   This is, of course, a list of *potential* users. Actual usage might be limited by a number of factors, including:

(a) The decision maker may not feel that it is worth making a detailed examination of the accounts of company in relation to the potential risk. For example, a supplier of stationery might estimate the likely maximum amount owing at any one time by a customer to be £50, and decide that the risk of default does not justify the trouble and expense of detailed analysis of the accounts.

(b) The decision maker may have access to alternative sources of information, particularly by virtue of their special relationship with the company. For example, an employee who sees that sales levels are falling does not need to consult the published accounts in order to foresee difficulties for the company.

(c) Decision makers may lack the ability to understand published accounts which, as we shall see, can require considerable technical skills! However, it should be borne in mind that each user may have access to a skilled 'adviser' group. For example, employees may be 'advised' by their trade union, the general public may be 'advised' by journalists or politicians.

We have seen many types of potential use for published accounts. There are a number of potential conflicts between different types of user need, the principal one being between:

(a) *Objectivity,* particularly important where accounts are used for regulatory purposes. The taxation authorities, for example, will have an obvious interest in minimizing the amount of subjective judgement involved in the preparation of accounts.

(b) *Realism,* being the need to give economically meaningful and realistic information. This involves unavoidable predictions and estimates.

Traditionally, accountants have put an emphasis on objectivity in preparing accounts. However, in recent years there has been an increasing awareness of the deficiencies of traditional accounts for decision-making purposes.

Conclusions

The preparation of published accounts is one aspect of the accountant's work. Such accounts have a range of potential users, and thus are a multi-purpose document. Unavoidably, published accounts represent a compromise between a variety of user needs. Individual users, therefore, require a thorough understanding of accounting principles in order to appreciate the relevance of a set of accounts to their individual needs.

Questions

Because of the introductory nature of this chapter, no questions are included. Points raised in this chapter are important to an appreciation of issues raised in questions accompanying a number of subsequent chapters.

2 The accounting framework

Objectives

The broad objective of this chapter is to explain the way in which the accounting system of a business works. Specifically we consider:

(b)   The basic 'accounting equation' shown in balance sheet.
(b)   The way in which details of transactions are recorded in the 'double entry' book-keeping system.
(c)   How the data summarized in the double entry book-keeping system is reported in the two basic accounting reports, the profit and loss account and the balance sheet.
(d)   The practical problems of allocating items of income and expenditure to the appropriate accounting periods.
(e)   The meaning, nature and significance of 'accounting concepts'.
(f)   Why the accounts do not, and cannot, be expected to show the 'value' of a business.

Example 2.1

(a)   On 1 January 1986 Kenneth paid £60 000 into a business bank account.
(b)   On 2 January 1986 he borrowed £40 000 from Edith, being an interest-free loan.
(c)   On 31 January 1986 he paid £50 000 for storage facilities.
(d)   On 31 March 1986 he paid £40 000 for 2000 widgets, which he planned to resell.
(e)   On 30 November 1986 he sold 1500 widgets for £36 000 to Richard on credit terms.
(f)   On 31 December 1986 Richard paid £36 000 to clear his account.

The basic accounting equation

Any business will need to acquire certain resources in order to operate. The resources owned by the business are called *assets*. The acquisition of assets can be financed in one of two ways:

(a)   The owners of the business can use their own money in the business. This is often called the owners' *equity*.
(b)   Finance can be borrowed from other people. The amounts owing are known as *liabilities*.

The *balance sheet* is an accounting statement that tells us what resources the business possesses, and how the acquisition of those resources has been financed. In its simplest form, this 'accounting equation' can be expressed as:

$$Equity + Liabilities = Assets$$

Example 2.1 shows a series of simple transactions relating to a business. If we consider the effect of each of these on the balance sheet of the business:

(a) On 1 January Kenneth pays into the business bank account £60 000 of his own money. Figure 2.1 shows how his balance sheet will appear following this transaction. The balance sheet tells us that the business possesses one asset, the amount of £60 000 at the bank, and this amount has been derived from the owner of the business.

Kenneth – Balance Sheet as at 1 January 1986

	£		£
Equity	60 000	Bank	60 000

Figure 2.1

(b) On 2 January Kenneth borrows £40 000. Thus, as shown in Fig. 2.2, the asset 'Bank' is increased by £40 000 while the loan is shown as a liability of £40 000. Thus the accounting equation continues to balance.

Kenneth – Balance Sheet as at 2 January 1986

	£		£
Equity	60 000	Bank	100 000
Loan	40 000		
	100 000		100 000

Figure 2.2

(c) On 31 January Kenneth buys an asset, the storage facilities, for £50 000. Thus, as shown in Fig. 2.3, the asset 'Storage' is increased by £50 000 and the asset 'Bank' is reduced by £50 000.

Kenneth – Balance Sheet as at 31 January 1986

	£		£
Equity	60 000	Storage facilities	50 000
Loan	40 000	Bank	50 000
	100 000		100 000

Figure 2.3

Note that in listing the assets we have shown the storage facilities above the bank balance. This is because it is customary to *marshal* the assets in *inverse order of liquidity*, meaning that the assets shown first are those which are furthest from being turned into cash.

(d) On 31 March 1986 Kenneth pays £40 000 for goods which he intends to resell. Accountants use the word *purchases* to describe the goods acquired for resale, and while they are held by the business these are referred to as *stock*. Thus, as shown in Fig. 2.4, we show an increase in the asset 'Stock' and a decrease in the asset 'Bank', being £40 000. Note that we continue to marshal our assets in inverse order of liquidity.

Kenneth – Balance Sheet as at 31 March 1986

	£		£
Equity	60 000	Storage facilities	50 000
		Stock	40 000
Loan	40 000	Bank	10 000
	100 000		100 000

Figure 2.4

(e)   On 30 November 1986 Kenneth sells goods which had cost £30 000 for £36 000, on credit terms. Thus, as we can see in Fig. 2.5, the asset stock has decreased by £30 000 while the asset 'Debtor' increases by £36 000; the difference between the two movements is a *profit* of £6000, representing the extent to which income from selling goods exceeds the related expenses. This profit belongs to the proprietors, and is therefore added on to the amount of equity shown in the balance sheet. Thus the equation continues to balance.

Kenneth – Balance Sheet as at 30 November 1986

	£		£
Equity – b/fwd	60 000	Storage facilities	50 000
Profit on sale	6 000	Stock	10 000
	66 000	Debtor	36 000
Loan	40 000	Bank	10 000
	106 000		106 000

Figure 2.5

(f)   On 31 December 1986 Kenneth receives payment from Richard of £36 000. This, as shown in Fig. 2.6, increases the asset 'Bank' and decreases the asset 'Debtor'.

Kenneth – Balance Sheet as at 31 December 1986

	£		£
Equity	66 000	Storage facilities	50 000
		Stock	10 000
Loan	40 000	Bank	46 000
	106 000		106 000

Figure 2.6

This simple example illustrates how a balance sheet can be drawn up at any point in time showing the resources owned by the business and how these have been financed; the example also illustrates the way in which each transaction that occurs alters the figures that make up the balance sheet while overall the accounting equation continues to balance.

Double entry book-keeping

So far we have illustrated the accounting equation by constructing a series of balance sheets, each reflecting the impact of a single transaction. This is clearly impracticable as a normal method for recording the transactions of the business, for two reasons in particular:

(a) Repeated construction of balance sheets would be cumbersome and unwieldy mechanism.

(b) The two occasions in our example when income was earned and related expenditure was consumed both involved transactions occurring at a single identifiable point in time.

In practice, many types of income and expenditure are spread over a period of time, and it is only practical to ascertain the profit which has been earned during a period.

In practice, therefore, balance sheets are only produced at fixed intervals, most commonly of one year. A record of transactions is kept in the 'ledger', the name given to a collection of *accounts*.

Together the accounts show where the resources of the business have gone to and have come from. Each page of the ledger shows an 'account' for one particular aspect of the position of the business. A line is drawn down the centre of the page; on the left-hand side are shown the *debit* items, while on the right hand side are shown the *credit* items. We debit an account where that aspect absorbs the resources of the business, and credit an account where the aspect provides resources to the business. Thus any increase in the assets of a business will be recorded as a debit in the relevant account because resources are absorbed in that form, while any increase in equity or liabilities will be recorded as a credit in the relevant account, indicating where the business has derived resources from.

As we have already seen, a business also derives resources from earning *income* and consumes resources in incurring *expenses*. Therefore the ledger will include accounts for each type of income and for each type of expenditure. Figure 2.7 summarizes how we account for increases in each type of item; decreases would be treated conversely.

Debit	*Credit*
Increases in:	Increases in:
Assets	Equity
Expenses	Liabilities
	Income

Figure 2.7

In order to illustrate the working of the ledger, we will return to the business 'Kenneth', introduced in Example 2.1. In Fig. 2.6 we showed Kenneth's balance sheet as at the end of 1986. At the beginning of 1987 each of these balance sheet items would be represented by an account in the ledger, with the amount at that date recorded as a 'balance brought down', normally abbreviated to 'bal b/d'. Figure 2.8 shows how the records would be made in the ledger.

Equity

	1 Jan 87 Bal b/d	66 000

Loan – Edith

	1 Jan 87 Bal b/d	40 000

Storage facilities

1 Jan 87 Bal b/d	50 000	

Stock

1 Jan 87 Bal b/d	10 000	

Bank

1 Jan 87 Bal b/d	46 000	

Figure 2.8 Recording the opening balances in the ledger

Each type of asset has been recorded as a debit balance, showing the form in which the resources of the business are currently held, while the credit balances on the equity and loan accounts together show where the resources have been derived from.

Our next stage is to consider how we record transactions in the ledger as they occur. For this purpose, Example 2.2 shows Kenneth's transactions during 1987.

Example 2.2

During 1987 Kenneth remained in business. He entered into the following trans-actions:

(a) On 31 January 1987 he bought 2 500 widgets for £50 000 from Berengar on credit terms.
(b) On 31 March 1987 he arranged overdraft facilities with the bank, and paid the amount owing to Berengar.
(c) On 31 October 1987 he sold 2200 widgets to Conrad for £55 000 on credit terms.
(d) On 31 December 1987 he paid £2000 to his employee Leopold, for work done during 1987.

If we consider each of the transactions in Example 2.2:

(a) When the business buys goods for resale, this means that resources have been absorbed by the expense account *purchases*, which is debited, and having been supplied on credit terms are derived from the creditor Berengar, who is credited. Note that while in the balance sheet all creditors are shown together as one total amount, in the ledger they are shown individually by name, giving a record of who money is owed to.
(b) The fact that overdraft facilities are arranged does not itself involve any transfer of resources, and therefore will not involve any entry in the ledger. The payment of £50 000 to Berengar involves a transfer from the bank account, which is credited, while resources are absorbed by clearing the liability, so that Berengar's account is debited.
(c) When the business sells goods on credit terms, resources are derived from the

income items 'sales', which is credited; while since the sale is on credit terms, resources are absorbed by the asset 'debtor' which is debited. As with creditors, debtors are shown as a single item in the balance sheet but individually by name in the ledger.

(d)   The payment of £2000 to Leopold represents a transfer from the bank, which is credited, to cover the expense wages, the account for which is debited. Note that we do not record the individual to whom wages are paid.

Figure 2.9 shows how these items are recorded.

Equity

		1 Jan 87 Bal b/d	66 000

Loan –

		1 Jan 87 Bal b/d	40 000

Storage facilities

1 Jan 87 Bal b/d	50 000		

Stock

1 Jan 87 Bal b/d	10 000		

Bank

1 Jan 87 Bal b/d	46 000	(b) 31 Mar 87 Berengar	50 000
		(d) 31 Dec 87 Wages	2 000

Purchases

(a) 31 Jan 87 Berengar	50 000		

Berengar

(b) 31 Mar 87 Bank	50 000	(a) 31 Mar 87 Purchases	50,000

Sales

		(c) 31 Oct 87 Conrad	55 000

Conrad

(c) 31 Oct 87 Sales	55 000		

Wages

(d) 31 Dec 87 Bank	2 000		

Note – the letters alongside each entry relate to the paragraph of Example 2.2 which gives rise to the entry.

Figure 2.9   Recording the transactions in the ledger

We have not got in the ledger a record of how the business stood at the beginning of 1987, and the effects of all the transactions which have occurred during 1987. At this stage it is normal to work out the net debit or credit balance on each account, and list this in a statement called the *trial balance*. The trial balance for our example Kenneth is shown in Fig. 2.10. The trial balance has two major functions:

(a) It serves as a check on the accuracy of the accounts. Since the figures transferred from the opening balance sheet balance and all subsequent transactions involve equal debit and credit entries, then we would expect the total of debit and credit balances to be equal. If they are not, there must have been an error.

(b) It is a useful summary of the information in the ledger, on the basis of which the accounting statements can be prepared.

Kenneth – Trial Balance at 31 December 1987

	Dr	Cr
Equity		66 000
Loan		40 000
Storage facilities	50 000	
Stock	10 000	
Bank		6 000
Purchases	50 000	
Sales		55 000
Conrad	55 000	
Wages	2 000	
	167 000	167 000

Figure 2.10

The basic accounting statements

We have already introduced one of the basic accounting statements, the balance sheet. This shows the assets owned by the business and how their acquisition has been financed, at a particular point in time. The other basic accounting statement is the *profit and loss account*, sometimes called an income statement, which shows the profit earned or loss incurred by a business during a period of time. In simple terms, the profit or loss of a business will consist of the resources earned, known as *income*, less the resources consumed, known as *expenses*.

As we have already seen in Fig. 2.7 above, debit balances in the ledger can represent either assets or expenses while credit balances can represent equity, liabilities, or income. At the end of an accounting period we transfer all the balances which represent income or expenses to the profit and loss account, which is an account in the ledger. After making these transfers the balance shown on the profit and loss account will represent the profit or loss for the period; this balance will be transferred to the account representing the owners' equity in the business.

Having made these transfers, the balances in the ledger will show the equity, liabilities and assets of the business as reported in the balance sheet. These balances are then 'carried down' to the beginning of the next accounting period.

One complication that arises in drawing up the accounts relates to goods purchased for resale. Some of these goods will be consumed during the accounting period and therefore be an expense to be shown in the profit and loss account, while some will be held at the balance sheet date and should therefore be recorded as an asset 'stock'. To account for these items it is necessary to compute the cost of stock held at the year end; this is normally done by physically counting the stock and working out the cost. The opening stock and the purchases during the year are then transferred to the profit and loss account, while the closing stock is deducted from the expenses in the profit and loss account and carried down as an asset in the stock account.

For our example 'Kenneth' we know that his closing stock consists of 800 widgets costing £20 each, and so £16 000 in total. (These quantities can be checked by adding up total stock bought less sold in Examples 2.1 and 2.2.) We can then complete Kenneth's accounts for 1987 as shown in Fig. 2.11:

(a) The balances on the stock, sales, purchases, and wages accounts are all transferred to the profit and loss account.
(b) The closing stock of £16 000 is credited to profit and loss and debited to the stock account.
(c) For each account, each side is added up; where the totals are not equal, the difference between the two is inserted as a 'balance carried down' (bal c/d) so that the two sides balance. The balance is then brought down on the correct side at the beginning of the new accounting period.

Equity

		1 Jan 87 Bal b/d	66 000
(c) 31 Dec 87 Bal c/d	75 000	31 Dec 87 P &L	9 000
	75 000		75 000
		(c) 1 Jan 88 Bal b/d	75 000

Loan –

(c) 31 Dec 87 Bal c/d	40 000	1 Jan 87 Bal b/d	40 000
		(c) 1 Jan 88 Bal b/d	40 000

Storage facilities

1 Jan 87 Bal b/d	50 000	(c) Bal c/d	50 000
(c) 1 Jan 88 Bal b/d	50 000		

Stock

1 Jan Bal b/d	10 000	(a) 31 Dec 87 P & L	10 000
(b) 31 Dec 87 P & L	16 000	(c) 31 Dec 87 Bal c/d	16 000
	26 000		26 000
(c) 1 Jan 88 Bal b/d	16 000		

Bank

1 Jan 87 Bal b/d	46 000	31 Mar 87 Berengar	50 000
31 Dec 87 Bal c/d	6 000	31 Dec 87 Wages	2 000
	52 000		52 000
		1 Jan 88 Bal b/d	6 000

Purchases

31 Jan 87	50 000	(a) 31 Dec 87 P & L	50 000

Berengar

31 Mar 87 Bank	50 000	31 Jan 87 Purchases	50 000

Sales

(a) 31 Dec 87 P & L	55 000	31 Oct 87 Conrad	55 000

Conrad

31 Oct 87 Sales	55 000	31 Dec 87 Bal c/d	55 000
1 Jan 88 Bal b/d	55 000		

Wages

31 Dec 87 Bank	2 000	(a) 31 Dec 87 P & L	2 000

Profit and loss

(a) 31 Dec 87 Stock	10 000	(a) 31 Dec 87 Sales	55 000
(a) 31 Dec 87 Purchases	50 000	(b) 31 Dec 87 Stock	16 000
(a) 31 Dec 87 Wages	2 000		
(c) Equity	9 000		
	71 000		71 000

Figure 2.11 Entries made in Kenneth's accounts at the year end

The balances carried down in the ledger represent the assets, liability and equity of the business as at the end of an accounting period, and therefore are the items shown in the balance sheet. Figure 2.12 shows the balance sheet for Kenneth as at 31 December 1987.

Kenneth – Balance Sheet as at 31 December 1987

Equity	75 000	Storage facilities	50 000
		Stock	16 000
Loan	40 000		
Bank	6 000	Debtor	55 000
	121 000		121 000

Figure 2.12

The balance sheet is an extract of information from the ledger, and does not form part of the double entry system as such. By contrast, the profit and loss account is part of the double entry system. However, it is normal to include in the accounts a copy of the profit and loss account. This is presented in a rather different form than shown in the ledger, falling into three sections:

(a) Sales are shown, then the cost of goods sold is deducted, to arrive at the 'gross profit'. The cost of goods sold is computed as:

> Cost of opening stock of goods
> *plus*
> Cost of goods purchased and cost of work done on those goods
> *Less*
> Cost of closing stock of goods.

This part of the profit and loss account is known as the *trading account*.

(b)   Any other form of income is added to gross profit, then all expenses of the business are listed and the total is deducted from income to give *net profit*.

(c)   In the case of a limited company or partnership, a third section, known as the *appropriation account*, shows how profit is shared out.

Figure 2.13 shows the profit and loss account for our example Kenneth.

Kenneth – Profit and Loss Account for the year ended 31 September 1987

	£	£
Sales		55 000
less:		
Stock 1 Jan 87	10 000	
Purchases	50 000	
	60 000	
Less Stock 31 Dec 87	16 000	
Cost of sales		44 000
Gross profit		11 000
less Expenses:		
Wages		2 000
Net profit		9 000

Figure 2.13

Figure 2.14 shows an overview of the accounting system. Two new points emerge:

(a)   In practice, transactions are normally summarized in *books of prime entry* prior to entry in the ledger. For example, cash transactions may be summarized in a *cash book*, sales in a *sales day book*, and purchases in a *purchase day book*. Special entries are recorded in a *journal*.

(b)   Between the extraction of a trial balance and the preparation of accounts, adjustments will be necessary. The reasons for these are considered in detail below.

Problems of income and expense allocation

In Fig. 2.14 we have seen that normally certain adjustments have to be made between extraction of the trial balance and presentation of the accounts. There are three main reasons for such adjustments becoming necessary:

(a)   Some types of item may have to be allocated between the profit and loss account and the balance sheet. An example is the way in which purchases have to be separated into cost of sales and stock carried forward.

(b)   Some movements of resources are not evidenced by any form of transaction, and

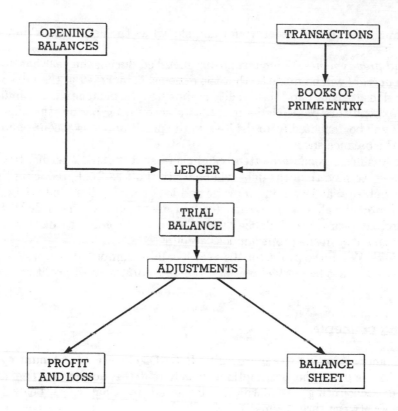

Figure 2.14

therefore cannot be 'captured' by the double entry system. An example is 'depreciation' considered below.

(c)   Some aspects of the position of a business may only become clear after the balance sheet date when preparation of the accounts has commenced. For example, the amount of taxation payable cannot be estimated until the profit for the year has been computed.

In practice, the effects of such adjustments are normally calculated in a set of working schedules used to prepare the accounts, and only entered into the double entry system after the final accounts have been presented. Thus the ledger is a working document up until the extraction of the trial balance, used as a mechanism to collect details of transactions during the accounting period; thereafter the accounts are prepared and the adjustments are entered in the ledger as a matter of record.

Matters which give rise to adjustments include:

Depreciation. This is the method for charging the part of the cost of a fixed asset consumed during an accounting period to the profit and loss account. The effect of the depreciation charge is to transfer part of the cost of fixed assets from the balance sheet to the profit and loss account. Often the original cost of an asset is shown in the balance sheet, with the accumulated 'provision for depreciation' shown as a deduction to give the 'net book value', being the amount at which the fixed asset is currently shown in the balance sheet.

Stock. We have already seen how the cost of purchases not yet sold is deducted from the purchases in the profit and loss account and shown as the asset 'stock' in the balance sheet.

Accruals and prepayments. When an expense incurred during the year has not yet been paid for, an *accrual* will be made so that the expense is included in the relevant item in the profit and loss account and the liability is shown in the balance sheet. Similarly when an item of expenditure paid relates to a future accounting period, the amount of the *prepayment* will be deducted from the item in the profit and loss account and shown as an asset in the balance sheet.

Debtors. In business, goods are often bought and sold on credit terms. If a customer proves unlikely to pay, then the debt will be written off as 'bad', reducing the balance sheet asset 'debtors' and creating a profit and loss account item 'bad debts'. When a debt is of doubtful value, a 'provision for bad debts' is often recorded, shown as a deduction from debtors in the balance sheet. Any increase or decrease in the provision is reflected by an entry in the profit and loss account.

Appropriations. When the profit for the year has been computed, the way in which the profit is 'shared' must be worked out, and the *appropriations* of profit recorded in the accounts.

Accounting concepts

In the UK an accounting standard, 'SSAP 2—Disclosure of Accounting Policies', discusses the issue of the assumptions which underlie accounts. (The nature and authority of accounting standards is discussed in Chapter 3 below.) SSAP 2 distinguishes between three terms:

Fundamental accounting concepts are the broad basic assumptions which underlie business accounts.

Accounting bases are the methods used by accountants to apply accounting concepts. For example, as we shall see in Chapter 4 below, there are a number of methods for computing depreciation in the accounts.

Accounting policies are the specific accounting bases chosen by a business for its accounts.

SSAP 2 requires companies to disclose their accounting policies' significant items in the notes to their accounts.

The significance of accounting concepts to users of accounts is that they help to explain the significance and limitations of accounting information. SSAP 2 identifies four fundamental concepts:

Going concern. Accounts are normally prepared on the assumption that the enterprise will continue in operational existence for the foreseeable future. The significance of this assumption is that the balance sheet does not attempt to show what assets would realize if disposed of on a forced sale. Note that if the circumstances of a business indicated imminent liquidation, then accountants would depart from this convention and show the assets on a 'break up' basis.

Accruals (also known as *matching*). Revenue and costs are shown in the accounts as they are earned or incurred, not when cash is received or paid. As far as possible, expenditure is 'matched' with related income. Thus profit for the year does not necessarily equal any inflow of cash. Sometimes very small non-profit-making organizations do not follow this convention, simply reporting cash flows in an income and expenditure account.

Consistency. There is consistency of accounting treatment of like items within each accounting period and from one period to the next. This convention helps promote comparability of accounting statements and also promotes objectivity. It is, however, open to criticism as restricting management's ability to portray the economic reality of each set of circumstances as they see it.

Prudence (also known as *conservatism*). Income is only recognized in the accounts when earned and when it is the subject of a firm legal entitlement, while losses are provided for as soon as they appear likely to occur. This concept introduces a form of bias into the accounts. It means that the reported profit does not represent the most objective estimate, but is biased towards prudence.

SSAP 2 does not claim to present a full list of significant concepts. Indeed, writers on accounting theory claim to have identified over 200 concepts. Other major ones are:

Materiality. The amount of detail necessary in the preparation and presentation of accounts is that which is relevant to decisions which are likely to be made. Thus excessive costs should not be incurred in providing an unnecessarily detailed analysis.

Substance over form. The commercial substance of a transaction should be recognized in the accounts rather than its legal form. This is a difficult concept to apply in some cases, since it is not always easy to define the commercial substance of a transaction. Leasing, considered in Chapter 9 below, is an example of such a problem.

Business entity. The accounts cover the affairs of the business and exclude the private affairs of the proprietor. This can be an important point to bear in mind when looking at a set of accounts. For example, a business which appears financially weak looking at the balance sheet may be supported by a proprietor with substantial personal resources.

Money measurement. All the resources of the business are measured in money. This can cause confusion because money is also an important resource of the business in the form of cash and bank balances. It is also an important limitation because the significance of the monetary unit changes over the years, particularly in times of inflation.

Historical cost. Items in the accounts are recorded at their original cost until consumed. Note that historical cost is likely to be different from 'value', which represents the current amount for which an asset might be bought, sold or otherwise yield benefits.

Periodicity. Accounts are presented regularly and at fixed intervals. It is interesting to reflect that the Italian merchants who first employed double entry book-keeping kept a separate set of accounts to cover each business venture, and profit was only computed at the end of a venture. Many of the problems of accounting arise because of the need to allocate items of income and expenditure between accounting periods before the consequences of transactions have been full experienced.

It should be emphasized that these concepts do not represent iron laws which are irreversible. Frequently they conflict, and sometimes arguments are put forward for their admendment. Their significance is that they help us to understand how accounting practices have developed.

Accounts and economic reality

Accounts try to portray the economic circumstances of a business. If accounts were able to portray full economic reality, then we would expect:

(a)   The balance sheet would show the 'worth' of a business at a point in time.
(b)   The profit and loss account would show how the activities of a business have increased or decreased its 'worth' over a period of time.

In fact, neither of these objectives is achievable in practice. There are two broad reasons for this:

(a)   The individual resources of a business are shown in the accounts at their historical cost, not their current value.
(b)   The business as a whole has a value different from the total of individual assets. This difference is called *goodwill*, whether positive or negative, and can arise from a variety of causes such as trading connections, employee skills and a range of 'contacts'.

The concept of 'worth' or 'value' is in itself necessarily a subjective one; users of accounts expect 'hard' objective information. These factors do not mean that accounts cannot be used as a basis for making economic decisions. They do mean that users need a thorough understanding of the nature and limitations of accounting information.

Conclusion

In this chapter we have introduced the traditional accounting framework. We have seen how the collection of data on transactions is linked to the accounting statements. Some basic accounting concepts have been introduced, together with an explanation of the basic limitations of accounting.

Questions

2.1   Parker has decided to set up in business as a wholesaler of television sets. During the month of December 1986 he enters into the following transactions:

(a)   On 1 December 1986 he pays £30 000 into a business bank account to launch the business.
(b)   On 3 December 1986 he borrows £20 000, interest-free, from Cranmer.
(c)   On 5 December 1986 he pays £35 000 for shop premises.
(d)   On 7 December 1986 he buys 200 television sets, costing £100 each, on credit terms from Ridley.
(e)   On 11 December 1986 he sells 50 television sets at £120 each for cash.
(f)   On 20 December 1986 he sells 120 television sets at £125 each on credit terms to Gardiner.
(g)   On 28 December 1986 he pays the amount owing to Ridley.

Prepare Parker's balance sheet as at the end of the above transactions.
2.2   Record the transactions of Parker above in a double entry system, showing a profit and loss account for December.
2.3   Most financial statements have been prepared in accordance with four basic concepts, the 'going concern', 'accruals', 'consistency' and 'prudence' concepts.

You are required to:

(a) define and explain the meaning of these four concepts;

(b) state and define one relevant alternative to each of these four concepts (i.e. four alternatives); and

(c) explain the possible effects on the financal statements of using the alternative concept.

(CertDipFA, June 1984)

2.4 While you were at a recent management conference you heard two delegates discussing the relevance of a company's balance sheet as produced in the annual accounts. One delegate stated: 'of course it shows the net worth of the business. How can you believe otherwise? Doesn't it show all the assets a company owns and deducts from them the liabilities . . .'

(a) Do you agree with the above speaker?

(b) Why?

(CertDipFA, December 1982)

3 The regulatory framework

Objectives

The basic objective of this chapter is to explain the regulatory framework within which published company accounts are presented. In detail we consider:

(a) The function of a regulatory framework.
(b) The types of regulatory authority governing UK published accounts.
(c) A brief summary of some specific UK company law disclosure requirements.
(d) The role of the auditor.
(e) The factors influencing those who formulate accounting regulations.

Function

The regulatory framework we will describe is that which applies to limited liability companies. Some other forms of commercial entity, such as building societies, are subject to separate but similar systems of regulation. Sole traders and partnerships fall totally outside this regulatory framework. It is interesting to reflect that professional firms of accountants, who play a major part in the formulation and application of accounting regulations, are formed as partnerships and therefore do not have to publish any form of accounts themselves.

In the UK, company law requires all limited companies to file annual audited accounts with the Registrar of Companies, where they can be inspected on payment of a modest fee (currently £1) by anyone who wishes. These accounts also have to be circulated to all shareholders. This requirement originates for two reasons:

(a) In a company the board of directors is responsible for the management of the company. Thus accounts are necessary for them to report on the affairs of the company to the shareholders, who are the proprietors.
(b) A limited company enjoys the privilege of limited liability. The filed accounts enable those having dealings with the company to see the financial position of the entity with which they are dealing.

In recent years, views on the range of responsibilities of the business enterprise have expanded, and to some extent this has broadened the range of aspects of the position of a company expected to be covered in the accounts. In particular, the interests of both employees and society as a whole have been given more attention by accounting regulators.

From the point of view of the company itself, the preparation of accounts would generally be necessary even if there were no regulatory framework, in order to present financial information to those, such as shareholders and lenders, who have claims upon the company. Thus the regulatory framework can be of use to the company itself, because it strengthens the credibility of the financial statements.

Types of regulatory authority

The Companies Act 1844 was the first piece of legislation to specify accounting requirements for companies. Successive Acts varied those requirements. The Companies Act 1948 pulled together and extended existing requirements, later being added to by the Companies Act 1967. Companies Act in 1976 and 1980 added little to these disclosure requirements, but in 1981 a further Companies Act substantially overhauled accounting requirements, bringing these into line with the provision of the EEC Fourth Directive. Finally, the Companies Act 1985 codifies the Acts from 1948 to 1981 into one single statute.

Statements of Standard Accounting Practice (SSAPs)

These are issued jointly by the six major UK accounting bodies. Because four of these bodies together have a virtual monopoly of the audit of limited companies they are able to exercise considerable influence to ensure that companies comply with SSAPs, threatening to comment critically in the audit report on any non-compliance.

Figure 3.1 shows the stages in the evolution of an accounting standard, which is handled by a joint committee of the professional bodies known as the 'Accounting Standards Committee' (ASC).

Take each stage in Fig. 3.1:

(a) The ASC identifies a topic which requires consideration.
(b) The ASC then commissions a reasearch study on the topic.
(c) On the basis of the research study, a preliminary draft of a statement is prepared.
(d) The next stage involves private consultation with interested parties on the preliminary draft. Increasingly consultation at this stage has been more widespread, even involving official publication.

Identify topic
↓
Research
↓
Preliminary draft
↓
'Private' consultation
↓
Exposure draft
↓
Consider comments
↓
Draft SSAP to individual professional bodies
↓
Individual bodies each issue SSAP

Figure 3.1 Formulating an accounting standard

(e)   Following private consultation an exposure draft (ED) is issued, containing a formal proposal for a statement. These exposure drafts are very widely circulated, particularly through the professional accounting press.

(f)   The ASC then consider comments in depth, following which a statement will normally be proposed.

(g)   The proposed statement is submitted by the ASC to each of the six sponsoring professional bodies.

(h)   SSAPs are issued on the authority of each individual accounting body. This is no empty formality, since at this stage one of the individual bodies can exercise an effective veto by insisting on a change as a condition of acceptance.

This is a full and exhaustive consultation process, indicating the importance that can be attached to the formulation of an SSAP.

Generally company law is confined to detailing the content of accounts, while SSAPs focus on accounting treatment to be adopted although also including disclosure requirements.

The *International Accounting Standards Committee* (IASC) has been set up by professional accounting bodies from over 60 countries to formulate 'International Accounting Standards' (IASs). These are normally applied by each national accounting standard-setting body incorporating their provisions into domestic accounting standards so that they are not applied directly to companies.

The European Community, as part of the objective of harmonizing company law, has sought to develop common accounting requirements through 'Directives'. These are applied by domestic legislation enacted by national legislatures and do not require direct application by companies.

The Stock Exchange imposes certain accounting requirements on listed companies, as discussed in Chapter 5 below.

Specific company law requirements

All UK company law requirements have now been codified into the Companies Act 1985. These requirements were previously extensively revised by the Companies Act 1981, which introduced the requirements of the EEC Fourth Directive into UK law.

The overriding requirement of the Act is that accounts should show a *true and fair view*. Any additional information required to achieve that objective beyond that specified in the Act must be disclosed and, if necessary for the presentation of a true and fair view, other specific requirements of the Act should be departed from. In the latter case full disclosure of the circumstances should be made.

The accounts should disclose 'corresponding amounts' for the previous year.

The Act requires companies to choose one of the specific formats shown in the Act for the balance sheet and the profit and loss account. Figure 3.2 shows one format for the balance sheet. An alternative format shows all assets totalled, and capital reserves, and liabilities totalled. Where a horizontal format is used, assets are shown on the left and liabilities on the right.

The profit and loss account formats are illustrated and explained in Chapter 5 below.

Appendix A to this book shows how a company might present accounts in compliance with the Act, while Appendix B offers a summary of the detailed disclosure requirements of the Act.

	£	£	£
A. CALLED UP SHARE CAPITAL NOT PAID		x	
B. FIXED ASSETS			
I *Intangible Assets*			
1. Development costs	x		
2. Concessions, patents, licences, trade marks and similar rights and assets	x		
3. Goodwill	x		
4. Payments on account	x		
		x	
II *Tangible Assets*			
1. Land and buildings	x		
2. Plant and machinery	x		
3. Fixtures, fittings, tools and equipment	x		
4. Payments on account and assets in course of construction	x		
		x	
III *Investments*			
1. Shares in group companies	x		
2. Loans to group companies	x		
3. Shares in related companies	x		
4. Loans to related companies	x		
5. Other investments other than loans	x		
6. Other loans	x		
7. Own shares	x		
		x	
TOTAL OF B		x	
C. CURRENT ASSETS			
I *Stocks*			
1. Raw materials and consumables	x		
2. Work in progress	x		
3. Finished goods and goods for resale	x		
4. Payments on account	x		
	x		
II *Debtors*			
1. Trade debtors	x		
2. Amounts owed by group companies	x		
3. Amounts owed by related companies	x		
4. Other debtors	x		
5. Called up share capital not paid	x		
6. Prepayments and accrued income	x		
	x		
III *Investments*			
1. Shares in group companies	x		
2. Own shares	x		
3. Other investments	x		
IV *Cash at bank and in hand*	x		
TOTAL OF C	x		

	£	£	£
D. PREPAYMENTS AND ACCRUED INCOME		x	
TOTAL OF D AND C		x	
E. CREDITORS: AMOUNTS FALLING DUE WITHIN ONE YEAR			
1. Debenture loans	(x)		
2. Bank loans and overdrafts	(x)		
3. Payments received on account	(x)		
4. Trade creditors	(x)		
5. Bills of exchange payable	(x)		
6. Amounts owed to group companies	(x)		
7. Amounts owed to related companies	(x)		
8. Other creditors including taxation and social security	(x)		
9. Accruals and deferred income	(x)	(x)	
F. NET CURRENT ASSETS (LIABILITIES) (C + D – E)			x
G. TOTAL ASSETS LESS CURRENT LIABILITIES (A + B + F)			x
H. CREDITORS: AMOUNTS FALLING DUE AFTER MORE THAN ONE YEAR			
1. Debenture loans	(x)		
2. Bank loans and overdrafts	(x)		
3. Payments received on account	(x)		
4. Trade creditors	(x)		
5. Bills of exchange payable	(x)		
6. Amounts owed to group companies	(x)		
7. Amounts owed to related companies	(x)		
8. Other creditors including taxation and social security	(x)		
9. Accruals and deferred income	(x)		
			(x)
I. PROVISIONS FOR LIABILITIES AND CHARGES			
1. Pensions and similar obligations	(x)		
2. Taxation, including deferred taxation	(x)		
3. Other provisions	(x)		
			(x)
J. ACCRUALS AND DEFERRED INCOME			(x)
			£x
K. CAPITAL AND RESERVES			
I. *Called up share capital*			x
II. *Share premium account*			x
III. *Revaluation reserve*			x
IV. *Other reserves*			
1. Capital redemption reserve fund	x		
2. Reserve for own shares	x		
3. Reserves provided for by the articles of association	x		
4. Other reserves	x	x	
V. PROFIT AND LOSS ACCOUNT			x
			£x

Figure 3.2

Role of the auditor

Since 1967, company law has required all limited companies to appoint a qualified auditor. Members of the following professional bodies are currently approved by the UK government to perform company audits:

(a)   The Institute of Chartered Accounts of Scotland.
(b)   The Institute of Chartered Accountants in England and Wales.
(c)   Institute of Chartered Accountants in Ireland.
(d)   The Chartered Association of Certified Accountants.

In addition, transitional arrangements which permitted those already in practice as auditors at the time of the relevant legislation to continue their profession continue to apply, although with the passage of time the number of such persons clearly diminishes.

The auditor is appointed by the shareholders in general meeting, and must be re-elected at each annual general meeting. The directors may only appoint an auditor when a casual vacancy arises. An auditor can only be dismissed by a vote of the shareholders, and has extensive rights to argue the case against dismissal.

The auditor must not be a director or employee of the company, while the professional bodies require that the auditor should not be a shareholder or excessively dependent on one client.

Thus we can see that company law has been carefully designed to ensure and protect the independence of the auditor.

The Companies Act 1985 requires the auditor to report specifically to shareholders on whether the accounts give a true and fair view and comply with the requirements of the Act. In addition, the auditor is required to report on whether:

(a)   Proper books of accounts have been kept by the company.
(b)   Proper returns have been received from branches.
(c)   The accounts agree with the books and records.
(d)   All information and explanations necessary for the audit have been received.

The professional bodies also require, in most circumstances, disclosure of failure to comply with SSAPs.

The duties of the auditor may be expanded, but not reduced, by private agreement with the company.

Auditor's Report to the Members of Griselda Ltd

We have audited the financial statements on pages 7 to 23 in accordance with approved Auditing Standards.

In our opinion the financial statements, which have been prepared under the historical cost convention as modified by the revaluation of land and buildings, give a true and fair view of the state of the company's affairs at 31 December 1986 and of the profit and source and application of funds for the year then ended and comply with the Companies Act 1985.

Trelfor & Co.
Chartered Accountants
15 March 1987

Figure 3.3   Example of an audit report

A typical example of a company audit report is shown in Fig. 3.3. Note the following points:

(a) The report is addressed to shareholders.
(b) The reference to 'approved auditing standards', which are issued by the professional accounting bodies.
(c) It is common for the report to refer to the broad accounting convention within which the accounts have been prepared.
(d) The specific reference to the 'true and fair view' and the Companies Act compliance are as required by law.
(e) The date indicates the most recent evidence which the auditors can have considered when preparing their report.

The auditor might, in rare circumstances, feel it necessary to draw attention to some particular point in the accounts. Such an 'emphasis of matter' might be shown in a separate paragraph in the report, commencing with some such words as 'we draw attention to . . .'

Where an auditor cannot wholeheartedly support the accounts, four broad categories of 'audit qualification' arise:

(a) There may be uncertainty on some matter which is material but not fundamental, in which case the auditor might express an opinion as 'subject to' the uncertainty.
(b) Where an uncertainty is fundamental, the auditors might declare themselves as 'unable to form an opinion' on the accounts.
(c) Where the auditors disagree with an accounting practice, if the matter is material but not fundamental they will express their opinion as 'except for' the matter concerned.
(d) In the case of a fundamental disagreement the auditors might express the view that the accounts do *not* give a true and fair view, etc.

The four types of audit qualification are summarized in Fig. 3.4.

	Material but not fundamental	Fundamental
Uncertainty	'Subject to . . .'	'Unable to form an opinion . . .'
Disagreement	'Except for . . .'	'Does not give . . .'

Figure 3.4 Forms of Qualified Audit Report

A difficult question that arises relates to auditor liability. We have seen the published accounts have a wide range of potential users, and the question arises as to what extent any such relying on the audit report has a claim for negligence against the auditor. Traditionally, auditors have relied upon the defence of 'privity of contract', arguing that they have no contract with users other than the shareholders. However, the 'Hedley Byrne' case established the principle that auditors have a duty of care to users who they know will use the accounts, and it is likely that the courts would now interpret the range of users with a good claim more widely than this. There is a current fashion for users to make increasing legal claims against auditors, a source of concern both to the audit profession and their insurers!

An auditor may also serve a company in other roles, such as accounts preparation, tax advice or financial advice. It is important to recognize that these roles are separate and subject to specific agreement with the directors rather than the shareholders. In practice, most audit firms send a 'management letter' to the directors at the conclusion of each audit advising on points arising during the audit; this can help the auditor's work in future years if accounting systems are improved in response.

Large organizations often employ an 'internal auditor', answerable directly to management. Such an appointment cannot be a substitute for the legal obligation to appoint an independent, qualified external auditor. However, it can have the following benefits:

(a) Improvements in the internal control system can result in a cut in external audit costs.

(b) The internal auditor may be used to assess all aspects of company performance, rather than the narrow financial compliance objectives of the external auditor. Indeed, sometimes an internal audit department will employ non-accountants, e.g. an engineer to check on energy usage.

(c) The internal audit department provides the organization with a useful reservoir of accounting skills to call on in times of emergency.

Factors influencing accounting regulations

Figure 3.5 represents a way of looking at the accounting process.

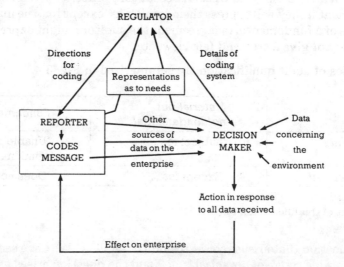

Figure 3.5

The box represents the enterprise. Within the enterprise the directors have to prepare a report on their view of the business, which they 'code' and transmit to a decision maker. The decision maker will take a decision based on the report from the business, plus other sources of data on the enterprise and data concerning the environment. The decision will have an impact on the business. The role of the accounting regulator is to issue directions on how the message should be coded, which will affect both the reporter in the coding and the decision maker in the interpretation.

We have already considered the wide range of potential users of published accounts in Chapter 1 above. Each user constitutes a potential decision maker. Thus we can see that there might be a wide range of parties affected by accounting regulations.

The drafting of accounting regulations may at first sight seem to be a technical problem, involving decisions on how best to portray the economic reality of the position of a business. To achieve greater consistency in such regulations it has been argued that a 'conceptual framework' should be evolved. However, for practical purposes the search for such a framework has been unsuccessful. A major problem is that accounts are produced to satisfy very different types of needs. In particular, there is conflict between those, such as the tax authorities, who need to maximize objectivity, and those, such as potential investors, who need economically realistic information with all the un-avoidable judgements and prediction that entails.

Academics studying the process of accounting regulation have become increasingly aware of *economic consequence* issues, being the effect of accounting regulations on the creation and distribution of wealth. As a result of these issues, heavy pressures are brought to bear on the accounting regulators by affected parties, and there are well-documented cases in both the USA and the UK of these pressures influencing the content of accounting standards. Where, as in the UK, a large part of the determination of accounting practices is in the hands of the accounting profession rather than the government, then these pressures can be particularly effective. This *politicization* of the accounting standard-setting process means that accounting standards cannot be accepted as necessarily representing the collective view of accountants on the most useful way of presenting accounting information. The well-informed analyst may well adjust accounts to reflect such biases.

Conclusion

The regulatory framework within which accounts are prepared is complex. To under-stand the significance of a set of accounts, the user must have a thorough understanding of the rules which have governed preparation of the accounts. At the same time, the validity of those rules for the purpose of the user should be critically assessed and the accounts interpreted accordingly.

Questions

3.1   Large organizations—especially public limited companies—have both internal and external auditors.

Itemize the differences between internal and external auditors.

Why is it necessary to have internal auditors when the company/organization already employs an external firm of auditors?

(Cert. Dip. in Accounting & Finance, June 1983)

3.2   *You are required to* state and explain the role and responsibilities in the production of published financial statements of:

(a)   the directors of a company;
(b)   the accountant of an organization; and
(c)   the external auditor of a company.

(Cert. Dip. in Accounting & Finance, June 1984)

Note: Some questions in later chapters will call for an awareness of the regulatory framework as part of the answer.

4 The balance sheet – assets

Objectives

We have seen that the balance sheet, in its simplest form, shows on one side the resources of the business, known as assets, and on the other side the sources from which the resources have been derived. The objective of this chapter is to consider the various types of asset and the special problems of accounting for each type. Specifically we consider:

(a) The various types of asset.
(b) Tangible fixed assets.
(c) Intangible assets.
(d) Stock and work in progress.
(e) Investments.
(f) Monetary assets.

Types of asset

The Companies Act 1985 uses the term *fixed asset* to cover those assets which 'are intended for use on a continuing basis in the company's activities'. In order to classify an asset as fixed, three conditions must be met:

(a) It must be held for the long term, normally taken to indicate a period of one year.
(b) It must be owned with the intention that it be used in the business.
(c) It must be of a material amount.

In practice it is not normal to classify items of small value as fixed assets, although a large group of such items might be so classified.

The 1985 Companies Act shows fixed assets under three main headings:

(a) Tangible fixed assets. These are items with a physical existence, such as property, plant, machinery, fixtures and motor vehicles.
(b) Intangible assets. These are rights to benefits enjoyed by the company which do not have a physical existence. Examples include patent rights and goodwill.
(c) Investments. These are interests in other businesses owned for the long term.

Traditionally, accountants have tended to confine use of the term 'fixed asset' to tangible fixed assets.

The other major category is that of *current assets*. A current item would normally be regarded as one that is expected to be converted into cash within one year. Thus an examination of the current items in a balance sheet is the normal starting point when considering the liquidity of a business. In practice, all items which circulate within the normal operating cycle of a business are normally classified as current, even where such items will not convert into cash within one year.

Tangible fixed assets

When a fixed asset is acquired, the cost must be recorded in the accounts. 'Cost' will include all costs involved in acquiring the asset and making it usable. For example, if a freehold property is purchased then the related legal fees and stamp duty will form part of the cost. Some times a business will construct a fixed asset for its own use; in that case the proportion of material, wage and overhead costs relating to the construction will be recorded as the cost of the fixed asset.

A practical problem that can arise is in distinguishing between maintenance costs relating to a fixed asset, which should be written off as an expense in the profit and loss account, and improvement costs, which should be regarded as an addition to the cost of the fixed asset.

Most fixed assets will have their value consumed, at least to some extent, during the period that they are owned by the business. It is therefore necessary to have a procedure for recording in the profit and loss account the cost of the portion of fixed assets consumed during a year. This is known, as we have already seen, as *depreciation*.

SSAP 12, 'Accounting for Depreciation', offers this definition of depreciation: 'The measure of the wearing out, consumption, or other loss of value of a fixed asset whether arising from use, effluxion of time or obsolescence through technology and market changes.'

Note that the word 'value' is here used to mean the amount at which an asset is carried in the accounts. It is important to emphasize that accountants do not in any way claim that depreciation is, or can be, a valuation process.

It is easy to see how both usage and the passage of time can be responsible for the consumption of a fixed asset. The term *obsolescence* refers to the risk of an asset losing value, although still functioning, because it has become out of date. The two causes of obsolescence are:

(a) *Technology*, as when an alternative asset is developed which is so clearly preferable that there is no further use for the existing asset.
(b) *Market changes*, when there ceases to be a demand for the product or service which the machine is employed for.

Each year it is necessary to make an estimate of the depreciation charge. There are a number of methods, considered in detail below, for depreciating fixed assets. All depreciation methods involve making some estimate of the life of an asset, either in terms of time or usage. Example 4.1 gives an example of the kind of estimates that might be made.

Example 4.1

Wolfe Ltd buys a new box-making machine for £8100 on 1 January 1985. The machine is expected to have a four-year life, at the end of which it is expected to be sold for £1600.

The machine is expected to manufacture 10 000 boxes in 5000 running hours.

During the year to 31 December 1985 the machine produced 3000 boxes in 1480 running hours.

There are two major types of time-based depreciation:

(a)   Straight line, where the asset is written off evenly over its useful life. The annual charge is computed as:

$$\frac{1}{n} \times (c-s)$$

where n=number of years' life
c=cost
s=scrap value when asset is taken out of use.
The computation for our example is shown in Fig. 4.1a.

In practice, the scrap value of an asset is often so small as to be ignored. In that case, straight-line depreciation is often expressed as a percentage to be applied to original cost, computed as:

$$\frac{1}{n}$$

For our example, the rate would be:

$$\frac{1}{4}=25\%$$

(a)   *Straight-line method*

$$\tfrac{1}{4} \times (8100 - 1600) = \underline{1625}$$

(b)   *Reducing balance*

$$\text{Rate} = 1 - 4\sqrt{\frac{1600}{8100}} = 33\tfrac{1}{3}\%$$

	W.D.V. b/fwd	Charge for year	W.D.V. c/fwd
	£	£	£
1985	8100	2700	5400
1986	5400	1800	3600
1987	3600	1200	2400
1988	2400	800	1600

(c)   *Units of production*

$$\frac{3000}{10\,000} \times (8100 - 1600) = \underline{1950}$$

(d)   *Production hours*

$$\frac{1480}{5000} \times (8100 - 1600) = \underline{1924}$$

Figure 4.1   Computation of depreciation charges

(b)   Reducing balance, where the objective is to charge a relatively high proportion of the total depreciation in the early years of an asset's life, reducing the charge as years go by. This is achieved by applying a consistent rate of depreciation to the amount at which the asset is carried in the accounts net of depreciation already written off (often referred to as the *written down value*). The rate is computed as:

$$1 - n \sqrt{\frac{s}{c}}$$

Figure 4.1b shows how this formula would be applied to our example and also shows how the depreciation charge on this basis would work out in each year.

Whichever method of depreciation is used, a problem arises when assets are acquired part way through a year:

(a)   To avoid unnecessary computation, a full year's depreciation is provided in the year of acquisition and none in the year of disposal.
(b)   To achieve a more precise result, depreciation is scaled down both in the acquisition and disposal years to an amount proportional to the part of the year in which the asset is owned.

Under examination conditions, students would be well advised to take the second approach if sufficient detail is given, unless told otherwise by the examiner.

Usage-based depreciation is computed by the formula:

$$(\text{Cost} - \text{Scrap value}) \times \frac{\text{Usage in year}}{\text{Total expected usage}}$$

In order to apply this formula it is necessary to find some measure of usage. Two common approaches are:

(a)   Units of production. This basis is illustrated for our example in Fig. 4.1c.
(b)   Production hours. This basis is illustrated for our example in Fig. 4.1d.

The directors of a company, when formulating an accounting policy for depreciation, will first have to choose between a time-based and a usage-based approach. Arguments might include:

(a)   Consideration of whether usage or time should be regarded as the prime factor in the consumption of the asset. For example, a leasehold building would normally be depreciated on a time basis.
(b)   Availability and economy of a measure of usage. For some types of asset such a measure may not be available, while in other cases the cost of measurement might be excessive.
(c)   Links with the cost accounting system. Where detailed records are kept of machine hours spent in producing units of output it may be convenient to management to use this information in the financial accounts.
(b)   Sensitivity of the accounts. Usage-based depreciation shows a higher depreciation charge when the level of activity is high, and vice versa. If management wish to 'smooth' reported profits this might make a usage basis attractive.

Arguments between different time bases might include:

(a)   Straight line is easier to apply.

(b)   Straight line is conceptually attractive in that depreciation is allocated strictly in relation to the passage of time.

(c)   Reducing balance is attractive where the asset is of a type where repair costs increase sharply in the latter years of use.

Arguments between the two usage-based measures we have shown include:

(a)   'Units of production' is only possible where a machine has a single type of output; in that case it is easy to apply, because normally records of output will be kept for control purposes.

(b)   'Production hours' is conceptually attractive because it relates depreciation directly to usage. By contrast, 'units of production' reflect how efficiently the machine has been used, so that 'inefficient' use would reduce the depreciation charge.

The Companies Act require separate disclosure of the cost and the accumulated depreciation relating to each type of fixed asset. The reason for showing cost and accumulated depreciation separately, rather than writing off depreciation directly against cost, can be illustrated by the example in Fig. 4.2. If depreciation were directly written off against cost, then we would see that each company had motor vehicles shown at £50 000 and assume that each company was therefore in a similar position. By showing cost and accumulated depreciation separately we gain two benefits:

(a)   We can recognize that in fact company A has a far greater original investment in vehicles than company B, and that company A is more likely to have to replace vehicles in the near future.

(b)   Depreciation inevitably involves estimates; company A's depreciated cost is more subject to error in estimate than company B's because of the relative proportion depreciated.

	Company	
	A	B
	£000	£000
Cost	250	60
Accumulated depreciation	200	10
Written-down value	50	50

Figure 4.2 Motor vehicles

The Companies Act 1985 requires disclosure:

(a)   In relation to the cost of each category of fixed assets, the amount brought forward, additions, disposals and the amount carried forward.

(b)   In relation to the accumulated depreciation on each category of fixed assets, the amount brought forward, additions, disposals and the amounts carried forward.

SSAP 12, in addition, requires an accounting policy note showing the basis of depreciation and estimated life for each kind of asset.

These disclosure requirements are illustrated in Appendix A on pages 219 and 217.

It is important to note that depreciation is not claimed to provide a mechanism either for showing the *value* of fixed assets or enabling *replacement*.

Value is a subjective concept; it can only be established in objective monetary terms by an arm's length transaction. The depreciated cost of an asset will not necessarily relate to the amount for which the asset could currently be purchased, since prices may have changed since the time of the original purchase. Equally, depreciated cost will not necessarily relate in any way to the amount at which an asset could be sold; indeed, where fixed assets are specially designed or adapted for the needs of the business, then they may have a very low resale value from the day when they are purchased.

The availability of resources for the replacement of fixed assets is a matter which management must plan for; it does not relate directly to the accounting provision of depreciation, which is a mechanism for the allocation of cost between accounting periods. There may be an indirect link in that the provision of depreciation reduces the amount of reported profit, and since reported profit is often taken as an indicator of the maximum amount that the proprietors can safely withdraw from the business by way of dividend or drawings, the depreciation charge may result in resources being retained in the business. However, there is no reason to assume that resources retained in the business will be held in a liquid form available for fixed asset replacement; they may well, for example, have been invested in other fixed assets.

So far we have considered the position where fixed assets are recorded at historical cost. In practice, many companies have developed the practice of revaluing some of their fixed assets. In a limited company any increase in the amount at which a fixed asset is shown will be recorded as a *capital reserve*, considered in detail in Chapter 5 below.

When a fixed asset is revalued, SSAP 12 provides that depreciation must be provided on the revalued amount. If at any time a company changes its estimate of asset life or changes the depreciation method used, then the part of the cost of the asset not written off at the date of change must be written off over the new estimated life by the new method.

Identifiable intangible assets

We have already defined intangible assets as rights or benefits enjoyed by a company which do not have a physical existence. However, such assets my have an identifiable existence, and any costs involved in their acquisition should be 'capitalized', that is recorded as the cost of acquiring the fixed asset concerned. These identifiable intangible assets will be depreciated over their estimated useful lives like any other fixed assets; the term 'amortization' is often used in place of 'depreciation' in this context.

One particular type of intangible asset which has caused accountants some difficulty is that arising from research and development expenditure. This is the subject of an accounting standard, SSAP 13. There are two basic approaches to such expenditure:

(a) A 'deferral' approach, whereby such costs are treated as an asset and are then amortized over the period that related income is earned. This is in line with the 'accruals' concept.
(b) A 'write-off' approach, whereby such costs are treated as an expense of the accounting period in which they are incurred. This treatment is justified by reference to the 'prudence' concept, since it is argued that there is likely to be uncertainty as to whether such costs will in fact generate future income.

SSAP 13 draws a distinction between 'research', being original investigation undertaken in order to gain new scientific or technical knowledge, and 'development', being the use of scientific or technical knowledge to produce some form of improved commercial output. All research expenditure must be written off in the year incurred. Companies are allowed to choose between a 'write-off' and a 'deferral' policy for development expenditure, being required to apply whichever policy is chosen to all development expenditure. Where a deferral policy is chosen, then development expenditure may be carried forward to future periods and amortized providing that the following conditions are all met:

(a) Costs must relate to a clearly defined project.
(b) Costs on the project must be separately identifiable.
(c) The outcome of the project must be assessed with 'reasonable certainty' as to technical feasibility and commercial viability.
(d) Future revenues must be 'reasonably expected' to cover all costs.
(e) Adequate resources to complete the project must be available.

Unidentifiable intangible assets

We have already seen in Chapter 2 above, that the value of a business as a whole at any point in time will differ from the total of the value of the individual indentifiable tangible and intangible assets; the difference is generally referred to as *goodwill*. Positive goodwill can arise for a variety of factors, such as established connection or reputation with customers, a trained and loyal workforce, or trading connections of other sorts. In some cases the value of a business as a whole will be less than the total of the value of individual identifiable assets, so that 'negative goodwill' might arise. We would not expect 'negative goodwill' to be common, because a business in this position might be expected to cease trading and realize the individual assets.

The traditional accounting framework provides no mechanism for the identification of goodwill during the course of normal trading transactions, and indeed it is difficult to imagine how any such mechanism could in practice be operated. However, goodwill is quantified when one business acquires another business as a going concern. In such a case it is necessary to ascertain the value of each of the identifiable items in the accounts of the acquired business at the acquisition date and record this amount in the books of the acquiring business; the difference between the purchase price paid and the total of the value of the identifiable items, referred to as 'purchased goodwill', then remains to be accounted for. By contrast, goodwill not quantified in this way is often referred to as 'inherent goodwill'.

SSAP 22, 'Accounting for Goodwill', lays down as normal practice that purchased positive goodwill should be written off in the year of acquisition. The reason for this is that purchased goodwill is then treated in the same way as inherent goodwill must, of necessity, be treated. The write off is taken direct to reserves rather than being shown on the face of the profit and loss account, since this does not represent an expense of the particular year concerned.

SSAP 22 does permit an alternative approach, whereby purchased goodwill is regarded as an intangible asset and is depreciated over its estimated useful economic life. A company is allowed to choose between these accounting treatments for each individual acquisition of purchased goodwill.

Negative goodwill is more difficult to account for satisfactorily. When this arises, SSAP 22 recommends:

(a)   That the values attributed to individual identifiable items should be scrutinized carefully to ensure that these have been fairly stated.

(b)   Consideration should be given to the question of whether there are in fact potential liabilities for which specific provision should be made.

Following such consideration, any remaining negative goodwill should be credited to a capital reserve.

In practice, there is no practical way for accountants to prescribe a single, objective, meaningful form of accounting treatment for goodwill, and users of accounts would be well advised to eliminate all accounting entries relating to goodwill from consideration in comparing company accounts.

Stock and work in progress

The term *stock* embraces all goods acquired or produced for consumption or sale by the business. The term *work in progress* covers goods in the course of production. As we have already seen, the total stock and work in progress at the end of an accounting period is deducted from the 'cost of sales' (or other relevant expense) figure in the profit and loss account and is shown as an asset in the balance sheet. Thus the amount at which stock and work in progress is computed has a significant effect on reported profit. In the UK the accounting treatment of stock and work in progress is the subject of an accounting standard, SSAP 9.

The physical quantity of stock is normally determined at the end of an accounting period by means of a physical count known as the *stocktake*. Sometimes a business will have a stock recording system, so that the amount of stock can be ascertained at any point in time; in such a case, it is normal to confirm that the system is working properly by doing a test count of stock at least once a year.

Having determined the physical quantity of stock, the next problem is to attribute to stock a monetary amount. SSAP 9 requires that stock and work in progress, other than long-term contract work in progress considered in detail below, should be shown at the: 'total of the lower of the cost and net realisable value of the separate items . . . or of groups of similar items'.

	Cost	Net realisable value (NRV)	Lower of cost and NRV
	£	£	£
Trousers	2300	2700	2300
Shirts	800	300	300
Braces	300	360	300
	3400	3360	2900

Figure 4.3   Men's outfitters – stock

By *net realizable value* is meant the amount for which goods could be sold less all costs to be incurred in order to achieve a sale. Figure 4.3 illustrates how this rule might be applied to a business. Note how the amount at which stock is shown is the total of the lower of cost and net realizable value of each group of items; to take the lower of total cost and total net realizable value would mean setting off losses on stock with a lower

NRV against expected gains on stock where NRV is higher, a breach of the prudence concept. At the same time, SSAP 9 rejects the use of *replacement cost* where this is lower than cost or NRV, on the grounds that this would transfer reported profit to a future accounting period although no actual loss has arisen.

SSAP 9 defines *cost* as the expenditure incurred in the normal course of business in bringing a product or service to its present location and condition. 'Cost' includes two elements:

(a) *Cost of purchase*, being the cost of buying goods.
(b) *Cost of conversion*, being the cost incurred in working on the product.

Thus to compute the cost of manufactured goods and work in progress it is necessary to allocate all expenses of manufacture over units of production. Example 4.2 shows a simple example of a manufacturing business.

Example 4.2

Clinton commenced business on 1 January 1986 as a manufacturer of widgets. At 31 December 1986 his trial balance showed:

	£	£
Sales		240 000
Purchases	186 000	
Factory wages	35 000	
Factory overheads	20 000	
Selling costs	20 000	
Administration costs	18 000	
Plant – Cost	50 000	
Debtors	20 000	
Creditors		10 000
Bank	1 000	
Equity		100 000
	350 000	350 000

Plant is to be depreciated at 20 per cent on the straight-line basis. During the year 80 widgets were sold, 100 were produced, and raw materials for 120 were bought.

The profit and loss account for Clinton is shown in Fig. 4.4. To prepare this, two types of stock have to be considered:

(a) **Raw materials.** We are told that sufficient raw materials to produce 120 widgets have been purchased, while only 100 widgets have actually been produced. Thus sufficient raw materials to produce 20 widgets must remain in stock. Raw material stock is therefore shown as:

$$\frac{\text{Number of widget materials in stock}}{\text{Total widget materials purchased}} \times \text{Cost of purchases}$$

i.e.

$$\frac{20}{120} \times £186\,000 = £31\,000$$

(b)   Finished goods. The cost of producing finished goods embraces all manufacturing costs including plant depreciation. We are told that 100 widgets have been produced but only 80 have been sold. Thus 20 must remain in stock. Stock will then be shown as:

$$\frac{\text{Stock of widgets}}{\text{Total widgets produced}} \times \text{Cost of goods produced}$$

i.e.

$$\frac{20}{100} \times £220\,000 = £44\,000$$

Clinton – Profit and Loss Account for the year ended 31 December 1986

	£	£
Sales		240 000
Less		
Purchases	186 000	
Less Stock of raw materials	31 000	
Cost of raw materials consumed	155 000	
Factory wages	35 000	
Factory overheads	20 000	
Plant depreciation	10 000	
Cost of goods produced	220 000	
Less Closing stock of widgets	44 000	
Cost of sales		176 000
Gross profit		64 000
Selling costs	20 000	
Administration costs	18 000	
		38 000
Net profit		26 000

Balance Sheet as at 31 December 1986

	£		£
Equity – b/fwd	100 000	Plant – Cost	50 000
Profit	26 000	Depreciation	10 000
c/fwd	126 000		40 000
Creditors	10 000	Stock (31 000 + 44 000)	75 000
		Debtors	20 000
		Bank	1 000
	136 000		136 000

Figure 4.4

Allocation of costs has been made simple in our example because only one type of product is manufactured. Where several types of product are produced it is necessary to decide on a basis for allocating indirect production costs to different types of output; this issue is considered in more detail in Chapter 10 below.

SSAP 9 states that the proportion of overheads regarded as part of the cost of stock should assume normal production levels. For example, if a business were closed down by a strike for a large part of a year it would be unreasonable to allocate all the year's overheads to goods actually produced.

The SSAP 9 requirement to allocate all production costs to stock is a good example of the application of the accruals concept, in that all the costs of production are matched with related sales.

A major problem is ascertaining the cost of stock arises when a business has purchased a number of identical items for different prices at different points in time. Consider our Example 4.3. It is easy to see the number of typewriters Trundle has in stock:

Purchased	1/1	100	
	4/1	80	
	13/1	80	260
Sold	9/1	60	
	19/1	70	130
In stock			130

However, it is more difficult to say what the cost of the 130 machines has been. Normally no record of which individual items has been sold will be available, so that some assumption has to be made as to the order in which items are sold.

Example 4.3

Trundle Ltd commenced in business as a dealer in typewriters on 1 January 1987. In the month of January the following transactions in one particular type of machine occurred:

1 January Purchased 100 machines at £50 each, total cost £5000
4 January Purchased 80 machines for £52.25 each, total cost £4180
9 January Sold 60 machines
13 January Purchased 80 machines for £53.50, total cost £4280
19 January Sold 70 machines

One common basis is to make the *First in—First out* (FIFO) assumption, that the goods sold are taken from the oldest stock. Figure 4.5 shows how this might be applied to our example 'Trundle Ltd'. At any point in time the cost of stock can be computed as relating to the most recent purchases which together make up the total quantity of stock held.

Another approach is 'Last in—First out' (LIFO), whereby goods sold are assumed to come from the most recent batch acquired until that is consumed, then from the previous batch and so on. This is illustrated in Fig. 4.6. Note that in principle it is not possible, with LIFO, to ascertain which costs must be allocated to stock without knowing the order in which sales and purchases have taken place. However, a crude version of LIFO can be applied when detailed data is not available by assuming that all purchases in a period preceded all sales, and examiners often set questions which can only be answered by making this assumption.

	Stock quantity	Cost per unit £	£	Amount £
1 Jan 87 Purchase	100	50		5 000
4 Jan 87 Purchase	80	52.25		4 180
Total cost to 4 Jan 87	180			9 180
9 Jan 87 Sale	(60)	50		(3 000)
Cost of stock at 9 Jan 87	120			6 180
13 Jan 87 Purchase	80	53.50		4 280
Cost of stock at 13 Jan 87	200			10 460
19 Jan 87 Sale	(40)	50	2 000	
	(30)	52.25	1 567.50	
				3 567.50
Cost of stock at 19 Jan 87	130			6 892.50

Made up of:
13 Jan 87 Purchase of 80 @ 53.50		4 280.00
4 Jan 87 Purchase of 50 @ 52.25		2 612.50
		6 892.50

Figure 4.5   First In – First Out (FIFO)

	Stock quantity	Cost per unit £	Amount £
1 Jan 87 Purchase	100	50	5 000
4 Jan 87 Purchase	80	52.25	4 180
Total cost to 4 Jan 87	180		9 180
9 Jan 87 Sale	(60)	52.25	(3 135)
Cost of stock at 9 Jan 87	120		6 045
13 Jan 87 Purchase	80	53.50	4 280
Cost of stock at 13 Jan 87	200		10 325
19 Jan 87 Sale	(70)	53.50	(3745)
Cost of stock at 19 Jan 87	130		6 580

Made up of:
13 Jan 87 Purchase of 10 @ 53.50		535
4 Jan 87 Purchase of 20 @ 52.25		1 045
1 Jan 87 Purchase of 100 @ 50		5 000
		6 580

Figure 4.6   Last In – First Out (LIFO)

In comparing FIFO and LIFO it should be borne in mind that in times of rising prices FIFO charges earlier costs, which will be lower, to the profit and loss account while showing the more recent (and therefore higher) costs in the balance sheet. Conversely, LIFO charges the more recent, higher costs in the profit and loss account and shows the earlier, lower costs in the balance sheet. Bearing this in mind, the following points arise:

(a)   Assuming that reports based on the most recent cost figures are likely to be more relevant to user decisions, then FIFO gives a more useful balance sheet figure and LIFO gives a more useful profit and loss figure.

(b) LIFO results in a lower reported profit figure. Thus it is likely to prove popular in those countries, such as the United States, which accept LIFO for tax purposes. By contrast in the UK, where LIFO is not accepted for tax purposes, it is rarely used.

(c) FIFO is simpler to operate than LIFO, because no analysis of detailed stock movements is necessary. FIFO also represents the order in which stock is likely to be used in practice.

(d) LIFO can give a distorted picture where stock levels dip and costs relating to stock acquired long in the past are brought into the profit and loss account.

In the UK SSAP 9 has expressed the view that LIFO is not regarded as desirable.

Both FIFO and LIFO can be cumbersome to apply when a system of continuous recording of stock movements is in force, for two reasons:

(a) It is necessary to look back through the records to ascertain which cost figure should be applied to each batch of stock issued.

(b) Sometimes a batch of stock issued will draw on more than one purchase batch, so that more than one cost figure will apply to the issue.

A way round this problem is to use *Average Cost* (AvCo) as shown in Fig. 4.7. With average cost, the cost of each batch of stock acquired is added on to the cost of stock already held. When stock is issued, the cost per unit is computed as:

$$\frac{\text{Total cost of stock held}}{\text{Number of units held}}$$

This gives the average cost, weighted by reference to the number of units acquired.

	Stock quantity	Cost per unit £	Amount £
1 Jan 87 Purchase	100	50	5 000
4 Jan 87 Purchase	80	52.25	4 180
Total cost to 4 Jan 87	180		9 180
9 Jan 87 Sale	(60)	9 180/180	3 060
Cost of stock at 9 Jan 87	120		6 120
13 Jan 87 Purchase	80	53.50	4 280
Cost of stock at 13 Jan 87	200		10 400
19 Jan 87 Sale	(70)	10 400/200	(3 640)
Cost of stock at 19 Jan 87	130		6 760

Figure 4.7 Average Cost (AvCo)

Long-term contract work in progress is subject to special rules. SSAP 9 defines a 'long-term' contract as one which extends over a period in excess of twelve months. Such work in progress is shown at:

Cost plus *attributable* profit less *foreseeable* losses

By 'attributable' profit is meant the portion of the total expected profit which has been earned so far, while 'foreseeable' losses are total losses expected to be made on a contract. Attributable profit is only taken when the work is sufficiently advanced to justify predicting the outcome.

Where a business undertakes long-term contract work it is common practice to agree with the customer that payments on account will be made as each stage of the contract is completed. These *progress payments* receivable are deducted from the related work in progress asset figure.

The application of these principles can be illustrated by Example 4.4.

Example 4.4

Hod Ltd – Contracts in progress at 31 December 1985

	A	B	C	D
	£000	£000	£000	£000
Cost of work to 31 December 1985	60	30	100	10
Estimated further costs to complete	40	10	60	190
Value of work completed at 31 December 1985	100	40	90	15
Total contract price	150	60	140	300
Progress payments receivable to 31 December 1985	50	–	80	–
Contract commenced	1 Jan 85	1 Oct 85	1 Feb 85	1 Dec 85
Completion date (expected)	31 Dec 86	28 Feb 86	30 Nov 86	31 Dec 87

Taking each contract in turn:

A. This contract is long term, and is expected to yield a total profit of £50 000 (i.e. total price less costs to date plus costs to complete). Since 60 per cent of costs have already been incurred, attributable profit will be:

$$60\% \times £50\,000 = £30\,000$$

Note that we do not take as attributable profit the difference between the value of work completed and related cost, being £40 000. This is because in practice profit may be unevenly earned over the contract, and it would not be prudent to allocate profit this way.
B. This contract is for a period of less than one year. It is therefore shown at lower of cost and net realizable value, i.e. cost £30 000.
C. The total foreseeable loss on this contract is:

	£000	£000
Contract price		140
Less		
Cost incurred	100	
Cost to complete	60	
		160
Loss		(20)

D. This contract appears profitable, but at such an early stage it would not seem prudent to compute attributable profit.

Figure 4.8 shows how contract work in progress for our example would be computed.

| | Long-term contracts | | | |
	A	C	D	Total
	£000	£000	£000	£000
Cost	60	100	10	170
Attributable profit	30	–	–	30
Foreseeable loss	–	(20)	–	(20)
Progress payments	(50)	(80)		(130)
	40	–	10	
Total long-term contract WIP				50
Other contract WIP – B at cost				30
Total contract WIP				80

Figure 4.8 Hod Ltd – Contract work in progress as at 31 December 1985

SSAP 9 requires disclosure of accounting policies relating to stock and work in progress, and an analysis of categories of stock. This disclosure is illustrated in Appendix A on pages 217 and 220.

Investments

An investment in another business may take one of two forms:

(a) It may involve acquisition of part of the equity of the investee, in which case the return it yields will consist of a share of profits.

(b) It may involve a loan to the investee, the return being by way of a fixed rate of interest.

Sometimes both types of investment will be made in the same business.

An investment may be made either on a long-term basis or a short-term basis. The Companies Act 1985 provides rather different rules for the amount at which each type of investment is shown:

(a) Long-term investments should be shown at cost less any provision for diminuition in value which is expected to be permanent.

(b) Short-term investments should be shown at the lower of cost and net realizable value.

The Companies Acts also require disclosure of the split between investments listed on the Stock Exchange and other investments, and where investments are listed the market value must be disclosed in the notes.

Where an investment involves more than 10 per cent of the investor's own assets, or more than 10 per cent of the investee's equity, details of the investment must be disclosed.

It should be noted that where a company buys and sells blocks of shares in another company, a problem arises in deciding which costs to attribute to shares retained. This is similar to the problem of attributing costs to stock considered above, and the same methods, such as FIFO and LIFO, are used to allocate costs.

Where an investment in another company gives control or substantial influence, special procedures are used, discussed in Chapter 9 below under the heading 'Group accounts'.

Monetary assets

By 'monetary assets' we mean amounts of money which are held by or owed to the business. Examples include trade debtors, amounts lent to other businesses (a form of 'investment') and bank balances.

Monetary assets are normally shown in the accounts at their monetary amount. The major exception to this principle is where there is some doubt as to whether a borrower will actually pay, in which case it might be considered prudent to make some provision against the asset. Example 4.5 shows the kind of information a company might have available on debtors.

Example 4.5

At 1 January 1986 Ashby Ltd had total debtors of £51 000, against which a provision for doubtful debts of £800 had been estimated at the end of 1985.

During 1986 bad debts totalling £1400 were written off, and a sum of £150 was received from a debtor who had been written off as a bad debt during 1984.

At 31 December 1986 total debtors were £64 500. It was decided to write off a debt of £300 as bad, and to increase the provision for doubtful debts to £1700.

Compute:

(a)   The total amount charged against profit for bad and doubtful debts in 1986.
(b)   The debtors' figure to be shown in the balance sheet as at 31 December 1986.

		£	£
(a)	**P & L charge:**		
	(1) Bad debts written off in year		1 400
	(2) *Less* Bad debts recovered		(150)
	(3) Bad debt written off at year end		300
	(4) Provision carried forward	1 700	
	(5) *Less* Provision brought forward	800	
	Increase in provision		900
			2 450
(b)	**Balance sheet:**		
	Debtors at year end		64 500
	(1) *Less* Write off		300
			64 200
	(2) *Less* Provision at year end		1 700
			62 500

Figure 4.9

The solution to Example 4.5 is shown in Fig. 4.9. To explain the terms used:

(a)   During an accounting period, debtors who are considered unlikely to pay may be written off as bad debts. The total amount will be shown as an expense in the profit and loss account.

(b) Sometimes a debtor who has been written off as bad will pay unexpectedly. Such 'bad debts recovered' will be treated as a reduction of the bad debt expense in the profit and loss account.

(c) At the end of an accounting period it is normal practice to review the list of debtors and to write off any considered 'bad' which have not been written off during the year.

(d) In reviewing the list of debtors some may be considered 'doubtful', in that there is uncertainty as to whether or not they will pay. It is unsatisfactory to write off such debts as 'bad', since to do so would eliminate from the ledger the record of the amount owing. On the other hand, it is also unsatisfactory to show such debtors as an asset in the accounts, since they may not ever be received. The solution is to leave a record of the debtors in the ledger, but to deduct from the total debtors figure a 'provision for doubtful debts'. At the end of each accounting period the amount of the provision is recomputed, and any increase or decrease is shown as an addition to or deduction from the profit and loss charge for bad debts.

Such provisions may be 'specific', computed by reference to an analysis of individual debtor balances, or 'general', computed as a proportion of total debtors.

Conclusion

The balance sheet shows all the resources acquired by a business, called 'assets'. Assets are normally recorded in the accounts at cost, less:

(a) A deduction to represent the proportion of the asset that has been consumed in the business.

(b) Any deduction necessary to show that the value of the asset is now less than cost.

Questions

4.1 The cost of a machine purchased by Northeast Cape Ltd on 1 April 1978 is £50 000. It is estimated that the machine will have a £5000 trade-in value at the end of its service life. Its life is estimated at 5 years; its working hours are estimated at 30 000; its production is estimated at 500 000 units. During the period to 31 December 1978 the machine was operated for 6000 hours and produced 120 000 units. The profits of Northeast Cape Ltd before the depreciation charge amountd to £10000.

You are required to:

(a) Compute the depreciation charge on the machine for the year ending 31 December 1978 by
 (i)   the straight-line method,
 (ii) the service hours method,
 (iii) the productive output method.
(b) Comment on the effect the different methods have on the profit figure.

(Cert. Dip. FA, June 1979)

4.2 Larchmont Ltd was established on 1 January 1983 to manufacture a single product using a machine which cost £400 000. The machine is expected to last for four years and then have a scrap value of £52 000. The machine will produce a similar number of goods each year and annual profits before depreciation are expected to be in the region of £200 000. The financial controller has suggested that the machine should be depreciated using either the straight-line method or the reducing balance method. If the latter method is used, it has been estimated that an annual depreciation rate of 40 per cent would be appropriate.

Required:

(a) Calculations of the annual depreciation charges and the net book values of the fixed asset at the end of 1983, 1984, 1985 and 1986 using:
(i) the straight-line method,
(ii) the reducing balance method.
(b) A discussion of the differing implications of these two methods for the financial information published by Larchmont Ltd for the years 1983–6 inclusive. You should also advise management which method you consider more appropriate bearing in mind expected profit levels.

Note: Ignore taxation.

(AIB, April 1983)

4.3   Two companies, the Smith Co. and the Jones Co., complete in the scrap metal warehousing business and are approximately the same size. In 1976 both coincidentally encountered seemingly identical operating situations resulting in the following information:

Opening inventory 10 000 tons costing £50 per ton.
Total purchases for the year 50 000 tons, of which 20 000 tons cost £70 per ton, and 30 000 tons cost £90 per ton. 45 000 tons were sold at average prices of £100 per ton, and other expenses in addition to the cost of goods sold but excluding taxation amounted to £700 000. The tax rate is 60 per cent and Smith operates the FIFO method whereas Jones uses LIFO.

You are required:

1.   Compute net income for the year for both companies.
2.   Discuss the effect of these two methods on reported profits and the working capital position of the business.

(Cert. Dip. FA, December 1977)

4.4   Stoker and Coke Ltd are coal merchants. During 1981 they sold 120 000 tons of coal. The original price was £90 per ton which rose on 1 April to £110 per ton. 40 000 tons were sold at the lower price. The rise in the selling price for coal reflected an increase from the colleries from £75 to £95 per ton. However, shrewd purchasing by Stoker who expected a price increase meant that they purchased 30 000 extra tons at the old price, in addition to the coal sold. A further 60 000 tons was purchased at the new price.

The stock on hand at 1 January 1981 was 10 000 tons which cost £620 000. During the year stocks never fell below 10 000 tons before the price rise nor 20 000 tons after the price rise—although the latter stock level was reached twice—in September and on 31 December 1981. Distribution and selling costs amount to 6 per cent of sales, and administration costs amount to £80 000 per month.

During the past Stoker and Coke Ltd have always used the FIFO method of stock costing for accounting purposes, but Mr Coke was told that the LIFO system provides more realistic accounting information.

You are required to:

1. Calculate the net profit (ignore taxation) under both method for the year ended 31 December 1981.
2. Comment upon the different results produced by the two methods.

(Cert. Dip. FA, December 1982)

4.5 Cavour Ltd is a firm of building contractors. The following information is provided relating to their uncompleted contracts at 31 December 1980:

Contract	A	B	C	D
Date contract commenced	1.1.80	1.2.80	1.8.80	1.10.80
Expected completion date	30.4.81	31.3.81	31.1.81	31.3.82
Cost of work to 31 December 1980	159 000	57 000	15 000	4 000
Estimated further costs to completion	36 000	15 000	2 000	62 000
Value of work certified to 31 December 1980	200 000	50 000	18 000	—
Contract price	260 000	65 000	21 000	75 000
Progress payments received and receivable at 31 December 1980	175 000	40 000	—	—

Required:

1. A statement showing your calculations of the separate values to be placed on each contract at 31 December 1980. The statement should show the profit or loss, if any, included in each of the valuations. You should include in the statement appropriate narratives to explain the treatments chosen.
2. A statement of the information in respect of the four contracts which would appear in the balance sheet of Cavour Ltd at 31 December 1980.

Note: Your calculations should take account of the requirements contained in Statement of Standard Accounting Practice 9.

(AIB, September 1981)

4.6 Conjuring Consultants are project consultants mainly engaged in designing and supervising long-term contracts.

The firm commenced business on 1 November 1978, and prepares its accounts to 31 October each year. The work on hand at each of the year ends was:

	1979 £	1980 £	1981 £
Direct labour and other costs	60 000	84 000	120 000
Overheads (calculated at 50% of the direct costs)	—	—	60 000
Valuation as per the balance sheet	£60 000	£84 000	£180 000

The profits per the accounts were:

	£
Year to 31 October 1979	54 000
Year to 31 October 1980	66 000
Year to 31 October 1981	78 000

The Chairman of Conjuring Consultants has told his bankers that the figures accurately reflect the company's profitability.

Do you believe that these accounts show a true and fair view?
If not, what would you suggest to be the correct profits for each of the years and why?

(Cert. Dip., December 1981)

4.7   Canvas Limited

Canvas Limited was incorporated in December 1975 to trade in a single product called 'Como'. The company began trading on 1 January 1976. Purchases and sales for the five years to 31 December 1980, when the company discontinued 'Como' in favour of a more profitable line, were as follows:

	Purchases		Sales	
	Units	Price per unit £	Units	Price per unit £
1976	100	400	80	500
1977	100	450	80	550
1978	100	500	80	600
1979	100	550	80	650
1980	—	—	80	700

Required:

(a)   Using (i) the first in—first out (FIFO) basis and (ii) the last in—first out (LIFO) basis of stock valuation, calculate the gross profit of Canvas Ltd for each of the five years to 31 December 1980. You should present your answer in columnar format.

(b)   Compare the results of your calculations and consider the relative merits of FIFO and LIFO as bases for valuing stock during a period of inflation.

(AIB, September 1981)

5 Sources of finance

Objectives

The objective of this chapter is to consider the various sources from which the business can derive its resources, and the way in which the accounts report this. Specifically, we consider:

(a) Accounting for the equity of the business, being resources derived from the proprietors.
(b) Equity as a source of finance.
(c) Various types of long-term borrowing.
(d) Various types of short-term borrowing.
(e) Other liability items in the accounts.
(f) 'Off balance sheet' sources of finance.
(g) Factors influencing the business in its choice of sources of finance.

The proprietors' interest

There are three major types of commercial entity:

(a) *The sole trader*. This is a private individual in business on their own account. Following the 'business entity' concept discussed in Chapter 2 above, the accounts of a sole trader will be prepared on the basis of showing only the business assets and liabilities. However, the sole trader has no legally separate business identity and is fully liable personally to meet all the obligations of the business.

(b) *Partnerships*. A partnership is made up of a group of 'persons carrying on a business with a view to profit' (as defined in the Partnership Act 1890). A partnership does not have a separate legal identity of its own, so that each partner is personally liable for all the obligations of the partnership. The Limited Partnership Act 1907 does permit some partners to restrict their personal liability in strictly controlled conditions, but in practice such limited partnerships are rare.

(c) *Limited liability companies*. A company is an 'artificial legal personality', having a legal existence independent of those involved in it. Normally liability is limited to the amount that the owners have to pay for their shares, so that once the shares have been paid for no further liability can arise. Sometimes a company will be limited 'by guarantee', so that the liability of members will be restricted to the amount they have undertaken to subscribe to the company if called upon to do so.

In the case of the sole trader, accounting for the proprietors' interest in the business is a simple matter in that each year we show the amount brought forward, add to this any amounts introduced during the year and any profit earned, deduct any drawings and any loss incurred, and so are left with the amount carried forward. However, in the case of both partnerships and limited companies there are a number of complications, considered in detail below.

Partnerships

A partnership requires a more detailed analysis of the equity than a sole trade for two reasons:

(a) It is necessary to distinguish between amounts permanently committed to the business as 'capital accounts', amounts left in the business on a day-to-day basis as 'current accounts', and amounts lent to the business over and beyond the obligation to subscribe capital being 'loan accounts'.
(b) It is necessary to record an account in the name of each partner for each part of the equity.

Each year the division of profits between partners will be recorded in the appropriate account. A partnership agreement will record the profit-sharing arrangements. Often this will include three element:

(a) An agreed rate of interest will be paid on the capital subscribed by each partner.
(b) A fixed sum will be allocated to each partner representing a form of remuneration for their services.
(c) The remaining profit or loss will be divided between the partners in some agreed profit-sharing ratio.

On dissolution of the partnership any surplus or deficit on realization of the asset is shared among the partners in profit-sharing ratio, then the cash balance should exactly cover the amount recorded in the accounts for each partner. Thus the accounts are used as a way of establishing the economic relationship between the partners. However, as we observed in Chapter 2, in practice historical cost accounts do not give a realistic view of the economic worth of the business both because assets are shown at cost rather than value and because the value of goodwill is not recorded in the accounts. As long as the same partners share profits in the same way this does not matter, because on dissolution the actual value of assets and goodwill will be realized and the increase or decrease recorded in each partner's personal account. But if there has been any change in the make-up of the partnership or the profit-sharing ratios, then the accounts will fail to reflect a fair division of the equity among the partners, because the realized surplus or deficit on dissolution shared out among the partners at the time may have been partially earned prior to the change in partnership arrangements. For this reason it is common to revalue both the tangible assets and the goodwill at each change in partnership arrangements, sharing any surplus or deficit on the old profit-sharing basis. The new partnership accounts can then commence in two ways:

(a) Assets can be carried forward at the new valuation.
(b) The historical cost principle can be adhered to by writing off the revaluation amount in the *new* profit-sharing ratio to the partners.

Limited companies

The equity of a limited company is analyzed into the *nominal value* and *share capital* and various *reserves*. Reserves may be *capital* or *revenue*. Let us now consider the significance of these terms.

A *share* represents a bundle of rights, which fall under two broad headings:

(a)   Rights to share in benefits distributed to shareholders.
(b)   Voting rights at company meetings.

A company may issue various categories of share, and the rights attaching to each category will be defined in the *Articles of Association*, the document which lays down the internal organization of the company. The two major categories of share issued are:

(a)   *Preference* shares, carrying a right to a fixed rate of dividend. Provided that realized profits are available, this preference dividend will be a fixed claim on the company which must b met before other dividends can be paid. *Cumulative* preference shares accumulate rights to dividend, so that if in one year realized profits will not cover dividends then preference shareholders are entitled to those arrears in future years if realized profits are earned. *Non-cumulative* preference shares do not accumulate dividend rights. Preference shares do not normally have any voting rights, except when the company proposes to change the rights attaching to them.

(b)   *Ordinary* shares. These shares receive whatever level of dividend the directors think it appropriate to *declare* out of realized profits. *Interim* dividends may be declared by the directors at any time during the year, while *final* dividends are proposed by the directors and must be approved at the annual general meeting, where shareholders may choose to reduce but are not allowed to increase the dividend. The factors that will influence dividend policy are discussed below. Each ordinary share normally carries full and equal voting rights at company general meetings. Sometimes the articles of association may create different classes of ordinary shares with different voting rights.

Pawkie Ltd – Balance Sheet as at 31 December 1986

	£
Ordinary shares of 25p	100
Retained profits	900
	1000
Net assets	1000

Figure 5.1

Each share has a *nominal* value, also referred to as *par* value. Dividends are expressed as a percentage of the nominal value, and companies are not allowed to issue shares for less than this amount. A shareholder who knows the nominal value of the shares they own can tell thereby what proportion of that class of share they own. For example, a shareholder who owned 60 shares in Pawkie Ltd (Fig. 5.1) sees that these shares have nominal value of:

$$60 \times 25p = £15$$

The balance sheet shows total shares issued at £100, so the shareholding represents $15/100 = 15$ per cent of the ordinary shares.

A company may wish to issue shares at an amount in excess of nominal value. For example, let us imagine that the balance sheet amount of the net assets of Pawkie Ltd represent the actual worth of the company, then given 400 shares in issue each share should be worth:

$$\frac{£1000}{400} = £2.50$$

Now supposing that we wish to raise a further £100 from issuing shares. If we issue these at nominal value, then net assets will be increased by £100 cash received, and 400 new shares will be issued, so that each share will now be worth:

$$\frac{£1100}{800} = £1.375$$

The effect of such a share issue would be to give the new shareholders a share in the surpluses accumulated by the old shareholders, who would receive no compensation. To avoid this problem, company law allows shares to be issued at a premium, in which case the difference between the issue price and nominal value is recorded in a *share premium* account. Taking our example, to raise £100 we might issue new shares at their fair value of £2.50 each so that the number of new shares issued will be:

$$\frac{£100}{£2.50} = 40$$

The nominal value of these shares will be 40 × 25p = £10, so that the remaining £90 received will be recorded as derived from share premium, as shown in Fig. 5.2.

Pawkie Ltd – Balance Sheet following share issue at £10 per share

	£
Ordinary shares of £1	
(100 + 10)	110
Share premium	90
Retained profits	900
	1100
Net assets (1000 + 100)	1100

Figure 5.2

It should be emphasized that we have here assumed that the balance sheet amount of assets equals their fair value in order to simplify the example; as we explained in Chapter 2, this will rarely be the case in practice.

Reserve is a technical term used by accountants to describe any part of the equity other than the nomnal value of the shares. Thus it is a historical record of where the resources of the business have come from an does *not*, as in everyday usage, represent a store of resources.

Revenue reserves represent accumulated realized profits out of which dividends have not yet been paid. *Capital* reserves represent other accumulated surpluses which belong to the shareholders. Examples of capital reserves include:

(a) The share premium account, discussed above.
(b) The capital redemption reserve, discussed below.
(c) The revaluation reserve, recording all surpluses arising on the revaluation of assets.

We have seen that dividends may only be paid out of realized profits. Thus the distinction between 'capital' reserves and 'revenue' reserves is an important one, since only the latter are *distributable* as dividends (Fig. 5.3). The reason for this is that company law aims to ensure that the resources originally injected by shareholders are retained in the business to cover any losses and provide some margin of safety for those who lend to it.

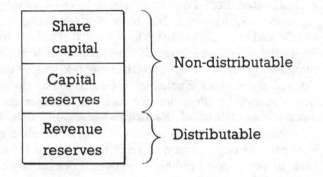

Figure 5.3   **Equity in a limited company**

A company may record the retained profits in more than one 'reserve' account. One common practice is to make occasional transfers from retained profits to some form of 'general' reserve. Such a reserve has no legal significance and is just as much a distri- butable reserve as 'retained profits', but in making such a transfer the directors are suggesting that they expect to retain these resources in the business for the long term.

Further confusion can arise because the Companies Acts do not include a specific requirement to identify 'distributable' and 'non distributable' portions of the reserves. Normally the title of each reserve will indicate its characters, but there can be minor exceptions.

Since 1981 companies have been allowed to make provision in their articles for the redemption of any type of shares, provided that at least some non-redeemable shares are in issue. Company law includes detailed requirements to ensure that any redemption of shares does not involve any reduction in non-distributable profit. To redeem shares the company will, of course, need to have sufficient cash resources available to purchase the shares, including any premium above nominal value payable on redemption. In addition, insofar as the nominal value of shares redeemed is not covered by the proceeds of a new share issue, a transfer must be made from revenue reserves to a non-distributable *capital redemption reserve*. The premium on redemption must be set off against revenue reserves, except tha *if* the premium on redemption is covered by the proceeds of a new share issue it may be set off against the share premium account to the extent it does not exceed the lower of:

(a)   Premiums received on the original issue of shares now redeemed.
(b)   The balance on the share premium account.

In addition, companies may, under the same strictly controlled conditions, purchase their own shares.

There are certain very strictly controlled conditions where companies might be permitted to cover redemption of shares from capital or enter into a capital reduction scheme. These are subject to stringent legal safeguards for creditors and fall outside the scope of this text.

Shareholders as a source of finance

Limited companies fall into two legal categories, public companies designated 'plc' and private companies designated 'Ltd'. Public companies have to comply with a number of restrictive and expensive requirements, but have the advantage that unlike private companies they are allowed to issue securities to the general public. In practice, a public company can only derive advantage from this permission if it is *listed* on the Stock Exchange, which involves compliance with another very expensive range of regulations designed by the Council of the Stock Exchange to ensure full disclosure, a wide market, and avoid unethical conduct by directors. To help the smaller company, the Stock Exchange has created an 'Unlisted Securities Market' with less cumbersome regulations, but even here costs of access are likely to run into six figures.

A listed company has the opportunity to raise new finance from the issue of new shares or loan stock to the general public; moreover, because of their marketability, institutional investors are likely to find investment in a company more attractive if the shares are listed. Methods by which a listed company might issue shares include:

(a) A *public issue* by prospectus. The *prospectus* is a widely advertised document which provides detailed information on the company and its plans, and is subject to detailed legal requirements. The company will normally be advised by an *issuing house*, such as a merchant bank, and arrange for *underwriters* to buy shares not taken up by the public. The costs involved in such an issue are very high.

(b) *Offer by tender.* As above a prospectus is issued inviting the public to name the price they are willing to pay. Shares will then be issued at a *striking price* to all who tendered at or above that price. This avoids underwriting costs but the amount to be raised cannot be predicted with certainty.

(c) *Offer for sale.* The shares are issued to the issuing house, which then offers them for sale to the public.

(d) *Placing.* This involves an adviser to the company, such as a merchant bank, finding buyers for a company's shares directly. The market mechanism is not involved, so unlisted companies can have their shares placed.

(e) *Rights issue.* The company offers shares to existing shareholders, in proportion to their existing shareholdings. The price is normally set below current market price to encourage shareholders to take up their rights or sell them to other investors. Any company may make a rights issue, but if the company is unlisted shareholders are unlikely to find a buyer for their 'rights', so that for an unlisted company the rights issue will only raise cash if shareholders are willing and able to subscribe for new shares personally.

An issue of ordinary shares has two types of cost to existing shareholders:

(a) Voting rights will be extended to new shareholders. Often, particularly in family-owned companies, existing shareholders are very reluctant to risk losing control of the company.

(b) The profits of the company have to be shared with a greater number of shareholders. Thus existing shareholders will only benefit if the return to be earned on new funds is equal to or greater than the return which can be earned on existing funds. One way to check this is to compute the earnings per share expected following a new share issue, comparing this with a predicted comparative earnings per share figure assuming no share issue (see Chapter 6 below on how to compute earnings per share)

A type of share issue that does not raise finance is the *bonus* issue, whereby shareholders are issued with new free shares in proportion to the number they already own. The nominal value of the issue is balanced by an equal reduction in one of the reserve accounts, and capital reserves may be used for this purpose. A bonus issue may have two purposes:

(a) Effectively, existing shares are split into smaller units, which may be more convenient to deal in.
(b) Where the issue is covered by distributable reserves, the company increases the non-distributable capital, thereby increasing confidence among creditors.

So far we have considered how a company can raise new finance from shareholders by issuing shares; the company can also raise finance from shareholders by retaining profit in the business. Looked at another way, the company's *dividend policy* can be formulated to distribute only a small portion of profits so that funds are retained for the expansion of the business.

In principle a company is only justified in retaining profits where the rate of return earned will exceed the rate shareholders could earn with the same funds for themselves. If a company retained a high proportion of profit, then we would expect future earnings to increase in proportion to the increased equity, so that an increased level of dividend can be offered in the future. The lower the proportion of profit paid out as dividend, the higher the rate of dividend growth that should be attainable.

Long-term borrowing

As we have seen, a listed company can issue long-term loan stock to the market in the same way as shares. All companies are allowed to raise loans privately or through institutional lenders. Long-term loans are often described as *debentures*, a term which simple means a liability acknowledged in writing. Debentures are normally *secured* on the assets of the company by a *charge*, which can be of two types:

(a) A *fixed charge* is a mortgage on specified assets which the company may not sell without permission of the mortgagee. In the event of default, the debenture holders may sell the asset, pay themselves out of the proceeds, and hand over the residue to the company.
(b) A *floating charge* normally relates to the fluctuating assets of the company, such as stock. In the event of default, the charge crystallizes, and after the claims of 'preferential' creditors (discussed in Chapter 10 below) have been met, then the proceeds of realization of the assets goes to the debenture holders.

A debenture will normally have a specified rate of interest, expressed as a percentage of *face value*. Often it will be issued at a *discount*, i.e. for less than the face value. The finance cost will then consist of the amount of interest payable each year plus the excess of face value which has to be repaid over the amount received at the time of issue. In the case of a *perpetual* debenture, which does not have any repayment date, the cost of borrowing will consist simply of the interest payments each year. However, in the case of a redeemable debenture the allocation of finance costs is more complex. Consider the simple example of a discounted redeemable debenture shown in Example 5.1. If we simply record finance costs as an expense in the year they occur, then we would show:

1986	Interest paid	£50
1987	Interest	50
	Surplus payable to redeem debenture	54
	Total cost	£104

Clearly it is unreasonable to allocate the discount part of the finance cost of a debenture entirely to the final year in this way. One way round this problem is to allocate the discount evenly over the years of the debenture. However, this approach is also open to criticism because it fails to recognize that the discount part of the finance cost does not have to be paid each year, but is effectively borrowed year-by-year until the capital repayment date.

		£
1 Jan 86	Sum borrowed	946
31 Dec 86	Finance cost 8%	76
		1022
	Less Interest paid	50
1 Jan 87	Amount outstanding	972
31 Dec 87	Finance cost 8%	78
		1050
	Less Interest paid	50
	Capital repaid	1000

Figure 5.4   Kungshaft Ltd

Figure 5.4 shows how we can allocate finance costs each year if we know the finance cost as a percentage of the sum borrowed. Each year the difference between the finance cost and the interest actually paid is added to the loan outstanding, so that in the final year the amount shown as owing is the face value of the debenture.

There is no formula for computing the finance cost as a percentage. This has to be found by trial and error or by iteration.

Example 5.1

On 1 January 1986 Kungshaft Ltd issue £1000 of 5 per cent debentures, redeemable on 31 December 1987, for £946, having computed that this results in a finance cost of 8 per cent.

Convertible loan stocks are of special type of debenture which carries the right to convert into shares on a specified date at a specified price. Normally the specified price will be set at a level somewhere above the current market price, giving the loan stock holders the opportunity to share in any gains arising from the company achieving a strong future performance. In exchange for this opportunity, lenders are likely to accept a lower rate of interest than they would otherwise expect.

In Chapter 2 above we saw that the balance sheet does not record the 'value' of assets. We can now consider whether the accounts necessarily present an economically realistic picture of long-term liabilities.

Example 5.2

Solna plc issued, in 1950, £10 000 000 of 4 per cent perpetual debentures. On 1 January 1986 the debenture holders were persuaded to accept £5 000 000 in cash to redeem the debentures, and this transaction was financed by a new issue of £5 000 000 10 per cent perpetual debenture stock at par.

Solna PLC Gain on redemption of debentures:	£
Nominal value per balance sheet	10 000 000
Less Cost of redemption	5 000 000
Surplus – reported as increased equity	5 000 000

Increase in finance costs:	£
New cost £5 000 000 × 10%	500 000
Old cost £10 000 000 × 4%	400 000
	£100 000

Figure 5.5

Consider the admittedly extreme picture given in Example 5.2. A company which issued perpetual debentures at the low market rates of interest prevailing in 1950 would continue to show those debentures at their nominal value until redemption. Figure 5.5 shows how, when debentures are redeemed in 1986 at a time of higher interest rates, an apparent gain is made in that year. Two points emerge:

(a)   The 'value' of a long-term liability fluctuates year by year in line with market rates of interest. When a liability is traded on the Stock Exchange a market figure for value can be identified, but nevertheless the balance sheet will continue to show the nominal value.

(b)   While the transaction shown in our example gives a nominal gain, in fact the company is worse off because the annual obligation to pay interest has increased.

The moral is that balance sheet figures for liabilities have to be interpreted cautiously, as with assets.

Short-term borrowing

The bank overdraft is a common form of short-term borrowing. This is nominally repayable on demand, but in practice the bank will normally agree an overdraft limit to cover a specified period of time, for which a commitment fee may be charged. Interest will then be charged on the amount actually borrowed, agreed as a certain percentage added to the bank's base rate. This form of finance has the following advantages:

(a) When the need for finance fluctuates, interest is only payable when money is actually borrowed.
(b) Providing a convincing proposition can be put to the bank, finance can be raised rapidly.
(c) When interest rates are high and expect to fall, then a long-term loan may commit the company to finance costs which will seem very burdensome if the predicted fall takes place. An overdraft can be used to tide over the company until interest rates fall.

Although an overdraft may in practice be renewed so regularly as to amount to a reliable form of permanent finance, the risk that the bank will require repayment in the short term remains. In recent years the banks have increasingly offered medium-term loans, perhaps up to ten yars, repayable by agreed instalments, which form a more secure form of bank finance.

Trade credit is another form of short-term borrowing, which can be exploited as a source of finance. Once cash discounts for prompt payment have been foregone, trade credit normally carries no interest cost. However, if payment of trade creditors is deferred excessively, then the company can lose supplier goodwill, and even have future supplies made condition on immediate cash payment. Thus excessive reliance on trade credit may be dangerous from the point of view of the commercial standing of the company.

Other liability items

In addition to the various forms of borrowing and trading liability considered above, a business may have other liabilities for appropriations such as taxation and proposed dividends shown in the balance sheet. In particular, the nature of various kinds of tax liability is considered in detail below.

Off balance sheet finance

This term is used to describe an arrangement whereby a business obtains the use of an asset in such a way that the asset, and consequently the related liability, does not appear in the balance sheet.

One way of obtaining the use of fixed assets is to hire instead of purchase. A company might hire an asset for a short period for operational reasons. However, sometimes an asset will be hired for the major part of its useful life under a lease agreement as an alternative to its acquisition; such an arrangement is effectively an alternative to purchasing the asset with borrowed funds, the regular rental payments being analogous to the repayment of capital and interest by instalments. The various ways of accounting for such arrangements are discussed in Chapter 9 below.

Another form of 'off balance sheet' finance arises from the practice of debt factoring. A debt factor may offer any combination of the following services:

(a) Advancing at the time of a sale a sum up to, say 80 per cent of the invoiced amount, which is then recovered when the debtor pays. Thus only debtors net of the advance appear in the balance sheet. An interest charge is made for the period while payment is awaited.

(b) The factor may also take over the administrative tasks of recording and collecting debtors.

(c) The factor may also offer insurance against default by agreed, specified debtors.

It is the first aspect of debt factoring that constitutes 'off balance sheet' finance.

Choice of financial structure

In examining company financial structure we revert to the basic principles of our balance sheet equation, that the resources of the business are obtained either from equity or from borrowing. The relationship between the two is known as *gearing*, and the higher the proportion of borrowing the higher a company is said to be geared. Some authorities would measure gearing by reference to the market value of equity and borrowings rather than the balance sheet amounts.

Gearing has two effects, illustrated by two companies shown in Example 5.3. The first effect is that higher gearing increases the risk that a comany will be unable to pay its debts. Thus A Ltd has no borrowing, and so could lose its total assets without defaulting on any obligation to lenders, while B Ltd will default on part of its obligations in the event of losing more than half its total assets. Consequently lenders are likely to be reluctant to lend further funds to a company that is already high geared.

The second effect of gearing is on the income available to shareholders. Consider the impact on profit available to shareholders of the three levels of trading profit shown in Example 5.3.

Example 5.3 Balance sheets

	A Ltd £	B Ltd £
Equity – ordinary shares of £1	1000	500
10% debenture	–	500
	1000	1000
Total assets	1000	1000

Consider earnings per share:

(a) Assuming profit before interest £100.
(b) Assuming profit before interest £80.
(c) Assuming profit before interest £120.

These are shown in Fig. 5.6.

(a) At the level of £100 both companies show the same earnings per share. This is not surprising since the return earned on trading assets is:

$$\frac{100}{1000} = 10\%$$

This is the same as the interest rate paid.

		A Ltd £	B Ltd £
(a)	Trading profit	100	100
	Interest	–	50
	Net profit	100	50
	Profit per share	$\dfrac{100}{1000} = 10\text{p}$	$\dfrac{50}{500} = 10\text{p}$
(b)	Trading profit	80	80
	Interest	–	50
	Net profit	80	30
	Profit per share	$\dfrac{80}{1000} = 8\text{p}$	$\dfrac{30}{500} = 6\text{p}$
(c)	Trading profit	120	120
	Interest	–	50
	Net profit	120	70
	Profit per share	$\dfrac{120}{1000} = 12\text{p}$	$\dfrac{70}{500} = 14\text{p}$

Figure 5.6

(b)   A 20 per cent fall in trading profit results in a 20 per cent fall in earnings per share for the ungeared company A Ltd, but a 40 per cent fall for the geared company B Ltd.
(c)   Conversely a rise in profit produces an equal rise in earnings per share for A Ltd but has twice the proportional impact for B Ltd.

Thus gearing magnifies the impact on shareholders of any fluctuation of trading profit. The potential impact of gearing can be measured by the *degree of capital gearing* which is:

$$\frac{\text{Profit before deduction of interest}}{\text{Interest}}$$

This factor, applied to the percentage change in trading profit, shows the fluctuation in profit attributable to shareholders. In our example, B Ltd has, under assumption (a), a degree of capital gearing:

$$\frac{100}{50} = 2$$

We have seen that a 20 per cent fall in profit leads to a fall in profit available to shareholders of:

$$2 \times 20\% = 40\%$$

In practice, a company would normally expect any project worth investing in to yield a rate of return in excess of the cost of borrowing. Thus a company's gearing will represent a compromise between the desire to increase the return enjoyed by shareholders and the desire to minimize risk.

Other factors influencing decisions on how to finance the business include:

(a)   The inherent risk of the project to be financed. The higher the risk, the less suitable the use of borrowings rather than equity.
(b)   Legal restrictions. For example, normally a company has a maximum level of

borrowing specified in the articles of association. Frequently these 'borrowing powers' are expressed as a multiple of share capital and reserves.

(c) Available security. For example, it will generally be easier to borrow money to acquire new premises than to finance research costs.

(d) Time cash required. Thus to meet a short-term requirement to finance working capital tied up in a single 'one-off' large order, a company would not wish to raise long-term finance.

(e) Proprietors' attitude. For example, if a family own the entire share capital of a company they may well be reluctant to lose control by issuing new shares to outsiders.

(f) Costs. These include both costs of raising finance and costs of employing finance.

Conclusion

We have seen how the balance sheet reports the various sources of finance, and we have considered the factors influencing a company's choice of financial structure. It is important to note that the balance sheet does *not* represent the economic value of equity or liabilities, and that it may exclude significant sources of finance.

Questions

5.1   Uncle Fred is concerned because he receives such small dividends from shares in a listed company. He has looked at the last annual report and seen that there is a large bank balance. In addition, the balance sheet shows the following items which he believes could be used to increase the dividend:

(a)   a large 'share premium account';
(b)   substantial 'unappropriated profits';
(c)   a large 'reserve for general contingencies';
(d)   a large 'provision for depreciation'.

You are required to prepare a brief explanation of the nature of these items suitable for Uncle Fred, indicating which of the items, if any, are relevant to his problem.

5.2   The following information relates to Bransford plc.

Recent Profit and Loss extract	£000
Profit before interest charges and taxation	1220
Interest charges	64
	1156
Taxation	520
	£636

Recent Balance Sheet extract		Recent market value of securities
	£000	£000
Ordinary share capital	1300	4850
Reserves	2600	
	3900	
8% borrowings	800	550
	£4700	

Required:

(i)   give two calculations which could be regarded as measures of capital gearing, giving brief reasons for your choices;

(ii) state, and briefly comment upon, two means by which a company might raise its gearing level.

(Cert.Dip. in Accounting & Finance, June 1982)

5.3   Waldron Superb Machines Ltd is planning an investment programme which will make a short-term drain on its financial resources but which is expected to be self-financing in the longer term. The Managing Director is reluctant to issue any further long-term debt securities or to introduce additional equity. He believes that the company has not fully exploited the scope for short and medium-term loan finance and has asked for your advice.

Required:

Prepare a report to the Managing Director of Waldron Superb Machines Ltd identifying the main sources of short and medium-term finance which his company could investigate, indicating the main characteristics of each.

(Cert.Dip. in Accounting & Finance, December 1983)

5.4   Mr Green has approached you for advice on how to launch a new business. He requires £60 000 to cover:

	£
Premises	40 000
Plant	15 000
Working capital	5 000
	60 000

You have prepared a cash budget, based on assumptions supplied by Mr Green which you regard as realistic, which confirms that an initial investment of £60 000 is adequate. The business is to be set up as a limited company.

Mr Green has £35 000 of his own money to invest in the business. He has been offered the following possibilities:

(a)   Mr White has offered to invest £30 000 in the new company. He proposes that Mr Green also invests £30 000, so that each investor has an equal share.

(b)   Black's Bank plc are willing to lend £28 000 on a five-year loan, repayable in equal annual instalments. The rate of interest will be fixed at 18 per cent. This rate is in line with current market interest rates, but financial commentators expect these rates to go down in the near future.

(c)   Yellow Properties Ltd, who currently own the premises Mr Green wishes to use, have offered to rent the property to him for two years at a rental of £5 000 per year if he prefers to rent instead of buying the property. However, they have made it clear that at the end of that time they will wish to offer the property for sale at the current market price with vacant possession.

Prepare a note of the factors which Mr Green should take into account in deciding between these possibilities.

6 The published profit and loss account

Objectives

The basic objective of this chapter is to explain the significance of the amounts reported in a published profit and loss account. Specifically we consider:

(a) The link between the profit and loss account and the balance sheet.
(b) The distinctions that accountants make between different types of item in the profit and loss account.
(c) The significance of each item shown in a published profit and loss account prepared in compliance with the Companies Act 1985.
(d) The significance of the earnings per share figure shown on the face of the published accounts, and related problem of computation.

The balance sheet link

Figure 6.1 shows the relationship between the opening and closing balance sheets and the profit and loss account for the year. The difference between opening and closing net assets is attributable to three broad reasons:

(a) Exchanges between the business and the proprietors.
(b) Revaluations, being restatements of the amounts at which assets are recorded in the accounts.
(c) Realized gains in the year, being the difference between income earned and related costs.

	£	£
Net assets at beginning of year		X
Assets injected by proprietors in year, e.g. share issue	X	
Less Resources withdrawn by proprietors in year, e.g. dividends	(X)	
		X
Net opening assets adjusted for amounts injected/withdrawn by proprietors		X
Amounts earned in period	X	
Resources consumed in period	(X)	
Total profit for year		X
		X
Revaluation surpluses/(deficits)		X
Net assets of end of year		X

Figure 6.1 Relationship between the balance sheet and profit and loss account

Because of this link, in each case where we have examined a balance sheet item we have also found ourselves considering any related profit or loss item. For example, the balance sheet figure for a fixed asset is directly linked to the profit and loss figure for depreciation. Thus we have already covered in earlier chapters the way in which individual items of income and expenditure are computed. In this chapter our concern will be the way in which profit and loss account information is presented.

SSAP 6 Extraordinary items and prior-year adjustments

Two extreme positions on the content of a published profit and loss account can be identified:

(a)   It can be argued that the profit and loss account should only include information on the trading activities of the business, with any non-trading gains or losses being shown as a direct adjustment to the owners' equity.

(b)   Alternatively an 'all-inclusive' view can be taken, whereby all gains or losses are shown in the profit and loss account.

SSAP 6 tries to achieve standard practice in this area. The ASC have also published an exposure draft, 'ED 36', with the same title, which proposes some developments of SSAP 6. SSAP 6 requires that unrealized surpluses on revaluation of fixed assets should be carried direct to reserves. All other gains or losses should be shown on the face of the profit and loss account. However, two types of item receive special treatment:

(a)   *Extraordinary items*, defined in SSAP 6 as:

Those items which derive from events or transactions outside the ordinary activities of the business and which are both material and expected not to recur frequently or regularly. They do not include items which, though exceptional on account of size or incidence (and which may therefore require separate disclosure), derive from the ordinary activities of the business. Neither do they include prior-year items merely because they relate to a prior year.

(b)   *Prior-year adjustments*, defined in SSAP 6 as:

Those material adjustments applicable to prior years arising from changes in accounting policies and from the correction of fundamental errors. They do not include the normal corrections and adjustments of accounting estimates made in prior years.

SSAP 6 requires that the profit and loss account should include the following elements:

(a)   A figure of profit or loss for the year arising from ordinary activities, excluding extraordinary items and prior-year adjustments, should be shown, together with related taxation.

(b)   A figure of extraordinary items net of related taxation should be separately identified in the profit and loss account. A note to the accounts should explain the nature and size of each extraordinary item.

(c)   Where there are prior-year adjustments these should be accounted for by restating prior years, so that the opening balance of retained profits will be adjusted accordingly. A statement of retained profits should be shown immediately following the profit and loss account, disclosing the impact on retained profits as previously reported of the adjustment. A note to the accounts should disclose the nature of each prior-year adjustment.

Wardes plc – Group Profit and Loss Account for the year ended 31 December 1986

	1986		1985	
	£000	£000	£000	£000
Turnover		12 260		12 140
Cost of sales		9 780		9 860
Gross profit		2 480		2 280
Distribution costs	640		610	
Administrative expenses	980		910	
		1 620		1 520
Trading profit		860		760
Share of profits of associated companies		310		290
		1 170		1 050
Investment income		110		90
		1 280		1 140
Interest payable		280		270
Profit on ordinary activities before tax		1 000		870
Tax on profit on ordinary activities		350		310
Profit on ordinary activities after tax		650		560
Minority interests		105		90
Profit before extra-ordinary items		545		470
Extraordinary items		110		(65)
Profit attributable to members of the holding company		655		405
Dividends		300		250
Retained profit for the year		355		155
Statement of group retained profit				
Retained profit for year		355		155
Retained profits as at January 1 1986:				
As previously reported	1 335		1 210	
Prior-year adjustment	210		180	
As restated		1 545		1 390
Retained profits as at 31 December 1986		1 900		1 545

Figure 6.2

The way in which a company might comply with these requirements is shown in Fig. 6.2 and discussed below in detail when considering the significance of each item in that example.

Another term which accountants have come to use is 'exceptional item', defined in ED 36 as: 'those items which whilst deriving from events or transactions that fall within the ordinary activities of the company, need to be disclosed separately by virtue of their size or incidence if the financial statements are to give a true and fair view'.

Such items will be included in arriving at the figure of profit or loss on ordinary activities. Both the Companies Act and SSAP 6 require that such items be disclosed in the notes to the accounts. ED 36 argues that it may sometimes be necessary to identify exceptional items on the face of the profit and loss account.

In practice, items included in the computation of profit or loss on ordinary activities are often referred to as falling 'above the line' while extraordinary items fall 'below the line'. An analyst might be expected to regard items 'above the line' as significant indicators of trends in the trading position, while items 'below the line' will only be significant insofar as they have an immediate effect in increasing or reducing the resources of the business. The computation of the widely quoted 'earnings per share' figure, discussed in detail below, is based on profit excluding extraordinary items. Thus the decision on whether or not an item should be classified as 'extraordinary' can have a material effect on the picture given by the accounts.

To illustrate the problems of classifying an item, let us consider the example of the costs that arise as a result of a decision to close a division of the business. Such closure costs would normally be an extraordinary item, since they are likely:

(a) To be material.
(b) Not to be part of ordinary activities.
(c) Not likely to recur regularly or frequently.

However, there may be circumstances where these assumptions do not apply. For example, a company with a number of operating divisions might regularly review the range of activities with a view to closing some and commencing others.

Because of the unavoidable element of management discretion in distinguishing between 'exceptional' and 'extraordinary' items, the analyst of a set of accounts should consider each item carefully and decide whether to reclassify it when interpreting the accounts.

Presentation of the published profit and loss account

Figure 6.2 shows an example of how a published profit and loss account might be presented in compliance with the Companies Act 1985 and SSAP 6. This is the 'Group' profit and loss account, embracing the holding company and also all the companies it controls, as explained in Chapter 9 below.

The first stage, down to 'trading profit', shows the minimum information required by company law where a 'type of operation' format is chosen. An alternative 'type of expenditure' format is also permitted, as illustrated in Fig. 6.3, but this is less commonly used. The term 'operating profit' might be used in place of 'trading profit'.

The next stage is to show income from *associated companies*, being other companies where the group does not have control but does have significant influence. The accounting treatment of these is explained in detail in Chapter 9 below. Some companies take the view that the term 'operating profit' should include income from these associated companies.

Next we add on investment income and deduct interest payable. The profit at this stage shows our total income from ordinary activities. At this stage is shown the tax on these ordinary activities.

The next item, 'minority interests', represents that part of profit which relates to other shareholders in companies which are controlled by the holding company but not totally owned by it. The term is examined in detail in Chapter 9 below.

We now come to 'extraordinary items'. These, as we have seen above, will be shown net of related taxation, and will be explained in a note to the accounts.

Finally, dividends are deducted to arrive at retained profit.

	1986		1985	
	£000	£000	£000	£000
Turnover		12 260		12 140
Changes in stock		120		90
		12 380		12 230
Raw materials	5 100		5 200	
Other external charges	180		170	
Staff costs	4 000		4 050	
Depreciation	1 900		1 800	
Other operating charges	340		250	
		11 520		11 470
Trading profit		860		760

Figure 6.3   Wardes PLC – alternative first section of the profit and loss account

Immediately following the profit and loss account, a statement of retained profits shows the effect of the 'prior-year adjustment', which will be fully described in a note to the accounts. The 1985 comparative profit and loss figures will also have been adjusted to reflect the new accounting policy or correct the fundamental error.

Earnings per share

A simple way to relate the figures in the profit and loss account to the individual shareholder is to compute a ratio of *earnings per share*. This ratio is considered in detail in 'SSAP 3: Earnings per share'. The standard requires all *listed* companies to disclose the earnings per share figure on the face of the profit and loss account, and gives detailed guidance as to the computation of the earnings per share figure.

SSAP 3 first requires disclosure of 'basic' earnings per share (EPS) computed by reference to shares actually in issue and ranking for dividend. The ratio is computed as:

$$\frac{\text{Profit after tax, and before extraordinary items, less minority interest and preference dividend}}{\text{Ordinary shares in issue and ranking for dividend}}$$

This is known as the 'net' basis. We will illustrate the computation of earnings per share by reference to Example 6.1 Lubin plc. Taking assumption (a) in that example:

$$1986 \frac{2\,500 - 100}{12\,000} = 20\text{p}$$

$$1985 \frac{2\,260 - 100}{12\,000} = 18\text{p}$$

This 'net' basis is criticized by some authorities on the grounds that the amount of 'irrecoverable ACT' (explained in Chapter 7 below), which has been included in the tax charge, is dependent on the level of dividend. They argue that it would be more meaningful to compute earnings per share on a 'nil' basis, adding back irrecoverable

ACT to profit so that all companies are comparable irrespective of the level of dividend. On this basis the 1986 earnings per share would be computed, following assumption (a) in our example, as:

$$\frac{2\,500 - 100 + 390}{12\,000} = 23.25\text{p}$$

SSAP 3 urges disclosure of earnings per share on the 'nil' as well as the 'net' basis where the difference between the two exceeds 5 per cent.

So far we have been concerned with the definition of earnings, and have defined this in two ways, the 'net' basis and the 'nil' basis. We now turn to the problems that can arise in identifying the number of shares when there is any change in share capital during the year. SSAP 3 lays down rules which depend on the nature of a new share issue as follows:

(a) *Issue at full market price.* A share issue of this kind increases the number of shares and at the same time introduces new resources into the business, and so improves earning capacity as from the date of the share issue. It is therefore appropriate to take the weighted average number of shares in the year of issue. Taking assumption (b) in our example, we compute this as:

$$
\begin{array}{lr}
\text{Pre-share issue} \quad 8/12 \times 12\,000\,000 = & 8\,000\,000 \\
\text{Post-share issue} \ 4/12 \times 13\,500\,000 = & \underline{4\,500\,000} \\
& \underline{12\,500\,000}
\end{array}
$$

On the net basis, earnings per share will be:

$$\frac{2\,500 - 100}{12\,500} = 19.2\text{p}$$

(b) *Bonus issue.* In this case the share issue does not involve the injection of any new resources into the business and so does not increase its earning capacity. All that has happened is that effectively the shares have been partially divided. Therefore we compute earnings per share on the basis of total shares following the bonus issue, and to ensure comparability we similarly adjust the comparative figure for EPS as the bonus issue had taken place in the previous year. Taking assumption (c) in our example, the number of shares following the bonus issue will be:

$$
\begin{array}{lr}
\text{Original number} & 12\,000\,000 \\
\text{1 to 10 issue} & \underline{1\,200\,000} \\
\text{New number} & \underline{13\,200\,000}
\end{array}
$$

So that the net EPS is:

$$1986 \quad \frac{2\,500 - 100}{13\,200} = 18.2\text{p}$$

$$1985 \quad \frac{2\,260 - 100}{13\,200} = 16.4\text{p}$$

(c) *Rights issue.* As we have already seen in Chapter 5 a rights issue is normally at a discount, so that it can be regarded as a mixture of a bonus issue and a full price issue. In computing our number of shares, we wish to treat the bonus element as covering the whole current year as well as the previous year, while including the full price element on a weighted average basis. In order to do this we compute the *theoretical ex rights price*, being:

$$\frac{\text{(Number of old shares} \times \text{Old market price)} + \text{(Proceeds of rights issue)}}{\text{Number of new shares}}$$

The old market price, known as the *actual cum rights price*, is taken as the share price actually prior to the rights issue. For our example, taking assumption (d), this will be:

Number of shares		*Price/cash*		£
2	×	2.10	=	4.20
1	×	1.80	=	1.80
3				6.00

$$\therefore \frac{£6}{3} = \underline{\underline{£2}}$$

Having ascertained this figure, then we compute the weighted average number of shares for the current year by the normal method, except that we multiply the number of shares prior to the issue by the factor:

$$\frac{\text{Actual cum rights price}}{\text{Theoretical ex rights price}}$$

Thus for our example:

Pre-issue	$12\,000\,000 \times 8/12 \times 2.10/2.00 =$	$8\,400\,000$
Post-issue	$18\,000\,000 \times 4/12$ =	$6\,000\,000$
		$14\,400\,000$

So that on the net basis the 1986 EPS will be:

$$\frac{2\,500 - 100}{14\,400} = 16.7\text{p}$$

The previous year's EPS figure still has to be adjusted. This is done by adjusting the figure previously computed by the factor:

$$\frac{\text{Theoretical ex rights price}}{\text{Actual cum rights price}}$$

Taking the net EPS for 1985 as computed in assumption (a) above, the adjusted EPS will be:

$$18\text{p} \times \frac{2.00}{2.10} = 17.1\text{p}$$

We have now considered the various complications that can arise in computing the basic earnings per share. However, the significance of the earnings per share figure can be materially affected when a company is committed to issuing new shares which will share in future earnings. In this case, SSAP 3 requires disclosure, in addition to basic EPS, of a *diluted* EPS figure which tries to show what the earnings per share would have been if the share issue had taken place at the beginning of the year. The mechanics of this can be quite complex, and SSAP 3 gives guidance on three examples which might arise:

(a) *Shares already issued but not yet ranking for dividend.* To compute the diluted earnings per share on this basis simply involves adding the new shares on to the number of shares so that, taking assumption (e) from our example, the diluted net EPS for 1986 will be:

$$\frac{2\,500 - 100}{12\,000 + 1\,000} = 18.5\text{p}$$

(b) *Convertible loan stock in issue.* In this case we compute diluted EPS by assuming full conversion, adding back related interest net of tax relief to earnings and adding the potential share issue of shares. Thus, taking assumption (f) in our example:

$$
\begin{array}{lr}
 & £ \\
\text{Interest } 2\,000\,000 \times 6\% = & 120\,000 \\
\textit{Less } \text{Tax @ 40\%} & \underline{48\,000} \\
\text{Increased earnings} & \underline{72\,000}
\end{array}
$$

$$\text{New shares} - \frac{\text{Total loan}}{\text{Price per share}} = \frac{2\,000\,000}{2} = 1\,000\,000$$

$\therefore$ 1986 diluted net EPS =

$$\frac{2\,500 - 100 + 72}{12\,000 + 1\,000} = 19\text{p}$$

(c) *Option to subscribe cash for shares.* This is the most difficult case of dilution to quantify, since we cannot know what increased level of earnings would be generated by investing the cash injected by the share issue. SSAP 3 suggests that earnings be estimated by assuming that cash would have earned the return available on 2½ per cent. Consolidated loan stock at the price ruling on the day before the first day of the accounting period. Thus taking assumption (g) in our example, additional earnings would be:

$$
\begin{array}{lr}
 & £ \\
\dfrac{£2\,000\,000}{25} \times 2.5 = & 200\,000 \\
\textit{Less } \text{Tax @} & \\
40\% & \underline{80\,000} \\
 & \underline{120\,000}
\end{array}
$$

So that diluted net EPS would be:

$$\frac{2\,500 - 100 + 120}{12\,000 + 1\,000} = 19.4\text{p}$$

Example 6.1

Lubin plc – Profit and Loss extracts for the year to 31 December 1986

	1986		1985	
	£000	£000	£000	£000
Profit before taxation		3370		3230
Taxation:				
Corporation tax	480		970	
Irrecoverable ACT	390	870	–	970
Profit after taxation		2500		2260
Extraordinary items		(220)		140
Profit after taxation and extraordinary items		2280		2400
Dividends:				
Preference	100		100	
Ordinary	840		840	
		940		940
Retained profit for year		1340		1460

On 1 January 1985 there were 12 000 000 ordinary shares of 25p in issue and ranking for dividend. In addition, the following assumptions are each made independently of the others:

(a) Throughout both years there was no further share issue.
(b) On 1 September 1986 a further 1 500 000 ordinary shares of 25p were issued at full market price.
(c) On 1 April 1986 a 1 for 10 bonus issue of ordinary shares was made.
(d) On 1 September 1986 a 1 for 2 rights issue was made at a price of £1.80 per share. The market price immediately prior to the issue was £2.10.
(e) On 1 January 1985, 1 000 000 new ordinary shares were issued. They will rank for dividend as from 1 July 1987.
(f) On 1 January 1986, £2 000 000 of 6 per cent convertible loan stock was issued. This is convertible into ordinary shares at £2 per share in the period 1991–3. Assume a marginal tax rate of 40 per cent.
(g) On 1 January 1986 'options to buy' 1 000 000 shares at a price of £2 per share at any time during 1988 were granted. The price of 2½ per cent consolidated stock on 31 December 1985 had been £25. Assume a marginal tax rate of 40 per cent.

The earnings per share figure is probably the most quoted figure from the accounts.

Conclusion

In this chapter we have considered the nature and significance of the information given in a company's published profit and loss account.

Questions

6.1 The financial director of Portland Ltd has prepared the following information with a view to drawing up the company's profit and loss account for the year to 30 June 1983:

	£000
Retained profit at 1 July 1982	7 200

Turnover	17 500
Cost of sales (Note 1)	10 800
Loss on closure of factory in Scotland	760
Administraton expenses (Note 2)	3 600
Distribution costs	1 200
Taxation (Note 3)	635
Dividends paid and proposed	100

Notes:

1.   The calculation of cost of sales includes opening stock of £1 000 000 and closing stock of £1 200 000, each valued on the marginal cost basis. The directors have since decided that the total cost basis gives a fairer presentation of the company's results and financial position, and the auditors agree with this assessment. Using the total cost basis, opening stock should be valued at £1 425 000 and closing stock at £1 840 000. You may ignore the effect on tax payable of this change in the method of stock valuation.

2.   Administration expenses include bad debts of £850 000. Bad debts are normally in the region of £100 000 per annum, whereas the figure for the current year includes a loss of £750 000 incurred when a major customer went into liquidation.

3.   The figure for taxation is made up of the following items:

	£000	£000
Tax payable on 'normal' trading profit		1180
Less Tax relief on bad debt arising from liquidation of a major customer	375	
Tax relief arising from l0ss on closure of factory in Scotland	170	545
		635

Required:

(a)   Define exceptional items and extraordinary items in accordance with the provisions of Statement of Standard Accounting Practice 6. Give two examples of each.

(b)   Prepare the profit and loss account and statement of retained earnings of Portland Ltd, not necessarily in a form suitable for publication but in accordance with good accounting practice and complying with the provisions of Statement of Standard Accounting Practice 6.

(AIB, September 1983)

6.2   Barry Public Limited Company is considering raising £12 million to finance an expansion programme. Its current balance sheet shows:

at 31 May 1982

	£000
Fixed assets	13 600
Net current assets	8 400
Share capital (£1 nominal shares)	10 000
Reserves	12 000

Its profit statement for the year ending 31 May 1982 shows:

Profit before tax	5 500
Less: Corporation tax	2 200
Profit after tax	3 300
Ordinary dividends	792

The additional investment is expected to generate £2 million additional pre-tax profit during the year ending 31 May 1983, and the anticipated tax rate will be 40 per cent. Without the additional investment, pre-tax profits should remain steady at the 1981—2 levels.

Several financing options are open:

(i) issuing debentures at 16 per cent per annum;
(ii) issue of 12 per cent preference shares;
(iii) rights issue at £6.00.

You are required to:

(a) compute the forecast earnings per ordinary share without any additional investment;
(b) compute the forecast earnings per share for each option (i) to (iii) individually; and
(c) comment on the gearing implications of the three options as shown in the respective profit and loss accounts and year-end balance sheets.

(Cert.Dip. in Accounting & Finance, June 1982)

6.3 Coningsby plc showed the following results for 1986 and 1985:

	1986		1987	
	£000	£000	£000	£000
Profit before taxation		1975		1820
Taxation		765		720
		1210		1100
Extraordinary item		190		—
		1020		1100
Dividends:				
Preference	200		200	
Ordinary	500		450	
		700		650
Retained profit		320		450

Share capital for Coningsby had moved:

	Ordinary shares of £1	10% preference shares of £1
At 1 Jan 85	12 000 000	2 000 000
Issue at full market price 1 July 85	1 500 000	—
At 31 Dec 86	13 500 000	2 000 000

The extraordinary item consisted of costs of £300 000, less related tax relief of £110 000, relating to closing down one of the manufacturing divisions of the company.

Required:

(a) Compute the earnings per share for 1985 and 1986. Also recompute the 1985 earnings per share as though the extraordinary item had been reclassified as exceptional.
(b) Briefly describe the requirements of SSAP 6 relating to the definition and

accounting treatment of exceptional items, extraordinary items and prior-year adjustments. Discuss the circumstances in which the accounting treatment of closure costs by Coningsby plc might, and might not, be justified.

6.4 The profit and loss account of Wildfell for the years ending 31 December 1986 and 31 December 1985 showed:

	1986		1987	
	£000	£000	£000	£000
Operating profit		3888		3320
Interest payable		250		250
Profit before tax		3638		3070
Taxation:				
Corporation tax	538		480	
Irrecoverable ACT	410		390	
		948		870
Profit after tax		2690		2200
Extraordinary items		(190)		–
Profit attributable to shareholders		2500		2200
Preference dividend	80		80	
Ordinary dividend	920		800	
		1000		880
Retained profit		1500		1320

The number of ordinary shares of £1 in issue during the period moved as follows:

At 1 Jan 85	10 000 000
Bonus issue 1 May 85	2 000 000
Rights issue 1 Sep 85	3 000 000
At 1 Jan 86	15 000 000

(i) The rights issue was a 1 for 4 issue at 1.20 per share. The share price immediately prior to the share issue was £2.20.

(ii) The interest payable was on £5 000 000 of 5 per cent convertible loan stock, convertible at £1.25 per share at any time in the years 1988–90. The marginal tax rate is 40 per cent in both years.

You are required:

(a) To compute the earnings per share figures for 1985 as they would be shown in the 1985 accounts.

(b) To compute the earnings per share figures to be shown in the 1986 accounts.

6.5 Brocmar plc has 10 million ordinary £0.50 shares in issue. The market price of the shares is £1.80. The Board of the company wishes to finance a major project at a cost of £2.88 million. Forecasts suggest that the implementation of the project will add £0.4 million to after-tax earnings available to ordinary shareholders in the coming year. After-tax earnings for the year just completed were £2 million, but this figure is expected to decline to £1.80 million in the coming year if the project proposed is not undertaken. A rights issue at a 20 per cent discount on the existing market price is proposed. Issue expenses can be ignored.

Required:

(a) To assist the Board in coming to a final decision you are required to present information in the following format:

Project not undertaken
 (i)   Earnings per share for the coming year
Project undertaken and financed by a rights issue
 (ii)   Rights issue price per share
(iii)   Number of shares to be issued
 (iv)   Earnings per share for the coming year
 (v)   The theoretical ex rights price per share
All workings should be separately shown.

(b)   What information other than that provided in the question is needed before the Board can make the investment decision?

(Cert.Dip. in Accounting & Finance, June 1983)

6.6   Ashcroft plc, a family-controlled company, is considering raising additional funds to modernize its factory. The scheme is expected to cost £2.34 million and will increase annual profits before interest and tax from 1 January 1984 by £0.6 million. A summarized balance sheet and profit and loss account is shown below. Currently the share price is 200p.

Two schemes have been suggested. Firstly, 1.3 million shares could be issued at 180p (net of issue costs). Secondly, a consortia of six city institutions have offered to buy debentures from the company totalling £2.34 million. Interest would be at the rate of 13 per cent per annum and capital repayments of equal instalments of £234 000 starting on 1 January 1985 would be required.

Ashcroft plc
Balance Sheet at 31 December 1983

	£ million	£ million
Fixed assets (net)		1.4
Current assets:		
Stock	2.4	
Debtors	2.2	
	4.6	
Creditors: amounts falling due within one year		
Creditors	2.7	
Corporation tax	0.6	
Proposed final dividend	0.2	
	3.5	
Net current assets		1.1
Total assets less current liabilities		2.5
Capital and reserves:		
Called-up share capital, 25p ordinary shares		1.0
Profit and loss account		1.5
		2.5

Ashcroft plc
Profit and Loss Account year ended 31 December 1983

	£ million
Turnover	11.2
Profit on ordinary activities before tax	1.2
Taxation on profit on ordinary activities	0.6
Profit on ordinary activities after tax	0.6
Dividends (net)	0.3
Retained profit for the financial year	0.3

Assume corporation tax is charged at the rate of 50 per cent.

Required:

(a)   Compute the earnings per share for 1984 under the debt and the equity alternatives.
(b)   Compute the level of profits before debenture interest and tax at which the earnings per share under the two schemes will be equal.
(c)   Discuss the considerations the directors should take into account before deciding upon debt or equity finance.

(Cert.Dip. in Accounting & Finance, June 1984)

7 Business taxation

Objectives

The basic objective of this chapter is to convey an understanding of the signficance of the various amounts reported in the accounts relating to taxation. Accordingly we consider:

(a)   A very brief outline of types of taxation affecting business income in the UK.
(b)   A brief outline of the corporation tax system.
(c)   The rules for accounting for advance corporation tax and deferred taxation.
(d)   A brief summary of the treatment of value-added tax in the accounts.

This is a brief chapter with strictly limited objectives. It does *not* attempt to provide a comprehensive view of business taxaton.

There are a number of ways in which a business will be concerned with the raising of revenue by the government, including:

(a)   Taxes may be levied in relation to certain services consumed by the business, such as rates or motor vehicle duties. Similarly, excise duties might be charged on items purchased by the business such as petrol. These will be shown as part of the expenses recorded in the profit and loss account.
(b)   The business may be required to deduct tax at source from payments made to other parties. An example is income tax deducted from employees' emoluments under the PAYE system. In such a case the expense incurred is shown gross in the accounts, while any amount deducted and not yet paid over at the accounting date will be shown in the balance sheet as a creditor.
(c)   The business may be required to collect indirect taxation on items sold to customers and pay this over to the appropriate authorities. The most common situation where this arises is in relation to value-added tax, considered in more detail below.
(d)   A liability to tax may arise on the income earned by the business and on capital gains relating to business assets. A company will itself be liable to *corporation tax* on such income and gains, so that a company's accounts must report the tax position in detail. On the other hand, sole traders and partnerships do not form independent legal entities, so that taxation on their income is a personal liability of the proprietors and will not be reflected in the business accounts; if a cheque for such a tax payment were drawn on the business bank account it would be recorded as 'drawings'.

Corporation tax

For taxation purposes, income is classified under six major headings, known as schedules, designated by the letters A to F. Within some schedules, certain subheadings known as 'cases', designated numbers, provide a further breakdown of categories. Each schedule and case has its own rules for the computation of income. Business income will, in the main fall under the headings:

Schedule D Case I Profits or gains of a trade
Schedule D Case II Profits or gains of a profession or vocation

For an individual the income from all sources is computed and totalled, from this is taken away personal allowance and certain other permitted deductions such as mortgage interest, and the net amount is then taxed at the following rates for 1985/6:

From	To	Rate (%)
0	16 200	30
16 201	19 200	40
19 201	24 400	45
24 401	32 300	50
32 301	40 200	55
40 200 and over		60

For most taxpayers the first rate, known as 'basic rate', will be the significant one.

For a company, corporation tax is charged at a single fixed rate on total income, without deduction of any form of personal allowance. The rates of tax are:

	Normal (%)	'Small companies' (%)
Year to 31 Mar 85	45	30
Year to 31 Mar 86	40	30
Year to 31 Mar 87	35	30

The small companies rate applies to companies with income less than £100 000, while companies with income up to £500 000 benefit from a rather complex system of marginal relief.

Where a company's financial year does not coincide with the fiscal year, then a weighted average tax rate is used. Thus a company with a 30 September 1986 year end would be taxed at the rate:

	%
6/12 × 40%	20
6/12 × 35%	17.5
	37.5%

Business income is normally computed by taking the profit as shown in the profit and loss account and adjusting this to exclude items which are not taken into account for tax purposes. Such adjustments include:

(a) Any form of capital expenditure or income.
(b) Political and charitable donations.
(c) Business entertainment costs, except for overseas customers.
(d) Any type of appropriation of profit. For example, in a company all dividends (including preference dividends) are not regarded as an expense, whereas interest on a business loan is an expense.
(e) Increases or decreases in a general bad debt provision; by contrast, specific bad debts actually written off or provided against are an allowable expense.

(f) Depreciation, in place of which 'capital allowances' and 'industrial buildings allowances' are given, being depreciation at standard rates laid down by the Inland Revenue.

(g) Income taxable under some other case or schedule. Apart from the special situation of dividends receivable from other companies, considered below, this is normally a purely technical adjustment for a company since such income will be separately computed and then added to the total of income to be taxed.

In addition to corporation tax on income, companies also pay corporation tax at a rate of 30 per cent on capital gains.

Between 1965 and 1973 shareholders in companies could be argued to be suffering taxation on company profits twice over, since profits available for dividend bear corporation tax levied on the individual shareholder and then the individual shareholder pays income tax on dividends received. In 1973 the UK adopted the 'imputation system', designed to ensure that company profits are only subject to taxation once by allowing shareholders to treat a proportion of the corporation tax on the profits of the company as a credit against their own income tax liability. The system is:

(a) Corporation tax is levied on the profits of a company and is payable nine months after the balance sheet date. This is known as *mainstream* corporation tax. Companies trading before 1 April 1965 can preserve the time lag between what was then the end of their base period and the then due date for payment, a period which could extend up to 21 months. Consequently some long-established companies may show two corporation tax liabilities, one for the current year and one for the previous year.

(b) When a company pays a dividend it is required to make a payment of 'Advance Corporation Tax' (ACT) which is computed as:

$$\frac{\text{ACT Rate}}{100 - \text{ACT rate}} \times \text{Amount of dividend}$$

In practice the ACT rate will be equal to the basic rate of tax.

(c) The shareholder receiving the dividend is liable to income tax on the cash amount of the dividend plus the related ACT, while the related ACT (known as *tax credit*) can be set off against the shareholder's own tax liability, and can also be reclaimed from the tax authorities if the shareholder's income falls below the tax thresholds.

(d) A dividend received by a UK company from another UK company is known as *franked investment income*. The tax credit on such income can be set off against the company's own liability to pay over ACT on dividends.

(e) ACT paid during a year can be set off against corporation tax on income of that year, up to a maximum of:

$$\frac{\text{Current ACT rate}}{100} \times \text{Taxable profit (excluding capital gains)}$$

'Unrelieved' ACT can be carried back against mainstream corporation tax for two years or can be carried forward indefinitely, within these limits.

Accounting for company taxation

The Companies Act 1985 requires the disclosure of the following points concerning the tax charge as shown in the profit and loss account:

(a)   The basis for computing UK corporation tax.
(b)   Details of any special circumstances affecting the tax liability.
(c)   The charge for UK corporation tax, and the extent to which that charge has been reduced by double taxation relief.
(d)   Any overseas taxation.
(e)   Any charge for UK income tax.
(f)   Each of the above should be identified separately for extraordinary items.

Two accounting standards deal with the accounting treatment of taxation, SSAP 8 and SSAP 15.

SSAP 8, 'The treatment of taxation under the imputation system in the accounts of companies', covers the following points:

(a)   Dividends received from other companies must be shown as part of profit before tax, grossed up to include related ACT. The related ACT should then be identified separately as part of the tax charge for the year.
(b)   Dividends paid and proposed should be shown at the net cash amount, excluding related ACT.
(c)   A forecast must be made as to whether ACT will be recoverable. For this purpose ACT can reasonably be predicted to be recoverable if it can be offset against a deferred tax liability (explained below) or can be predicted to be recovered against the following year's mainstream tax liability.
(d)   Where ACT is regarded as irrecoverable it must be written off as part of the tax charge shown in the profit and loss account.

Computation and presentation issues relating to ACT are covered in the detailed example below.

SSAP 15, 'Accounting for deferred tax', addresses another accounting problem relating to taxation. We have seen above that there are various differences between the profit or loss reported in the accounts and the income computed for tax purposes. These differences may be split into two categories:

(a)   Non-taxable or non-allowable items, such as dividends income or business entertaining.
(b)   *Timing differences*, being items of income or expenditure included in the accounts in one period and in taxable income in a different period.

Deferred taxation is the tax effect of these timing differences.

The following are the major types of timing difference currently arising in the UK:

(a)   Short-term timing differences. These relate to items treated on a cash basis for tax purposes and an accruals basis for accounts purposes. Examples include royalties and interest, both payable and receivable.
(b)   Accelerated capital allowances. These arise where capital allowances on plant are enjoyed in a different accounting period to the related depreciation write off. From 1972 to 1984, when capital allowances and plant were effectively at the rate of 100 per cent in the year of acquisition, such timing differences could be very substantial. Currently these high allowance rates are being phased out, so that in future capital allowances of 25 per cent on the reducing balance method will apply; these are likely to produce very much smaller timing differences.
(c)   Fixed asset revaluation surpluses. Taxation on such a surplus will only be incurred

if and when the asset is ever sold, so that a capital gain is recorded.
(d)   Roll-over relief. When a fixed asset is sold the company may sometimes, if the asset is replaced, 'roll over' the tax liability on any capital gain until disposal of the new asset.
(e)   Trading losses. These may be carried forward and relieved against future trading profits, thus attracting tax relief in a future year.

The potential deferred tax liability can be computed in two ways:

(a)   The liability method. This involves applying the current tax rate to accumulated timing differences. Thus whenever the tax rate changes, the opening deferred tax balance must be adjusted.
(b)   The deferral method. This involves applying the current tax rate to differences arising in the current year, and reversing previous years' timing differences at the rate applying when they first arose.

SSAP 15 recommends the liability method.

The major controversy relating to deferred tax is the extent to which provision should be made in the accounts. There are three broad approaches:

(a)   The flow-through approach, whereby deferred tax is ignored in the accounts and the actual tax charge as computed in the accounts is recorded as an expense in the profit and loss account.
(b)   Full deferral, whereby the full tax effects of timing differences are recorded in the profit and loss account and the full potential liability is shown in the balance sheet.
(c)   Partial deferral, whereby whether or not provision for timing differences is made depends on whether it is expected that taxation will actually become payable in the future. Taking our major kinds of timing difference:

(1)   Between 1972 and 1984 when 100 per cent first-year capital allowances were given it was common for a company with a steady, planned, replacement programme for plant to find that each year's new allowances more than covered reversal of previous timing differences. With the reduced rates of allowance this is less likely to occur in future except for a rapidly expanding company.
(2)   Timing differences relating to potential capital gains on fixed assets are conditional on disposal without replacement, a circumstance which might well be unlikely to arise in a going concern.

SSAP 15 opts for a partial deferral approach, provision to be required where on balance it is probable that taxation will actually become payable. The standard also requires disclosure of the full potential liability in a note to the accounts, with an explanation of how both the provided and the potential liability are composed.
A deferred tax asset can arise for two reasons:

(a)   Recoverable ACT may exceed the provision on the deferred tax account. As already discussed, such ACT should only be treated as recoverable where it can be offset against tax on the expected profits of the next accounting period.
(b)   Where the impact of timing differences is negative. SSAP 15 gives detailed guidance, to ensure that such a deferred tax asset is only recorded when there is good cause to expect the benefit to arise in the near future.

Example 7.1 gives a simple illustration of how taxation in the accounts might be arranged. The ACT paid during the year will have consisted of:

		£
ACT on dividend paid £35 000 × 30/70	=	15 000
Less ACT on dividend received 14 000 × 30/70	=	6 000
Paid—as per trial balance		9 000

Example 7.1

Janicula Ltd showed the following trial balance at 31 December 19–6, following the first year of trading:

	£	£
Share capital		950 000
Creditors and accruals		180 000
Operating profit		210 000
Interest receivable		50 000
Dividends received		14 000
Plant – cost	100 000	
– depreciation		20 000
Short-term loan	500 000	
Stock	110 000	
Debtors and prepayments	490 000	
Cash	180 000	
Interim dividend paid	35 000	
ACT paid	9 000	
	1 424 000	1 424 000

Notes:
(a) Of the interest £20 000 was accrued income, being actually received in 1987.
(b) First-year allowances of 50 per cent were enjoyed on plant purchased. Because of plans for expansion this is not expected to be a reversing difference.
(c) Corporation tax charge for the year is:

		£
Trading profit		210 000
Interest		50 000
Depreciation added back		20 000
		280 000
Less First-year allowance	50 000	
Interest not yet received	20 000	70 000
		210 000
@ 40%		£84 000

(d) Proposed dividend is £42 000. The ACT rate is 30 per cent.

The profit and loss account and balance sheet for Janicula Ltd are shown in Fig. 7.1. Taking each tax item in turn:

(a) ACT on the dividend received is computed as:

$$£14 000 × 3/7 = £6 000$$

Janicula Ltd – Profit and Loss Account

	£	£
Operating profit		210 000
Dividends receivable		20 000
Interest		50 000
Profit before tax		280 000
Taxation: Corporation tax for the year	84 000	
ACT on dividend received	6 000	
Deferred tax	8 000	98 000
Profit after tax		182 000
Dividend: paid	35 000	
proposed	42 000	77 000
Retained profit		£105 000

Balance sheet

	£	£
Plant		80 000
Current assets:		
Deferred tax	10 000	
Stock	110 000	
Debtors	490 000	
Loan	500 000	
Cash	180 000	
	1 290 000	
Current liabilities:		
Creditors	180 000	
Corporation tax	75 000	
Dividend	42 000	
ACT	18 000	
	315 000	
Net current assets		975 000
		£1 055 000
Share capital		950 000
Retained profit		105 000
		£1 055 000

Figure 7.1

Deferred taxation

	Provided £	Potential £
Short-term timing difference	8 000	8 000
Accelerated capital allowance	–	12 000
	8 000	20 000
Less ACT recoverable	(18 000)	(18 000)
	£(10 000)	£2 000

Figure 7.2 Notes to the accounts

This is added to the dividend and shown as part of the tax charge for the year.

(b) Deferred tax for the year relates purely to the short-term timing difference on interest, being:

$$£20\,000 \times 40\% = £8\,000$$

This is recorded in the profit and loss account and as part of the deferred tax balance shown in Fig. 7.2. In addition, there is a potential liability on accelerated capital allowances:

	£
	£
First-year allowance	50 000
Less Depreciation	20 000
Timing difference	30 000
@ 40%	£12 000

(c) The corporation tax for the year of £84 000 will have offset against it ACT actually paid in the year of £9000, leaving a current liability of £75 000.

(d) ACT payable on the proposed dividend is:

$$£42\,000 \times 30/70 = £18\,000$$

This is shown as a current liability and as a deduction from deferred tax.

(e) The deferred tax account now shows an asset. This is recorded as a 'current asset', because although only recoverable after more than one year it cannot be fitted into any other Companies Act heading. A deferred tax liability would be shown as payable after more than one year.

Value-added tax (VAT)

The workings of the value-added tax system can be illustrated by a simple example, shown in Fig. 7.3.

	Selling Price	VAT	Paid to Customs & Excise
	£	£	£
A Ltd, a producer of raw materials, sells £1000 worth to B Ltd, a manufacturer	1000	150	
A Ltd pays over tax			150
B Ltd produces a manufactured item and sells it to C, a private individual for £1800	1800	270	
B pays to Customs & Excise (270 − 150)			120
Tax paid			270

Figure 7.3

Supposing that A Ltd, a producer of raw materials, sells £1000 worth to a customer B Ltd. A Ltd will add VAT at the current rate of 15 per cent to the invoice, and will pay over this 'output tax' to the customs and excise authorities who administer VAT.

B Ltd performs work on these materials and sells them to an individual C for £1800, charging VAT at 15 per cent being £270. B Ltd has already paid £150 to A Ltd as 'input tax', so now pays over to the tax authorities a sum of £120, being output tax less input tax.

In practice, each individual sale is not matched with a related purchase. What happens is that each quarter the business pays over total output tax less input tax. The effect is that total VAT is borne by the final consumer, having been collected at successive stages as goods and services have changed hands.

Currently in the UK there are two rates of VAT, 'zero rate' and standard rate of 15 per cent. Normal purchases and sales are recorded at their net amount by a business, related VAT being recorded in a separate account which will be cleared by the quarterly settlement with customs and excise. Two major exceptions to this rule arise:

(a) Certain types of trade are 'exempt', so that VAT need not be charged but cannot be reclaimed. In such a business input tax will form part of related costs.

(b) Certain types of purchase cannot have related VAT reclaimed as input tax, motor cars used in the business being an example. In such a case related VAT is again accounted for as part of cost.

These principles are discussed in detail in SSAP 5, 'Accounting for value added tax'.

Conclusion

Taxation appears in the accounts of a company in a variety of ways because a company acts as a collector of tax and also incurs tax on its own income. An understanding of the distinction between these two roles helps us to understand the information on taxation shown in the accounts.

Question

7.1 Lancaster Ltd was incorporated and commenced business in January 1982. The following trial balance was extracted from the books at 31 December 1982.

	£	£
Share capital (ordinary shares of £1 each)		1 000 000
Trade creditors		264 500
Operating profit		315 000
Royalties		90 000
Dividends received		7 000
Fixed assets at cost (purchased January 1982)	200 000	
Provision for depreciation at 31 December 1982		40 000
Stock, debtors and cash	1 469 500	
Interim dividend paid	35 000	
Advance corporation tax	12 000	
	£1 716 500	£1 716 500

The following additional information is provided:

(1) Royalties consist of £65 000 received in cash and £25 000 outstanding at the year end.

(2)   The royalties outstanding give rise to a 'short-term' timing difference as defined by SSAP 15 entitled 'Accounting for deferred taxation'.

(3)   The directors intend to claim a first-year allowance of 100 per cent on the fixed assets purchased in January 1982. No provision for deferred taxation will be made in respect of the resulting timing difference as the directors are in possession of reliable evidence which supports their opinion that it will not reverse in the foreseeable future.

(4)   Corporation tax is payable at 52 per cent on taxable profits of £220 000.

(5)   The directors propose to pay a final dividend of 14p per share for 1982.

Required:

The profit and loss account of Lancaster Ltd for 1982 and balance sheet at 31 December 1982, not necessarily in a form of publication, but complying with the provisions in SSAP 15.

Note: Advance corporation tax should be taken as 3/7th for the purpose of your calculations.

(AIB, April 1983)

8 Additional statements in the annual report

Objectives

The basic objective of this chapter is to consider the statements, in addition to the balance sheet and profit and loss account, which we might find in a company's annual report. One of these, the audit report, has already been considered in Chapter 3 above. Those considered here are:

(a) The directors' report, a statement required by company law.
(b) The historical summary, as required by the Stock Exchange.
(c) The funds statement, as required by SSAP 10.
(d) The value-added statement, a piece of voluntary disclosure offered by some companies.
(e) The chairman's statement, a voluntary statement presented by most large companies.
(f) In addition, we briefly consider the interim accounts as required by the Stock Exchange.

The directors' report

In addition to the profit and loss account, balance sheet and notes thereon, the Companies Act 1985 requires presentation with the accounts of a directors' report including a range of additional information. Broadly this covers:

(a) A review of the development of the company and its subsidiaries during the year, and the typical activities of the company and its subsidiaries during the year.
(b) The amount recommended for dividend and the amount to be carried to reserves.
(c) Any significant changes in fixed assets during the year.
(d) Where significant, the estimated differences between the market value of land and buildings and the amount at which they are shown in the accounts.
(e) The names of all directors during the year and, for all directors in office at the year end, details of any shares or debentures in the company they held at the beginning of the year (or date of appointment if later) and at the year end; for this purpose the interests of spouses and infant children must be included.
(f) Where political and charitable donations together exceed £200, there must be shown:

(1) Separate totals for each.
(2) The recipient and amount of each political contribution over £200.

(g) Particulars of important post-balance sheet events, an indication of likely future

developments, and an indication of any activities in the research and development field.
(h)   Policies for the employment, training and career development of the disabled.
Companies with less than 250 employees are exempted from this requirement.
(j)   Extensive details must also be disclosed where a company has acquired or pledged
its own shares.

The historical summary

In 1964 the Chairman of the Stock Exchange requested listed companies to present
historical summaries of their accounts in the annual report, covering a number of years,
thus helping readers to observe trends in the company's position and performance.
Most listed companies do in fact publish such a summary, covering a period of five to
ten years. Such summaries have to be used with caution for two reasons:

(a)   Accounting policies may have changed substantially over the years.
(b)   Price level changes may make comparisons meaningless.

The funds statement

We have seen that the balance sheet shows the position of the business at a single point
in time, while the profit and loss account shows the results of the activities of the
business between two balance sheet dates. The basic objective of the funds statements,
also known as a 'statement of sources and applications of funds', is to show any changes
in the form in which the business holds resources. SSAP 10, 'Statements of Source and
Application of Funds', requires all companies with a turnover in excess of £25 000 to
present such a statement and lays down certain requirements as to the content of a
funds statement that are considered in detail below.

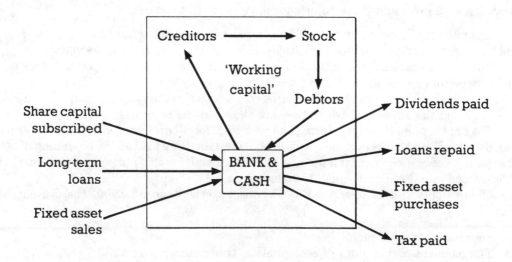

Figure 8.1   A view of the flow of resources through a business

Figure 8.1 illustrates in a simplified diagrammatic form the flow of resources through a business. The box in the centre gives a picture of the 'operating cycle' of a typical business, whereby creditors supply stock, which is supplied to debtors, who pay cash, which is used to pay creditors. Providing the business is trading profitably, these 'working capital' resources should constantly be increased as a result of trading, since we expect the selling price of goods to exceed the related costs of sale. Resources may also flow into the business from outside; three possible *sources* are shown in the diagram. There are also various possible *applications* which might absorb resources; four possible examples are shown in the diagram.

On the basis of this analysis of the way in which resources flow through a business we can see, in Fig. 8.2, the logic of the normal layout of a funds statement:

(a)   First of all we ascertain the inflow of 'funds' into the business from operations.
(b)   We add to this all other sources of 'funds'.
(c)   We deduct from this all applications of 'funds'.
(d)   The net movement can then be analysed into the component parts of 'funds'.

Sources of funds from operations	X
Plus Other sources of funds	X
Total sources of funds	X
Applications of funds	(X)
Net increase/(decrease) in funds	X
Analysis of changes in form in which funds are held	X

Figure 8.2   Simple layout of a funds statement

In this description there is a fundamental omission; we have failed to define the term 'funds' which is the focal point of the statement. We are in good company, since SSAP 10 makes the same omission! In practice, there are two broad approaches to the definition of 'funds':

(a)   The term can be used to embrace all the working capital items in the operating cycle. A funds statement based on this approach would include details of changes in all the items in the working capital box in Fig. 8.1 in the fourth section.
(b)   The term can be used, as in everyday language, simply to mean cash balances at bank and in hand. In this case the fourth section of the funds statement would analyse only changes in these cash balances, described in SSAP 10 as 'net liquid funds', movements in other working captal items being shown as 'applications' or 'sources'.

Both these approaches are found in practice, different companies taking different views as to the most meaningful approach. Below we will illustrate the presentation of a funds statement using an ingenious compromise suggested in the appendix to SSAP 10, whereby 'funds' are in effect defined as working capital, but within the section analysing working capital the movements in cash balances are separately identified and highlighted. It should be emphasized that this form of presentation is not *required* by SSAP 10.

The kind of information which is normally available to us when we prepare a funds statement is illustrated in Example 8.1 Pedro Ltd.

Given two consecutive balance sheets, the easiest way to give a view of the movement of resources might seem to be to list the increases or decreases in each balance sheet item. In fact most of the figures in our funds statement are derived in this way; however, there are a number of situations where this would give an inadequate or misleading view, either because a balance sheet movement is explained by two or more types of flow of resources or because a balance sheet movement does not reflect any real movement of resources at all.

Example 8.1

Pedro Ltd – Profit and Loss Account for the year ended 31 December 1986

	£000	£000
Sales		3000
Less Cost of sales		1800
Gross profit		1200
Administration costs	250	
Distribution costs	160	
		410
Operating profit		790
Loan interest		120
Profit before taxation		670
Taxation		235
Profit after taxation		435
Divided – proposed		210
Retained profit		225

Pedro Ltd – Balance Sheet as at 31 December 1986

	1986		1985	
	£000	£000	£000	£000
Fixed assets:				
Plant (Note 1)		5600		4100
Current assets:				
Stock	450		300	
Debtors	600		400	
Bank	–		841	
	1050		1541	
Current liabilities:				
Creditors	150		120	
Bank overdraft	55		–	
Taxation	235		256	
Dividends	210		190	
	650		566	
Net current assets		400		975
		6000		5075
12% debentures		1000		1500
		5000		3575

Ordinary shares of £1	1500	1000
Share premium	1000	300
Retained profits	2500	2275
	5000	3575

Note 1: Plant movements during the year were:

	Cost	Depreciation
	£000	£000
B/fwd	5000	900
Additions/charge for year	2900	800
Disposals	(800)	(200)
C/fwd	7100	1500

A loss on the sales of plant of 50 000 has been written off as part of cost of sales.
Note: During the year 500 000 new ordinary shares were issued at a price of £2.40 each.

Pedro Ltd – Statement of Sources and Applications of Funds for the year ended 31 December 1986

	£000	£000
Sources		
Profit before taxation		670
Adjustments for items not involving movement of funds:		
Depreciation	800	
Loss of sale of plant	50	850
Generated from operations		1520
Other sources		
Sale of plant	550	
Share issue	1200	
		1750
		3270
Applications		
Plant purchases	2900	
Debenture redemption	500	
Tax paid	256	
Dividend paid	190	
		3846
		(576)
Net increase/(decrease) in working capital:		
Increase in stock	150	
Increase in debtors	200	
Increase in creditors	(30)	
	320	
Movement in net liquid funds:		
Decrease in bank	(896)	
		(576)

Figure 8.3

		£000
1.	*Plant disposal*	
	Cost	800
	Depreciation	200
	NBV	600
	Loss on sale	50
	Sale proceeds	550
2.	*Tax Paid*	
	B f/wd	256
	Charge for year	235
		491
	Less C f/wd	235
	Paid	256
3.	*Dividends*	
	B f/wd	190
	Charge for year	210
		400
	C f/wd	210
	Paid	190
4.	*Share issue*	
	50 000 × 2.4 = £1 200 000	
5.	*Profit for year*	
	Retained profit increase	225
	Add Dividend	210
	Add Tax	235
		670

Figure 8.4 Workings

The presentation of a funds statement for Pedro Ltd is shown in Fig. 8.3 and the related workings are shown in Fig. 8.4. Taking each balance sheet movement in turn:

(a) *Fixed assets:* In our example the net balance sheet movement in fixed assets is explained in Note 1 to the accounts, and is attributable to three causes:

(1) Additions during the year. These are shown as an application of funds.
(2) Depreciation for the year. This represents a transfer from the fixed asset account to the profit and loss account, and does not involve any actual movement of funds. The depreciation charge is therefore shown on the face of the funds statement added back to profit to show funds generated from operations.
(3) Disposals during the year. The movement on the fixed assets account will represent the net book value of these disposals. In the funds statement we show the actual disposal proceeds as a source of funds and the profit or loss on disposal is treated in the same way as the depreciation charge. Working 1 in Fig. 8.4 shows the computation of these amounts.

(b) *Stock.* The increase in stock is shown in the working capital section of the funds statement.

(c) *Debtors*. Similarly the increase in debtors is shown in the working capital section of the funds statement.

(d) *Bank*. The fall in the asset 'bank', combined with the increase in the liability 'overdraft', is separately identified in the working capital section of the balance sheet as the fall in net liquid funds.

(e) *Creditors*. The increase in creditors is shown in the working capital section of the balance sheet.

(f) *Taxation*. Working 2 shows how we compute the actual tax paid during the year. This is then shown as an application of funds.

(g) *Dividends*. Similarly, working 3 shows how actual dividends paid are computed, then shown as an application of funds.

(h) *Debentures*. The fall in debentures is assumed to represent a repayment, shown as an application of funds.

(j) *Ordinary shares and share premium*. Working 4 shows how the increase in these two balance sheet items, taken together, represents funds derived from the share issue.

(k) *Retained profits*. The tax charge and dividend for the year, dealt with above, are added back to the increase in retained profit to give profit before tax, the opening figure in the funds statement.

Another commonly required form of adjustment required arises when a bonus issue of shares has been made; since such an issue involves no movement of resources, the increase in share capital and related fall in reserves are both ignored in preparing the funds statement.

Once prepared, the funds statement gives a useful picture of how resources have moved through the business. It is a particularly useful tool for explaining to the non-accountant why the profit for the year is not represented by an increase in the cash balance.

The value-added statement

A value-added statement aims to show the total wealth created by a business during an accounting period and the way in which this wealth has been shared out. In the UK the ASC strongly recommend the publication of a value-added statement in a discussion document, the *Corporate Report*, published in July 1975. In the *Corporate Report*, the suggested format fell into two parts:

(a) Sales were shown, with all 'bought in' items shown as a deduction, to give total 'value added' by the business.

(b) Application of value added were then shown, under the four main headings of 'Employees', 'Government', 'Providers of capital', and 'Retained in the business'.

Thus the value-added statement takes the data in the profit and loss account and sorts it into a different form, which focuses on the wealth produced by the business and its division among the wealth-producing team. The *Corporate Report* commended the statement as 'putting profit into a proper perspective as a collective effort by capital, management, and employees'. Advocates of the statement have claimed the following benefits:

(a) Presentation of a company's results in this way symbolizes management's acceptance of a broader range of responsibilities than simply to shareholders, and so may help to break down the 'adversary' approach in industrial relations.

(b) Value added is a <u>useful measure of company size in expressing the economic significance of the entity</u>.

(c) Value added is us<u>ed as the basis for a number of government statistics</u>, helping comparison with the company's own performance.

(d) Management can use the statement to <u>demonstrate the contribution made by the company both to government funds and to employees</u>.

We will illustrate the preparation of a value-added statement with the simple example 'Shelthorpe Ltd' presented in Example 8.2.

Example 8.2

The profit and loss account of Shelthorpe Ltd for the year ended 31 December 1986 showed:

	£000	£000
Sales		10 000
Stock 1 Jan 86	800	
Material costs	3 400	
Labour costs (including PAYE £9 000 000)	3 660	
	7 860	
Stock 31 Dec 86	1 000	
Cost of sales		6 860
Gross profit		3 140
Less Expenses	1 520	
Wages and salaries (including PAYE £190 000)	60	
Heat and light	440	
Depreciation	100	
Rent	80	
Rates	220	
Interest	60	
Sundry expenses		2 480
Profit before tax		660
Taxation		340
Profit after taxation		320
Dividend		100
Retained profit		220

The value-added statement for Shelthorpe Ltd is presented in Fig. 8.5. The figures in the statement are derived as follows:

(a) Turnover is as shown in the profit and loss account. Commencement of the value-added statement with the sales figure is invariable in published accounts, but for internal management reports it is <u>sometimes argued that it would be more useful</u> to <u>show the selling price of goods produced in the year as the opening figure so as to identify the value added by the manufacturing process in the year.</u>

Shelthorpe Ltd – Value-added Statement for the year ended 31 December 1986

	£000	£000
Turnover		10 000
Less Bought-in items		3 500
Value added		6 500

Applied as follows:

	£000	£000
Employees' remuneration		5 180
To providers of capital:		
Interest	220	
Dividend	100	
		320
To pay government:		
Corporation tax		340
To provide for maintenance and expansion of assets:		
Retained profits	220	
Depreciation	440	
		660
		6 500

Bought-in items comprise:

	£000
Material costs	3 400
Stock increase	(200)
Heat and light	60
Rent	100
Rates	80
Sundry	60
	3 500

Figure 8.5

(b) Bought-in items are made up as shown at the foot of Fig. 8.5. A number of these items present problems or arouse controversy as follows:

(1) The net stock increase in the year is shown as a deduction from material costs for the year. However, if the stock figure has been computed in compliance with SSAP 9, then it will include a proportion of allocated labour costs. Normally this is regarded as not sufficiently material to require adjustment.

(2) Rent is generally regarded as a bought-in cost. However, some authorities argue that rent is paid in order to enjoy the use of a capital asset and should be regarded as a form of payment to the providers of capital.

(3) Rates are here treated as a bought-in cost, this practice being justified by the view that a payment is being made for services provided by the local authority. The alternative view is that rates should be regarded as a form of taxation and included in the heading of value added allocated to pay government.

(c) Employee's remuneration is computed by taking the figures:

	£000
Labour costs	3660
Wages and salaries	1520
	5180

PAYE is included in these amounts, being regarded as a tax payable by employees and simply collected by the government. The alternative view would be to regard PAYE as part of the total taxation contribution to the government generated by the enterprise as a whole.

(d)   The amounts taken here as payable to providers of capital have been taken as interest and divided. Note that in this context we make no distinction between the providers of loan capital and equity capital.

(e)   The amount paid to government is taken in this case simply to include corporation tax.

(f)   The amount to provide for maintenance and expansion of assets includes both retained profits and depreciation. Arguments for treating depreciation in this way are:

(1)   Depreciation does not involve any cash flow and is therefore more properly regarded as an amount retained out of profit.

(2)   The depreciation charge depends on estimates of asset life and the depreciation method chosen. Thus a figure for bought-in costs which included depreciation would lack objectivity.

The alternative view is that depreciation should be treated as a bought-in cost. In support of this view it can be argued that depreciation is an allocation of the bought-in costs of fixed assets, and it is inconsistent to exclude one particular type of bought-in cost simply because of problems of allocation.

In practice, most companies treat depreciation together with retained profits. Some distinguish between 'gross' value added computed excluding depreciation from bought-in costs and 'net' value added, after deduction of depreciation.

Other problems in the computation of a value-added statement are:

(a)   The treatment of non-trading income. This would most commonly be shown as an addition to value added.

(b)   The treatment of fixed assets constructed by the business for its own use. Two possible approaches are:

(1)   Exclude all costs relating to the construction from the value-added statement.

(2)   Add the cost of the asset to turnover and then split the costs between bought-in items and amounts paid to employees.

(c)   Benefits in kind enjoyed by employees may be classified either as bought-in costs or as employees' remuneration. For example, a subsidy for a staff canteen can be argued to be an expense to promote business efficiency or as an employee benefit.

(d)   Payments to labour-only sub-contractors might, following legal form, be regarded as a bought-in cost or, following their commercial substance, might be regarded as employees' remuneration.

(e)   Excise duties are generally regarded as a bought-in cost but might be regarded as part of taxation.

The value-added statement can form a useful basis for a productivity bonus scheme, in that employees can be offered a share of increased value added produced. In such a case, deduction of depreciation to give net value added is likely to be appropriate, since otherwise there is a danger that the business will not realize the savings in labour costs that new capital investment can be expected to produce.

The chairman's statement

Most large companies include a 'chairman's statement' in the accounts, although there is no regulatory obligation to do so. It is important to bear in mind the content of the chairman's statement is not subject to audit.

The content of the chairman's statement varies. Frequently it will include a review of the performance of individual divisions of the business and an indication of performance since the balance sheet date; sometimes forecasts of future performance are also included. Research has shown that readers of accounts tend to give special attention to the chairman's statement, probably because of the light this kind of information can throw on future prospects.

However, the quality of information in the chairman's statement can vary enormously, and in some cases constitutes little more than a soap box from which the individual chairman can declare his views on the state of the nation!

Interim statements

The Stock Exchange listing agreement includes a requirement for listed companies to prepared a half-yearly interim report. The minimum information to be disclosed is:

(a) Turnover.
(b) Profit before taxation.
(c) Taxation on profits.
(d) Minority share of profit.
(e) Profit attributable to shareholders before extraordinary items.
(f) Extraordinary items.
(g) Profit attributable to shareholders.
(h) Dividends paid and proposed.
(j) Earnings per share.
(k) Comparative figures for the above for the corresponding previous period.
(l) Any supplementary information which the directors regard as necessary to appreciate the results for the period.

Conclusion

In this chapter we have considered a range of additional statements found in the annual report. We have also examined in depth the computation and uses of the funds statement and value-added statement.

Questions

8.1   Ridd Ltd—Balance Sheet at 31 March 1986

	1986		1985	
	£000	£000	£000	£000
Ordinary share capital issued		600		300
General reserve		150		—
Profit and loss account		573		663
		1323		963

Fixed assets

Land and buildings		165		165
Plant and equipment at cost	612		585	
Less Depreciation	(114)		(96)	
		498		489
		663		654

Current assets

Stock	105		168	
Debtors	282		399	
Bank	615		42	
	1002		609	

Less current liabilities

Trade creditors	(144)		(87)	
Corporation tax	(138)		(147)	
Dividends proposed	(60)		(66)	
	(342)	660	(300)	309
Net current assets		1323		963

There were no sales of assets or interim dividend paid during the year ended 31 March 1986. Corporation tax paid during the year was £145 000.

Prepare a sources and applications of funds (funds flow) statement for Ridd Ltd for the year to 31 March 1986.

8.2 Using the balance sheets show below, prepare a statement of sources and applications of funds during 1986.

Doone Ltd—Balance Sheet as at 31 December 1986

	31 Dec 85		31 Dec 86	
	£	£	£	£
Fixed assets				
Freehold property		72 000		72 000
Equipment at cost	394 800		494 400	
Less Depreciation	78 400		120 800	
		316 400		373 600
		388 400		445 600
Current assets				
Stock	94 800		114 000	
Debtors	33 200		46 800	
Bank	—		27 200	
	128 000		188 000	
Less current liabilities				
Creditors	(23 200)		(25 600)	
Bank	(15 600)		—	
Tax	(19 200)		(42 800)	
Dividend	(28 800)		(30 000)	
Working capital		41 200		89 600
		429 800		535 200

Ordinary share capital	240 000	240 000
Reserves	189 600	215 200
6% loan stock	—	80 000
	429 600	535 200

During the year, tax paid was £19 500 and an interim dividend of £3000 was paid. A piece of equipment costing £5000 and with accumulated depreciation of £3500 was sold for £500.

8.3   The following balance sheet had been prepared for Cohen Limited at 31 December 1979:

Balance Sheet at 31 December 1979

	£	£		£	£
Ordinary share capital (£ shares)		800 000	Freehold property at cost		400 000
10% redeemable preference share capital		300 000	Plant and machinery at cost	1 446 600	
			Less Depreciation	617 900	828 700
Reserves		625 500	Investments at cost		230 000
		1 725 500			
12% debenture, 1990		500 000	Current assets:		
			Stock	1 063 700	
			Debtors	682 300	1 746 000
Current liabilities:					
Trade creditors	476 200				
Taxation due 30 Sept 80	196 000				
Dividend	60 000				
Bank overdraft	247 000				
	979 200				
	£3 204 700				£3 204 700

The directors of Cohen Limited are concerned about the fact that the present overdraft is close to the facility allowed by the company's bank. The financial director has prepared the following estimated statement of funds for 1980:

Estimated Statements of Funds for 1980

	£	£
Sources:		
Profit before taxation		437 100
Add Items not involving the outflow of funds:		
Loss on sale of plant (note 1)		3 500
Depreciation		247 600
		688 200
Funds from other sources:		
Sale of investments (note 2)		175 000
Sale of plant (note 1)		2 000
Ordinary share capital (note 3)		240 000
		1 105 200

Applications:

Dividend paid—ordinary shares	60 000	
preference shares	15 000	
Redemption of preference shares (note 4)	300 000	
Taxation paid	196 000	
Purchase of plant and machinery	206 500	777 500
		327 700
Changes in working capital items:		
(Increase) in trade creditors	(43 400)	
Increase in debtors	59 700	
Increase in stock	103 500	
Increase in net liquid funds	207 900	327 700

Notes on the above accounts

(1) Plant which had cost the company £25 000 some years ago will be sold for £2000.
(2) This represents the proceeds arising from the sale of 20 000 shares which had cost the company £7.00 each in 1970.
(3) As the result of the share issue, the company's authorized and issued ordinary share capital will consist of one million ordinary shares of £1 each.
(4) The preference share capital is to be redeemed, at par value, on 1 July 1980.
(5) The freehold property is to be revalued during 1980. It is expected that a firm of professional valuers will place a figure of approximately £660 000 on the property, and this revised figure will be written into the books.
(6) Tax payable on the estimated profits for 1980, including the capital gain on the sale of investments, will be £203 800, and the directors propose to pay a final dividend of 10p on each ordinary share.

Required:

The estimated balance sheet of Cohen Limited at 31 December 1980, presented in vertical format and taking account of the above information. You should show clearly how the figure for reserves, appearing in the forecast balance sheet, has been calculated.

Note: Ignore advance corporation tax.

(AIB, September 1980)

8.4 The following data has been prepared for the managing director of a small packaging company as part of the planning process shortly after the financial year end.
    Summarized financial data relating to Penryn Limited:

Financial year	1980–1	1981–2	1982–3
Weeks	52	52	52
Year-end balance sheet data	£000	£000	£000
	Actual	*Actual*	*Forecast*
Net fixed assets	120	130	150
Stocks	107	124	170
Debtors	230	341	491
Bank loan*	59	49	39
Current liabilities[†]	100	203	150
Shareholders' capital	200	200	200
Retained profit	128	158	?
Cash position	30	15	?

*Repayable in equal instalments

†Primarily trade payables

Other information for financial years	£000	£000	£000
Fixed asset acquisitions‡	15	34	46
Turnover	1300	1587	1988

‡Disposals negligible.

The company has in the past paid out 40 per cent of its profits as dividends and the managing director intends to continue this practice and has already forecast £32 000 as dividends for the financial year 1982–3.

The managing director has now asked for a preliminary appraisal of the forecast on the company's cash flow, and at the first stage will ignore the impact of taxation as it has been of negligible importance in the past.

You are required to:

(a) Prepare a budget statement of source and application of funds for the year ending 31 May 1983, in a format suitable for presentation to the managing director.
(b) Provide a statement of the explanations and implications of the results shown in (a).
(c) Provide an analysis of two options available for improving the cash flow assuming the company is unwilling to raise further long-term debt finance.

(Cert.Dip. in Accounting & Finance, June 1982)

8.5 The summarized added-value statements shown below relate to a group which consists of three manufacturing divisions:

£000 year ended 31 August

	1979	1980	1981	1982	1983
Sales	230	240	350	360	470
Bought-in materials and outside services	105	110	165	170	225
Added value	125	130	185	190	245
Applied as follows:					
To employees	65	65	80	80	95
To government	10	15	5	20	15
To providers of capital	20	25	30	35	40
Retained (including depreciation 10, 10, 50, 50, 70)	30	25	70	55	95
	125	130	185	190	245

You are required to:

(a) describe, briefly, the purposes of an added-value statement and its advantages to shareholders compared with a profit and loss account;
(b) state and comment upon the arguments for and against including depreciation in the lower half of the statement; and
(c) describe, with numerical data and ratios if appropriate, how this summary could provide a basis for a productivity or profit-making scheme.

(Cert.Dip. in Accounting & Finance, June 1984)

8.6 Exhibit I and II detail the annual accounts of Advanced Techniques Public Limited Company.

Required:

Using the information given below, prepare a value-added statement for the company for the year ended 31 October 1981, identifying the main features and assumptions of your presentation.

Notes on Exhibits I and II

(a) An analysis of the trading profit and loss account reveals:

		£000
(i)	Manufacturing wages:	
	Net amount paid	4574
	PAYE and national insurance	1115
(ii)	All other wages, salaries and fees:	
	Net amount paid	1435
	PAYE and national insurance	560
(iii)	Material consumed	5110
(iv)	Power, light and heat	1321
(v)	Other production costs	2431
(vi)	Rates paid	1074
(vii)	Bank interest and charges	320
(viii)	Loan interest	792
(ix)	Administration costs	484
(x)	Research and development costs	140

(b) During the year the company constructed a new synthesis plant for their own use. The cost of the plant was:

	£000
Materials purchased	420
Engineering labour (including PAYE/NI)	374
Sub-contractors' labour	133
Services and other purchases cost	96
Total cost of the plant	1023

The total cost of the plant was capitalized.

(c) Bank charges amounted to £6000.

(d) Royalties are receipts resulting from patents developed by the company's research and development programme.

(e) The investments are trade investments.

(f) The company's value-added tax returns for the year show:

	Net of VAT £000	VAT £000
Sales at 15% rate	17 300	2 595
zero rate	7 040	–
	24 340	2 595
Inputs at 15% rate	9 420	1 413
zero rate	3 750	–
	13 170	1 413
Net VAT paid to the government		1 182

Exhibit 1
Advanced Techniques Public Limited Company
Profit and Loss Account for the year ended 31 October 1981

		£000
Turnover		£24 340
Operating profit		3 547
	£000	
After charging: Depreciation	1437	
Loan interest	792	
Directors: Fees	31	
Other emoluments	420	
Auditors' remuneration	55	
Add Royalty income	49	
Investment income	23	72
Profit before taxation		3 619
Less Corporation tax		1 333
Profit after taxation		2 286
Add Profit and loss a/c		
Balance brought forward		886
		3 172
Less Dividends:		
Preference—Paid	70	
—Proposed	70	
Ordinary —Proposed	840	
Transfer to general reserve	1000	1 980
Profit and loss account balance carried forward		£1 192

Exhibit II
Advanced Techniques Public Limited Company
Balance Sheet as at 31 October 1981

Share capital	£000		*Fixed assets*	£000		
				Cost	Depn	Net
Ordinary shares			Land/buildings	8 245	430	7 815
issued fully paid	3 500		Plant	8 620	3 126	5 494
10% preference shares	1 400		Sundry assets	413	127	286
	4 900			17 278	3 683	13 595
Reserves:						
Share premium	1 000					
General reserves	4 400					
Profit and loss a/c	1 192	6 592	Investments	242		
			Patents	385		627
Long-term loans		6 540				
Current liabilities:			Current assets:			
Creditors	2 065		Stock	3 950		

Accrued taxation	2 420		Debtors	6 130	
Dividends proposed	910		Cash	42	10 122
Bank overdraft	917	6 312			
		24 344			24 344

8.7   You have been employed by the Association of Fitters and Mechanics (AFM), a trade union, to advise them in their negotiations with an employer Ec Ac Ltd. The trade union wishes to argue that the workforce currently receive a small proportion of the total value added by the company, while it is expected that the company will try to argue the opposing case. *You are required to prepare:*

(a)   A value-added statement to be presented by the AFM in negotiations.
(b)   A statement showing how the employers are likely to argue that the value-added statement should be computed. (It is suggested that you show these two statements in columnar form side by side.)
(c)   A brief explanation of the arguments over the treatment of each item which is treated differently in the two statements.

The most recent profit and loss account for Ec Ac Ltd, together with other information, is given below:

	£000	£000
Sales		4780
Less Cost of sales:		
Stock b/fwd	550	
Purchases	3650	
	4200	
Stock c/fwd	600	3600
Gross profit		1180
Wages and salaries	410	
Rent	80	
Rates	70	
Electricity	120	
Catering costs	90	
Interest	110	
Depreciation	140	
Sundry bought-in items	60	1080
Net profit		100
Taxation		50
Profit after tax		50
Dividend		20
Retained profit		30

Wages and salaries include PAYE deductions of £100 000, while catering costs relate to subsidized staff canteen facilities.

(Loughborough University)

8.8   From the information provided you are required to prepare a 'source and application of funds' statement for the year ended 31 December 1988.
   Workings should be submitted.

The summarized balance sheets of Julius Limited as at 31 December 1987 and 31 December 1988 were as follows:

	1987 £	1988 £
Issued share capital	100 000	150 000
Share premium	15 000	35 000
Profit and loss account	28 000	70 000
Debentures	70 000	30 000
Bank overdraft	14 000	–
Creditors	34 000	48 000
Proposed dividends	15 000	20 000
Depreciation: Plant	45 000	54 000
Fixtures	13 000	15 000
	£334 000	£422 000
Freehold property, at cost	110 000	130 000
Plant and machinery, at cost	120 000	151 000
Fixtures and fittings, at cost	24 000	29 000
Stocks	37 000	52 000
Debtors	43 000	44 000
Bank balance	–	16 000
	£334 000	£422 000

The following additional information is relevant:

(i) There had been no disposals of freehold property in the year.

(ii) A machine tool which had cost £8000 and in respect of which £6000 depreciation had been provided was sold for £3000 and fixtures which had cost £5000 in respect of which depreciation of £2000 had been provided were sold for £1000. The profits and losses on these transactions had been dealt with through the profit and loss account.

(iii) No interim dividend has been paid.

(iv) The debentures were redeemed at par.

(v) 50 000 ordinary shares of £1 had been issued during the year at a premium of 40p per share.

9 Developing the traditional framework

Introduction

We have already considered the broad limitations of the traditional accounting framework. In this chapter we consider some specific problems that have risen in the context of that framework, and the ways in which accountants have tried to solve these problems.

The problems considered are:

(a) Group accounts. The traditional accounting framework fails to report fully on the implications of investments in other companies where the investor has a controlling or substantial influence. There are well-established accounting practices in this area, covered by the Companies Acts, SSAP 14, 'Group Accounts', SSAP 1, 'Associated Companies', and SSAP 22, 'Acquisitions and Mergers'.

(b) Foreign currency translation. Where a company enters into foreign currency transactions it is necessary, for reporting purposes, to translate those items into the 'home' currency. An agreed solution to this problem has only been found recently with the issue of SSAP 20, 'Foreign Currency Translation'.

(c) Off-balance sheet items. These are resources or commitments of the business which arise from special forms of legal agreement which do not give rise to conventional assets and liabilities. Examples considered here are leasing agreements and pension commitments.

(d) Current cost accounts. These are a special type of accounts adjusted to reflect the effects of inflation. Currently SSAP 16, 'Current Cost Accounts', covers this topic, but the subject is still controversial and liable to future change.

(e) Post-balance sheet events, covered by SSAP 17, and contingencies, governed by SSAP 18. These two standards give guidance on when such items should affect the accounts, or be otherwise disclosed.

It should be noted that these topics can become very complex and detailed. In this chapter we consider the major issues, but do not claim to give a comprehensive coverage.

Group accounts

When one company acquires shares in another company, the conventional accounting treatment would be to report the cost of the investment as an asset in the balance sheet. This can be misleading for two reasons:

(a) Where the investment represents a controlling interest in the investee company, then the investing company has effective control of all the assets and liabilties of the investee, but the conventional accounts fail to report these individual items controlled by the company.

(b)   Each year the conventional accounts will report the dividend received from the investee company. Where the investor has a significant influence on the investee, it would seem more appropriate to show the investor's share of the profit of the investee for the year, irrespective of whether that profit has been received as a dividend by the investor or retained to earn future profits by the investee.

Accountants have tried to solve this problem by the use of *group accounts* which are accounts designed to report the results and financial position of a holding company and its investee companies together. For the purpose of preparing group accounts, investments can be divided into three broad categories:

(a)   *Subsidiary* companies, where the investor controls more than half the voting equity of the investee and therefore controls the company.

(b)   *Associated* companies, where the investor owns a substantial but not a controlling interest in the investee and is in a position to exercise a significant influence on the management of the company.

(c)   Other investments, which are neither subsidiary nor associated companies.

The most common form of group accounts are *consolidated accounts*, which present the accounts of the holding company and its subsidiaries as though they were a single undertaking. The principles of preparing a set of consolidated accounts can be illustrated with the simple Example 9.1.

Example 9.1

On 31 December 1985, Lenthall plc acquired the entire share capital of Bradshaw Ltd. The accounts of the two companies at that date showed:

	Lenthall	Bradshaw
	£000	£000
Share capital	400	100
Retained profits	300	250
	700	350
Cost of investment in subsidiary	400	–
Fixed assets	560	200
Net current assets	180	190
	1140	390
Long-term loan	440	40
	700	350

To prepare a simple set of consolidated accounts, the accounts of each company concerned are prepared at the end of the year. The consolidated accounts for our example are then prepared in the following stages, and presented as in Fig. 9.1.

(a)   We add together the total of each kind of asset and each kind of liability; these are then shown on the face of the consolidated accounts under the appropriate headings.

(b)   The 'share capital' figure shown on the face of the consolidated balance sheet will be that of the holding company itself.

Lenthall plc – Consolidated Balance Sheet as at 31 December 1985

	£000
Share capital	400
Retained profits	300
	700
Goodwill	50
Fixed assets	760
Next current assets	370
	1180
Long-term loan	480
	700

Workings		
Goodwill	£000	£000
Cost of investment		400
Less Share capital acquired	100	
Retained profit acquired	250	
		350
Goodwill		50

Figure 9.1

(c)   The nature of consolidation goodwill has already been considered in Chapter 4 above. This is computed as:

Cost of investment to the holding company
Less:
The group share of the share capital and reserves of the subsidiary at the date of acquisition

The computation of goodwill for our example is shown in the workings at the foot of Fig. 9.1.

(d)   The consolidated retained profits will consist of:

Total retained profits of the holding company
Plus:
Holding company's share of retained profits of the subsidiary since the date of acquisition.

In Example 9.1 the accounts are being presented at the date of acquisition of the subsidiary, so that only the retained profit of the holding company will be included in the consolidated accounts.

Example 9.1 related to the situation where the holding company owns all the share capital of the subsidiary. Example 9.2. shows an instance where only part of the share capital of the subsidiary is owned by the holding company.

Example 9.2

On 31 December 1985, Downing Ltd acquired 80 per cent of the ordinary shares of Waller Ltd. The accounts of the two companies at that date showed:

	Downing	Waller
	£000	£000
Ordinary shares	200	50
Retained profit	180	150
	380	200
Cost of investment in subsidiary	190	–
Fixed assets	150	50
Net current assets	40	150
	380	200

Downing Ltd – Consolidated Balance Sheet as at 31 December 1985

	£000
Share capital	200
Retained profit	180
Minority interest	40
	420
Goodwill	30
Fixed assets	200
Net current assets	190
	420

Workings

	£000	£000
1. *Goodwill*		
Cost of investment		190
Less Share of share capital	40	
Share of reserves	120	
		160
		30
2. *Minority interest*		
Share of share capital		10
Share of reserves		30
		40

Figure 9.2

The part of the subsidiary not owned by the holding company is called the *minority interest*. When preparing the consolidated accounts, as shown in Fig. 9.2, we continue to add together all the assets and liabilities of the group. There are two differences from the previous example:

(a) It is necessary to compute the minority interest, being the minority proportion (in this case 20 per cent) of the equity of the subsidiary. The computation is shown in working 2 of Fig. 9.2. This minority interest is shown in the consolidated balance sheet immediately after group shareholders' funds.

(b) In this case the holding company, when computing goodwill, only takes into account 80 per cent of the pre-acquisition equity, because the other 20 per cent is part of the minority interest.

Both the examples we have considered so far have involved consolidation at the date when acquisition took place. Example 9.3 shows an instance of consolidation some time after the acquisition date. The preparation of the consolidated accounts is shown in Fig. 9.3. The consolidation is carried out as in the two previous examples but with the new problem that part of the retained profits relate to the *post-acquisition* period.

Rupert Ltd – Consolidated Balance Sheet as at 31 December 1985

	£000
Ordinary shares	500
Retained profits	886
Minority interest	176
	1562
Goodwill	12
Fixed assets	910
Net current assets	640
	1562

Workings

	£000	£000
1. *Goodwill*		
Cost of investment		240
Less Share of share capital	180	
Share of pre-acquisition profit (60% × 80 000)	48	228
		12
2. *Minority*		
Share of share capital		120
Share of profit (40% × 140 000)		56
		176
3. *Retained profits*		
In Rupert's accounts		850
Share of post-acquisition profits of Newcastle (60% × £60 000)		36
		886

Figure 9.3

The workings show that:

(a)   Goodwill is computed by reference to the group's share of *pre-acquisition* profits.

(b)   The minority interest is computed by reference to the whole of the retained profits in the subsidiary, because the distinction between 'pre-acquisition' and 'post-acquisition' profits has no relevance to the minority.

(b)   Consolidated retained profits consist of the total of the holding company's own retained profits plus the group share of the *post-acquisition* retained profit of the subsidiary.

Example 9.3

On 31 December 1981, Rupert Ltd acquired 60 per cent of the ordinary shares of Newcastle Ltd, which at that date had retained profits of £80 000. On 31 December 1985 the accounts of the two companies showed:

	Rupert	Newcastle
	£000	£000
Ordinary shares	500	300
Retained profits	850	140
	1350	440
Cost of investment in subsidiary	240	—
Fixed assets	610	300
Net current assets	500	140
	1350	440

It is important to emphasize the significance of identifying the pre-acquisition reserves of the subsidiary. This is because the pre-acquisition equity of the subsidiary has been purchased by the holding company, and only profits earned after the acquisition date can properly be regarded as part of the retained profits earned by the group. Two problems often arise in the computation of the pre-acquisition equity:

(a) When a dividend is paid by the subsidiary after the acquisition date out of pre-acquisition profits, the holding company should deduct the amount of dividend it receives from the cost of the investment. This is because the dividend received represents a payment back to the holding company of part of the resources it has invested in the company, and does not represent any profit earned since the acquisition. Sometimes the dividend received is credited to the profit and loss account in error, in which case an adjustment should be made on consolidation to rectify the position, i.e. the amount of dividend is deducted from retained profit, and deducted from the cost of investment.

(b) The amount at which the assets of a subsidiary are shown in the historical cost accounts at the acquisition date may not reflect their 'fair value'. SSAP 14 requires that at the date of acquisition the 'fair value' of the assets of the subsidiary acquired must be ascertained. This 'fair value' must then be introduced into the accounts of the subsidiary by a revaluation, or alternatively be introduced into the group accounts by a consolidation adjustment.

Example 9.4 shows how these two issues might arise.

Example 9.4

On 31 December 1984, Suckling Ltd acquired 75 per cent of the ordinary shares of Davenant Ltd, which at that date showed retained profits of £120 000 in the balance sheet; the balance sheet of Davenant Ltd at 31 December 1984 also included a proposed dividend of £20 000.

On 31 December 1985 the accounts of the two companies showed:

	Suckling	Davenant
	£000	£000
Ordinary shares	800	200
Retained profits	310	160
	1110	360

Cost of investment in subsidiary	320	—
Freehold property	250	100
Other fixed assets	310	150
Net current assets	230	110
	1110	360

During 1985 Suckling Ltd received its share of the proposed dividend and credited this to the profit and loss account. No further dividend was paid or proposed by either company in 1985.

At 31 December 1984 the valuation of all the assets of Davenant Ltd was reviewed. All assets were considered to be stated at fair value, except that the freehold property costing £100 000 was estimated to have a value of £140 000. This revaluation was not incorporated into the accounts. Davenant Ltd does not depreciate freehold property.

Suckling Ltd – Consolidated Balance Sheet as at 31 December 1985

		£000
Ordinary shares		800
Retained profits		325
Minority interest		100
		1225
Goodwill		35
Freehold property (250 + 100 + 40)		390
Other fixed assets		460
Net current assets		340
		1225

Workings

1. *Goodwill*

	£000	£000
Cost of investment		320
Less Dividend from pre-acquisition profits		15
		305
Less Share of share capital	150	
Share of pre-acquisition profit (75% × 120)	90	
Share of revaluation surplus (75% × 40)	30	270
		35

2. *Minority*

Share of share capital	50
Share of retained profit (25% × 160)	40
Share of revaluation surplus (25% × 40)	10
	100

3. *Retained profits*

In Suckling's accounts	310
Less Pre-acquisition dividend	15
	295
Share of post-acquisition profit (25% × 40)	30
	325

Figure 9.4

Figure 9.4 shows how a consolidated balance sheet would now be prepared for our Example 9.4. Taking each of our new adjustments:

(a)   The accounting treatment of the dividend received from the subsidiary (75% × £20 000) is corrected in the consolidation workings.

(b)   The revaluation of the freehold property is shown as an addition to the property of £40 000. The revaluation surplus will be a pre-acquisition capital reserve, divided between the holding company's share reflected in the computation of goodwill and the minority share treated as part of the minority interest. Had the revalued asset been a depreciating asset, it would also have been necessary to record depreciation of the revalued part of the asset each year. This would be done by writing off an appropriate portion of the fixed asset, allocating the group share of additional depreciation to post-acquisition retained profits and the minority share to the minority.

Other major issues that arise in the preparation of consolidated accounts are:

(a)   It is necessary to cancel out borrowings between group companies.

(b)   Where fixed assets or stock have been acquired by one group company from another, the cost shown in the balance sheet should be written down to original cost to the group, with the 'inter-company profit' on the sale eliminated from retained profits.

(c)   In addition to a consolidated balance sheet, a consolidated profit and loss account is also presented. This involves totalling the various items of income and expenditure of group companies. In addition to the balance sheet adjustments already considered, it will also be necessary to eliminate inter-company turnover and other charges, cancelled against related expenditure items in the other group company accounts.

We have already considered the term 'associated company', being a company where the investor has a significant influence and a substantial, but not controlling, investment. SSAP 1 gives detailed guidance on how to identify an 'associate'; broadly speaking, normally a holding between 20 and 50 per cent will be an associate. SSAP 1 requires that in the *consolidated accounts* such investments should be accounted for as follows:

(a)   In the profit and loss account the group share of an associate's profit before tax should be shown added on to group profit before tax, the group share of the associate's tax charge should be added on to the group tax charge, and the group share of the associate's extraordinary items and minority interest should be treated similarly.

(b)   Any dividend receivable from the associate is excluded from the group profit and loss account; thus the net effect of these adjustments is to increase the group retained profit by the group's share of the associate's retained profit for the year.

(c)   The group share of the retained profit of the associate since acquisition is added to the cost of the investment in the associate.

(d)   A note to the accounts should show how the total investment in the associate (consisting of original cost plus retained profits) is made up of three elements, being:

(1)   The group share of the associate's net tangible assets.

(2)   The group share of the associate's goodwill.

(3)   The difference between the group share of the associate's net assets at the date of acquisition and the cost of the investment, being a premium on acquisition similar in character to goodwill.

The application of these rules can be illustrated by Example 9.5.

Example 9.5

On 1 January 1985, Byron Ltd acquired 40 per cent of the equity of Eythin Ltd. Byron Ltd has other subsidiary companies but Eythin Ltd is the only associated company of the group. Consolidated accounts for the Byron Group before taking into account the results of the associate, together with the accounts of Eythin Ltd, for the year to 31 December 1985 show:

Balance sheets	Byron Group	Eythin Ltd
	£000	£000
Ordinary shares	1000	500
Retained profits	1640	900
Minority interest	170	—
	2810	1400
Investment in associate	600	—
Goodwill	270	120
Fixed assets	1150	680
Net current assets	790	600
	2810	1400
Profit and loss accounts		
Sales	2050	1000
Expenses	1640	680
Net profit	410	320
Taxation	140	120
Profit after taxation	270	200
Minority share of profit	70	—
Retained profit for year	200	200
Retained profit b/fwd	1440	700
Retained profit c/fwd	1640	900

The group accounts, prepared in accordance with SSAP 1, are shown in Fig. 9.5. Note that:

(a)   To prepare the consolidated profit and loss account simply requires us to add on the group share of the associate's profit and tax charge. The effect of this is to boost group retained profit for the year by the group's share of the associate's retained profit.

(b)   The group's share of the associate's retained profit since acquisition is added both to the retained profits and the investment shown in the balance sheet.

(c)   The computation of the detailed breakdown of the investment in the associate is shown in working 1.

A variation on normal consolidation practice arises when *merger accounting* is adopted. In this case the total retained profits, both pre- and post-acquisition, of the subsidiaries are shown as group retained profits. Such an approach has been legalized in the Companies Act 1981, under strictly controlled conditions. SSAP 22, 'Acquisitions and Mergers', provides that merger accounting can be used where the purchase consideration for the subsidiary consists mainly (at least 90 per cent) of shares in the holding company, and at least 90 per cent of the subsidiary is acquired. The logic of merger accounting is that the shareholders of the subsidiary become shareholders in the holding company, so that the interests of the two companies can be regarded as being 'pooled'. The detailed rules and mechanisms for applying merger accounting are complex and fall outside the scope of this book.

Byron Group – Balance Sheet as at 31 December 1985

	£000
Ordinary shares	1000
Retained profits (1640+80)	1720
Minority interest	170
	2890
Investment in associate (note 1)	680
Goodwill	270
Fixed assets	1150
Net current assets	790
	2890

Note 1 Investment in associate	£000
Share of tangible assets	512
Share of goodwill	48
Premium on acquisition	120
	680

Byron Group – Profit and Loss Account for the year to 31 December 1985

	£000
Sales	2050
Less Expenses	1640
	410
Share of profit of associate (40% × 320)	128
	538
Taxation (140+(40% × 120))	188
Profit after taxation	350
Minority interest	70
Retained profit	280

Workings

Investment in associate	£000	£000
Cost of investment		600
Share of post-acquisition retained profit (40% × 200)		80
Total investment in associate		680
Less Share of associate's assets: goodwill (40% × 120)	48	
Tangible assets (balancing figure)	512	
Total share (40% × 1400)		560
Premium on acquisition		120

Figure 9.5

Foreign currency translation

When a company enages in activities in a foreign country it will become involved with foreign currency transactions. In the case of ordinary purchase and sale transactions this does not pose any great difficulty to the accountant, because the foreign currency paid or received will have to be converted into the company's home currency, and can then be recorded in the accounts at the amount of home currency involved. However, the situation becomes more complicated when an asset purchased, or loan raised, in a foreign currency is still outstanding at the year end. Moreover, a company may have a foreign branch or subsidiary, with accounts which have to be included in the group accounts.

In these cases it is necessary to *translate* the foreign currency item into the home currency so that it can be included in the accounts for the year. The rate of exchange to be used will be either:

(a) The *historical rate*, being the rate of exchange applying at the date when the original transaction took place.
or
(b) The *closing rate*, being the rate of exchange applying at the balance sheet date.

SSAP 20, 'Foreign Currency Translation', considers two major approaches to the translation of foreign currency items:

(a) The *temporal* method. This approach translates items at the exchange rate ruling on the date when their value was established in the accounts. Thus monetary items are translated at the closing rate, because the monetary amount expresses their value at the balance sheet date. Non-monetary items will be translated at the historical rate, unless there has been a revaluation in which case the rate at the revaluation date will be used. In the profit and loss account, depreciation will be translated at the same rate as related fixed assets, while income and expenses during the year are normally translated at the average rate for the year. Proposed dividends and estimated tax for the year are translated at the closing rate.
(b) The *closing rate* method. This method applies the closing rate to all balance sheet items, except for the pre-acquisition equity which is translated at the historical rate. Profit and loss items may be translated either at the closing rate or at the average rate for the year.

SSAP 20 states that the method of translation to be used depends on circumstances. Where the accounts of a 'foreign enterprise' (i.e. branch or subsidiary) are being translated for incorporation into the group accounts, then normally the closing rate method should be used. The exception is that where the foreign company's home currency', then the temporal method must be used. The temporal method is also applied to individual items in a company's own accounts. It should be emphasized that SSAP 20 does *not* give a choice between the two methods, but instead lays down the rules as to when each should be used.

In the accounts of individual companies the temporal method should be used. Example 9.6 shows how a foreign currency translation problem might be presented.

Example 9.6

On 1 January 1985, Hardy Ltd, a UK company, acquired the entire share capital of Bligh Inc., a company registered and trading in Ozland, for a purchase consideration of $65 000 000. To help finance the purchase, a loan of $15 000 000 was raised in Ozland by Hardy Ltd on 1 January 1985.

On 1 January 1985, Bligh Inc. acquired all the plant currently shown in the balance sheet.

The accounts of Bligh Inc. for the year to 31 December 1985 showed:

Profit and loss

	$000	$000
Sales		69 000
Cost of sales		46 000
Gross profit		23 000
Depreciation	6 500	
Other expenses	9 200	
		15 700
Net profit		7 300
Retained profit 1 Jan 85		18 000
Retained profit 31 Dec 85		25 300

Balance sheet

	$000	$000
Plant – cost		65 000
– depreciation		6 500
		58 500
Current assets:		
Stock	25 200	
Debtors	21 000	
Cash	2 600	
	48 800	
Less Creditors	12 000	
Net current assets		36 800
		95 300
Long-term loan		30 000
		65 300
Ordinary share capital		40 000
Retained profit		25 300
		65 300

The exchange rate has moved as follows:

1 January 1985	$25 to £1
Average 1985	$23 to £1
At date stock acquired	$21 to £1
31 December 1985	$20 to £1

Figure 9.6 shows translation by the closing rate method. Note that pre-acquisition profits are translated at the rate applying at the date of acquisition. If there had been any post-acquisition profits prior to the current accounting year these would have been shown translated at the amount as translated in the previous year's accounts. Thus the

'balancing figure' in the translated balance sheet is the profit for the year. If we insert this figure into the profit and loss account, then the difference between this figure and the profit as translated is a gain or loss on translation.

The gain or loss on translation arises because amounts are translated at an exchange rate different to that applying when those items were first entered in the accounts. Under the closing rate method all assets and liabilities are translated at the closing rate, so that it is the *net investment* in a subsidiary that is subject to *exposure* to translation differences.

Profit and loss

	$000	$000	Translation factor	£000	£000
Sales		69 000	1/20		3 450
Cost of sales		46 000	1/20		2 300
		23 000			1 150
Depreciation	6 500		1/20	325	
Other expenses	9 200	15 700	1/20	460	785
		7 300			365
Translation difference		–			580
Net profit		7 300	**		945
Retained profit 1 Jan 85		18 000	**		720
		25 300			1 765

Balance sheet

	$000	$000	Translation factor	£000	£000
Plant – cost		65 000	1/20		3 250
Depreciation		6 500	1/20		325
		58 500			2 925
Current assets – stock	25 200		1/20	1 260	
debtors	21 000		1/20	1 050	
cash	2 600		1/20	130	
	48 800			2 440	
Less Creditors	12 000		1/20	600	
		36 800			1 840
		95 300			4 765
Long-term loan		30 000	1/20		1 500
		65 300			3 265
Ordinary share capital		40 000	1/25		1 600
Pre-acquisition profit		18 000	1/25		720
Profit for year		7 300	*		945
		65 300			3 265

*Balancing figure
**As per the balance sheet translation

Figure 9.6 Translation by the closing rate method

Figure 9.7 shows translation by the temporal method. As with the closing rate method, the equity in the balance sheet is translated:

(a) Pre-acquisition share capital and reserves at the historical rate.
(b) Post-acquisition reserves prior to the current year as translated at the last balance sheet date.
(c) Profit for the current year is a balancing figure.

Profit and loss

	$000	$000	Translation factor	£000	£000
Sales		69 000	1/23		3 000
Cost of sales		46 000	1/23		2 000
Gross profit		23 000			1 000
Depreciation	6 500		1/25	260	
Other expenses	9 200		1/23	400	
		15 700			660
		7 300			340
Translation difference		–			40
Net profit		7 300	*		300
Retained profit 1 Jan 85		18 000	**		720
Retained profit 31 Dec 85		25 300			1 020

Balance sheet

	$000	$000	Translation factor	£000	£000
Plant – cost		65 000	1/25		2 600
Depreciation		6 500	1/25		260
		58 500			2 340
Current assets – stock	25 200		1/21	1 200	
debtors	21 000		1/20	1 050	
cash	2 600		1/20	130	
	48 800			2 380	
Less Creditors	12 000		1/20	600	
Net current assets		36 800			1 780
		95 300			4 120
Long-term loan		30 000	1/20		1 500
		65 300			2 620
Ordinary share capital		40 000	1/25		1 600
Pre-acquisition profit		18 000	1/25		720
Profit for year		7 300	*		300
		65 300			2 620

*Balancing figure
**As per balance sheet translation

Figure 9.7 Translation by the temporal method

In the balance sheet all non-monetary items are translated at the historical rate and all monetary items at the closing rate. In the profit and loss account, when the profit for the year as computed in the balance sheet is introduced, we find there is a translation loss, compared to the translation gain under the closing rate method. This is because under the temporal method it is the net monetary items, which here constitute a net liability, which are exposed, compared to the net investment (an asset) under the closing rate method.

We have now seen how the two translation methods considered in SSAP 20 work and when each should be employed. The final question we have to consider is how translation differences should be treated in the accounts. The basic rule here is that when the closing rate method is used translation differences should be taken direct to reserves, while when the temporal method is used they should be taken through the profit and loss account for the year, shown as exceptional items if sufficiently material. The one exception that may arise to this rule is when the *cover* approach is used.

The 'cover' method may be applied when a foreign investment is financed by foreign currency borrowing. If we consider our example Hardy Ltd. (Example 9.6), in the company's own accounts there are two foreign currency items:

(a)   An investment of $65 000 000 in Bligh Inc. Under the temporal method, which has to be used in a company's own accounts, this will be translated as:

$$\$65\,000\,000 \times 1/25 = \pounds2\,600\,000$$

This will continue to be the amount at which the investment is translated, whatever the foreign currency movement.

(b)   A loan of $15 000 000. At the date raised, the loan will be translated as:

$$\$15\,000\,000 \times 1/25 = \pounds600\,000$$

While the balance sheet date the loan will be translated as:

$$\$15\,000\,000 \times 1/20 = \pounds750\,000$$

The increase in the liability method of £150 000 will be taken through the profit and loss account as a loss on exchange.

This may be regarded as unreasonable, in that the foreign currency loss on the loan might be considered to be compensated for by a related gain in the value of the investment. SSAP 20 therefore permits a company to adopt a 'cover' approach in its own accounts, whereby both the investment in foreign companies and related borrowings are translated at the closing rate, with the net translation difference taken direct to reserves. Such an approach is only permitted:

(a)   If the value of the investment is greater than the amount of the loan.
(b)   To the extent that translation differences on the loan are covered by translation differences on the investment.
(c)   Provided that the cover approach is applied consistently.

In the group accounts the accounting entries to apply the cover approach to investments in subsidiaries in the company's own accounts have to be reversed; otherwise the calculation of the goodwill on consolidation would be 'thrown out' by constant changes in the amount at which the cost of the original investment is translated. However, SSAP 20 permits translation differences on loans used to finance such investments to be set off against the consolidation translation differences and taken direct to reserves, provided that the 'closing rate' translation method is used and the other conditions for a 'cover approach' as outlined above are met.

Leasing and pension commitments

A *lease* is a contract whereby a *lessor*, who owns an asset, agrees to give the right to use the asset to a *lessee* for an agreed period of time in exchange for a specified rental. During the 1970s it became increasingly common for a company wishing to acquire a new fixed asset to enter into a leasing agreement, whereby a financial institution would buy the asset and lease it to the company wishing to use it for a period equal to its expected useful life; the agreed rental would be computed on a basis designed to reimburse the lessor for the total cost of the asset plus interest on the capital tied up in the agreement.

Example 9.7 shows how a business might be given a choice between two ways of acquiring an asset. Note that the commercial substance of either transaction is absolutely identical, in that the company acquires the use of an asset for its entire useful life in exchange for a cash outflow of £1000 at the end of each of the next five years. The legal form of each transaction is, however, very different.

Example 9.7

Lambert Ltd is considering acquiring an item of plant costing £3791. The item has an estimated five-year life with no residual value, and Lambert Ltd uses the straight-line method of depreciation.

Two methods of acquiring the asset are available:

(a)   Monk Ltd has offered to lend Lambert Ltd £3791, repayable by five equal annual instalments of £1000 payable at the end of each year. The implicit interest rate on the reducing balance is 10 per cent.

(b)   Albemarle Ltd has offered to buy the asset and lease it to Lambert Ltd for five years, at an annual rental of £1000 paid at the end of each year

When we consider the traditional accounting treatment for each of the transactions, shown in Fig. 9.8, we find that it differs substantially even though the economic reality is identical. In the case of a loan repayable by instalments, interest is normally allocated by reference to the amount outstanding at the beginning of the year. The workings to Fig. 9.8 show how the interest for each year is computed as 10 per cent of the amount owing at the beginning of the year. Where the asset is purchased, the profit and loss expense consists of:

(a)   The depreciation charge for the year
  plus
(b)   The interest charge.

By contrast, the expense under the lease agreement consists of each year's rental charge.

In the balance sheet the purchase of an asset involves showing the asset and the related loan, while the lease agreement does not involve any balance sheet entry.

There have been two major reasons for the increasing popularity of leasing:

(a)   From March 1972 until the 1984 Budget, 100 per cent first-year allowances were available to companies buying plant and machinery. In practice, many industrial companies did not have sufficient taxable profits to make use of these allowances. When a leasing agreement was entered into, the financial institution acting as lessor could claim the first-year allowance and would pass part of the cash flow benefit on to the lessee by way of a reduced finance charge. Thus leasing effectively acted as a mechanism where the benefit of accelerated capital allowances could effectively be 'sold'.

(b)   Under traditional accounting practice, lease commitments have not been directly identifiable from the accounts. Thus leasing has been a form of 'off-balance sheet' finance, whereas purchase of an asset financed by a loan would reveal an increase in gearing.

Profit and loss account – expenses relating to asset

	Purchase			Lease
	Depreciation	Interest	Total	Rental Charge
	£	£	£	£
Year 1	759	379	1138	1000
Year 2	758	317	1075	1000
Year 3	758	248	1006	1000
Year 4	758	174	932	1000
Year 5	758	91	849	1000
			5000	5000

Balance sheet

	Fixed asset – plant	Loan
	£	£
Year 1	3032	3170
Year 2	2274	2487
Year 3	1516	1735
Year 4	758	909
Year 5	—	—

Workings

	Amount owing – beginning of year	Interest (10%)	Repayment	Amount owing – end of year
	£	£	£	£
Year 1	3791*	379	(1000)	3170
Year 2	3170	317	(1000)	2487
Year 3	2487	248	(1000)	1735
Year 4	1735	174	(1000)	909
Year 5	909	91	(1000)	—

*This is the capital sum borrowed

Figure 9.8

   SSAP 21, 'Accounting for Leases and Hire Purchase Contracts', lays down detailed disclosure requirements relating to lease agreements. The standard divides lease agreements into two types:

(a)   A *finance lease* is one that transfers substantially all the risks and rewards of ownership of an asset to the lessee.

(b)   An *operating lease* is any other form of lease agreement.

SSAP 21 requires lessees to *capitalize* finance leases, recording the transaction as though it were the purchase of a fixed asset by means of a loan. Assets held under finance leases must be identified separately from other fixed assets, and the amount of finance lease obligations must be identified separately from other liabilities. Operating leases are accounted for in accordance with traditional accounting practice.

There should also be disclosed, both for finance leases and operating leases, an analysis of commitments to future rental charges analysed into:

(a)   The next year.
(b)   The next two to five years.
(c)   The amount payable thereafter.

The accounting requirements of SSAP 21 for lessors are broadly similar.

The requirements of SSAP 21 relating to the capitalization of finance leases can be seen as an interesting example of the application of the 'substance over form' concept.

Pension schemes fall into two broad categories:

(a)   Defined contribution schemes, whereby the pension paid out is directly linked to the contributions paid. Normally such schemes are covered by an independent external fund, and the pension contributions paid each year reflect the full cost to the employer.
(b)   Defined benefit schemes, whereby the pension paid is determined by some formula not dependent on total contributions; commonly such schemes specify some fraction of salary in the final years of employment. Although an external pension fund is normally set up to cover such schemes, the employer remains responsible for pension payments and must meet any shortfall in the fund.

In the case of defined benefit schemes it has also been normal practice for employers to regard the regular payments made into the pension fund as representing the cost for each year of employee pension arrangements. However, a number of problems can arise in this case. In particular:

(a)   An actuarial valuation of the pension scheme may disclose that the pension fund is not sufficient. The question then arises as to whether the employer should immediately provide for the unfunded liability.
(b)   A decision to improve pension benefits, applied retrospectively, may create an unfunded liability.

Again the question arises as to whether immediate provision should be made.

The accounting profession have not, as yet, been able to agree a solution to the problems of accounting for pension costs. In studying a company's accounts, therefore, it is necessary to be aware that there may be an undisclosed potential liability for pension costs, even where there is a funded pension scheme.

Current cost accounts

One problem that arises in using traditional accounting statements is that in times of inflation the accounts move further away from portraying the economic reality of the position of a business. This is because the 'value' of money is falling, so that the monetary unit of measurement does not have a constant value. There are two particularly important problems:

(a)   Expenditure will normally be incurred before related income is received, so that in the profit and loss account the amount of expenditure written off against income will be less than its 'value' at the date of consumption. For example, the depreciation charge is made up of the proportion of the historical cost of fixed assets consumed in the year; the current value of the fixed asset consumed is likely, in times of inflation, to be higher. Thus in economic terms, historical cost profit is overstated in times of inflation.

(b)   Assets and liabilities will be shown in the balance sheet measured at the monetary amount paid for them at the time of acquisition. In the case of *monetary* items, being items such as cash, loans, debtors and to creditors, which represent an entitlement or obligation fixed in monetary amount, this will represent their current value whatever happens to the value of money. However, in the case of *non-monetary* items, such as fixed assets and stock, in times of inflation their value will be understated by the historical cost amounts.

The combined effect of overstating profit and understanding the assets will be to report a greatly overstated return on capital employed. If not understood by the users of accounts, this could lead to serious errors of business judgement.

In the UK both the professional accounting bodies and the government have produced a number of proposals to solve this problem. These fall into two broad categories:

(a)   A change from money as the unit of measurement to a new 'current purchasing power' (CPP) unit. Currently, CPP accounting is not widely regarded as practical, but proposals for such a system have been put forward in the past and may emerge again in the future.

(b)   A change from historical cost to *value to the business* as the basis of measurement. This system is known as 'current cost accounting' (CCA) and is currently the subject of an accounting standard, SSAP 16.

SSAP 16 defines 'value to the business' as the *lower* of *replacement cost* and *recoverable amount*, while 'recoverable amount' is defined as the *higher* of *net realizable value* and *present value*. To understand the meaning and significance of this definition we must appreciate that any asset can have three types of 'value' depending on what we do with it:

(a)   *Buy it.* In this case the value of the asset will be represented by *replacement cost*, being the amount that would have to be paid to replace the asset.

(b)   *Sell it.* In this case the value of the asset will be represented by *net realizable value*, being the selling price less all costs of disposal.

(c)   *Use it.* In this case the value of the asset will be represented by *present value*, being the worth of the total future net inflows of cash arising from use of the asset.

'Value to the business' represents the loss the business would incur if deprived of an asset, and for this reason is often known as *deprival value*. The reason is that if a business were deprived of an asset, then the asset would be replaced if it could either be sold or used at a profit, so the loss would be equal to the replacement cost; otherwise the asset would not be replaced, so that the loss suffered would be the higher or what could have been gained from the sale or from the use of the asset, on the assumption that the most profitable course of action would have been pursued.

In practice, the most common measure of 'value to the business' will be 'replacement cost'.

If we consider the two common types of non-monetary asset:

(a)   Stock can normally be sold for more than cost. Otherwise there would be no point in staying in business!

(b)   A going concern would normally expect to continue to carry on trading profitably, so that fixed assets will be replaced when they are consumed on the assumption that future cash flow will exceed cash.

In practice, therefore, current cost accounts are normally prepared on the basis of replacement cost, and the method of preparing such accounts outlined below will proceed on this basis. However, one of the criticisms made of current cost accounting is that there may be situations where in practice 'replacement cost' grossly overstates 'value', and that there is generally no practical way of satisfactorily identifying and quantifying such situations.

SSAP 16 requires most listed, and certain large, companies to present a current cost profit and loss account and balance sheet; these are normally presented in a supplementary statement attached to the main, historical cost, accounts. The preparation of a set of current cost accounts in compliance with SSAP 16 is illustrated by Example 9.8.

Example 9.8

Luttrell plc – Profit and Loss Account for the year ended 31 December 1985

	1985	1985	1984	1984
	£000	£000	£000	£000
Operating profit		230		210
Less Interest		60		60
Profit before tax		170		150
Taxation		80		70
Profit after tax		90		80
Dividends:				
Paid	10		10	
Proposed	20		20	
		30		30
Retained profit		60		50

Luttrell plc – Balance Sheet as at 31 December 1985

	1985	1985	1984	1984
	£000	£000	£000	£000
Fixed assets:				
Plant – Cost		1000		800
Depreciation		180		80
		820		720
Current assets:				
Stock	300		280	
Debtors	410		370	
Cash	40		118	
	750		768	

Less Current liabilities:		
Creditors	208	196
Dividends	20	20
Taxation	80	70
	308	286
Net current assets	442	482
	1262	1202
10% debentures	600	600
	662	602
Ordinary shares of £1	300	300
Retained profits	362	302
	662	602

Notes:

1. Plant movements on the plant account during the year can be summarized:

	At 31.12.84	Acquisition in 1985	At 31.12.85
Acquired 1 Jan 84	800	—	800
Acquired 1 Jan 85	—	200	200
	800	200	1000

Depreciation movements on the depreciation account during the year can be summarized:

	Balance at 31.12.84	Charge for year	Balance at 31.12.85
On plant acquired 1 Jan 84	80	80	160
On plant acquired 1 Jan 85	—	20	20
	80	100	180

2. The average date for stock acquisition is 1½ months before the balance sheet date. Similarly debtors and purchases relate, on average, to transactions 1½ months before the balance sheet date.

3. Monetary working capital is regarded as consisting of debtors and creditors, which on average arose 1½ months before the balance sheet date.

4. Relevant indices moved:

	Stock and monetary working capital	Fixed assets
1 January 1984	79.2	60.0
Mid-November 1984	86.0	76.1
31 December 1984	90.3	80.0
Average 1985	94.6	100.0
Mid-November 1985	100.0	115.2
31 December 1985	104.0	120.0

The first stage in preparing a set of current cost accounts is to prepare a current cost balance sheet. For this purpose, all assets and liabilities have to be shown at their 'value to the business'. For monetary items this will be the same as historical cost. For non-monetary items, such as the plant and stock in our example, it will be necessary to restate the amount from historical cost to replacement cost. The most common method for computing replacement cost is to employ a *specific price index,* which measures movements in the prices of specific categories of goods. The UK government publishes 'Price Index Numbers for Current Cost Accounting' (PINCCA) which gives indices for most types of plant and stock. The estimated replacement cost of non-monetary assets is computed by multiplying historical cost by the factor:

$$\frac{\text{Index at balance sheet date}}{\text{Index at acquisition date}}$$

	HC	CCA factor	CCA
At 31 Dec 85	300	104/100	312
			300
Revaluation surplus			12
At 31 Dec 84	280	90.3/86.0	294
			280
Revaluation surplus			14

Figure 9.9 Stock workings

	HC Cost	HC Depr	CCA factor	CCA Cost	CCA Depr
Date acquired:					
1 Jan 84	800	160	120/60	1600	320
1 Jan 85	200	20	120/80	300	30
	1000	180		1900	350
	180			350	
Net book value	820			1550	
				820	
Revaluation surplus				730	
At 31 Dec 84					
Date acquired:					
1 Jan 84	800	80	80/60	1067	107
	80			107	
Net book value	720			960	
				720	
Revaluation surplus				240	

Figure 9.10 Fixed assets workings

Figure 9.9. shows how this calculation is made for stock. Figure 9.10 shows how it is made for plant; in the case of plant it is necessary to analyse both its cost and the related depreciation. Note that at the same time we also compute the opening replacement cost of plant and stock in order to find out the opening revaluation surpluses; we will need this information when we come to compute the *gearing adjustment*, considered in detail below.

Luttrell plc – Current Cost Balance Sheet as at 31 December 1985

	£000	£000
Fixed assets:		
Plant – cost		1900
Depreciation		350
		1550
Current assets:		
Stock	312	
Debtors	410	
Cash	40	
	762	
Less Current liabilities:		
Creditors	208	
Dividends	20	
Taxation	80	
	308	
Net current assets		454
		2004
10% debentures		600
		1404
Ordinary shares of £1		300
Current cost reserve		828
Retained profits		276
		1404

Figure 9.11

Figure 9.11 shows the current cost balance sheet. The one part which has not yet been explained is the make-up of the 'current cost reserve' and 'retained profits'; to understand this part of the balance sheet we must first prepare the current cost profit and loss account.

The objective of the current cost profit and loss account is to show the results of the operations of the business after allowing for the 'value to the business' of resources consumed during the year. Figure 9.16 shows how, in compliance with SSAP 16, a statement can be prepared which explains the difference between the historical cost and current cost profit.

The first stage is to find the 'current cost operating profit', being the CCA profit earned from operations. This is found by making three adjustments to the historical cost operating profit (i.e. profit before interest):

(a) The *depreciation adjustment*. This reflects the difference between depreciation based on the average replacement cost of plant consumed in the year and historical cost depreciation. Thus when indices are used, the depreciation charge for the year should be analysed to the time when related assets were acquired, and each part of the depreciation charge is multiplied by the factor:

$$\frac{\text{Average index for year}}{\text{Index at acquisition date}}$$

Figure 9.12 shows how the depreciation adjustment will be computed for our example Luttrell plc.

Acquired	HC	CCA factor	CCA
1 Jan 84	80	100/60	133
1 Jan 85	20	100/80	25
	100		158
			100
Depreciation adjustment			58

Figure 9.12 Calculation of the depreciation adjustment

	HC	Averaging factor	CCA
Closing stock	300	94.6/100	284
Opening stock	280	94.6/86	308
	20		24
Volume decrease			20
Price increase			44

Figure 9.13 Computation of the 'COSA' by the averaging method

	HC	Averaging factor	CCA
Closing MWC (410−208)	202	94.6/100	191
Opening MWC (370−196)	174	94.6/86	191
Monetary increase	28		
Volume change			0
MWCA			28
			28

Figure 9.14 Computation of the MWCA

(b) The *cost of sales adjustment* (COSA). This adjustment is intended to reflect the difference between the 'value to the business' of stock consumed and the historical cost. This is most commonly computed by the *averaging method*, illustrated by reference to our example in Fig. 9.13. The basis of the averaging method is that both opening and closing stock are adjusted from historical cost to average cost for the year by applying the factor:

$$\frac{\text{Average index for year}}{\text{Index at acquisition date}}$$

It then follows that since the difference between the opening and closing historical cost of stock represents the total increase or decrease, and the difference between the opening and closing stock both expressed at average price represents the volume increase or decrease, the difference between the two movements must be attributable to changing price levels; this will be the cost of sales adjustment.

(c)   The *monetary working capital adjustment* (MWCA). By 'monetary working capital' is meant the monetary assets and liabilities which are tied up in the operating cycle of the business. Basically, monetary working capital consists of trade debtors, trade creditors, and any part of bank and cash balances held to finance day-to-day operations. The adjustment reflects the fact that in times of rising prices an increase in debtors is necessary to finance a constant volume of sales and, conversely, an increase in creditors will arise with a constant volume of purchases. Figure 9.14 shows how the MWCA can be computed by the averaging method in the same way as the COSA. Note that when prices are rising the MWCA can decrease to increase historical cost profit, depending whether the net monetary working capital is an asset or a liability.

After computing these three adjustments, the first stage of the current cost profit and loss account has been completed and we have arrived at a figure of current cost operating profit. The second stage of the current cost profit and loss account is to find what part of current cost profit is attributable to shareholders. As we can see from Fig. 9.16 this follows conventional practice in deducting interest, then tax, then dividends. However, the CCA profit and loss account combines with the interest charge a new element, the *gearing adjustment*. This adjustment reflects the fact that part of the resources of the business are financed by borrowing so that, assuming a consistent policy of gearing, part of the increased finance required in times of inflation will come from borrowing rather than from shareholders. To compute the gearing adjustment it is necessary to compute:

(a)   The *net borrowing*. This consists of all monetary liabilities less monetary assets, excluding those items shown as part of monetary working capital.

(b)   The CCA equity. This consists of the historical cost share capital and reserves plus the CCA revaluation surpluses. It also includes proposed dividends, since these belong to shareholders.

Having computed these two figures, we can work out the *gearing proportion*, being:

$$\frac{\text{Average net borrowing}}{\text{Average net borrowing} + \text{CCA equity}}$$

The gearing adjustment will then be an abatement of the CCA operating adjustments, computed as:

$$\text{Gearing proportion} \times \text{Total CCA operating adjustments}$$

The computation of the gearing adjustment is illustrated in Fig. 9.15.

Having computed the CCA profit and loss account, we are now in a position to work out the movements on reserves in the current cost balance sheet.

The retained profits in the current cost account will show the retained profit as reported at the beginning of the year, adjusted for the retained CCA surplus or deficit in the year. Thus CCA retained profit consists of historical cost retained profit up to the date when CCA accounts are first presented, plus or minus the accumulated CCA surpluses or deficits after that date. The calculation of retained profit for our example shown in Fig. 9.17 assumes that 1985 is the first year in which CCA accounts have been presented.

Gearing proportion		*1985*		*1984*	
	£000	£000		£000	£000
Cash		(40)			(118)
Taxation		80			70
Debentures		600			600
Net borrowing		640			552
Shares	300			300	
Retained profits	362			302	
Proposed dividends	20			20	
Revaluation surplus	742			254	
CCA equity		1424			876
Equity + borrowing		2064			1428

Average net borrowing $\dfrac{640 + 552}{2} = 596$

Average equity + Borrowing $\dfrac{2064 + 1428}{2} = 1746$

$\therefore$ Gearing adjustment: $(58 + 44 + 28) \times \dfrac{596}{1746} = 44$

Figure 9.15   Computation of the gearing adjustment

Luttrell plc – Current Cost Profit and Loss Account for the year ended 31 December 1985

	£000	£000
Historical cost operating profit		230
Current cost operating adjustments:		
Depreciation	58	
Cost of sales adjustment	44	
Monetary working capital adjustment	28	
		130
Current cost operating profit		100
Gearing adjustment	(44)	
Interest	60	
		16
Current cost profit before taxation		84
Taxation		80
Current cost profit after taxation		4
Dividends:		
Paid	10	
Proposed	20	
		30
Current cost deficit transferred to reserves		(26)

Figure 9.16

Revaluation surpluses are normally shown under the heading *current cost reserve*. This reserve will be made up of:

(a)   *Unrealized surpluses*, being the revaluation surpluses on assets held at the balance sheet date. As shown in Fig. 9.17, each year the movements in revaluation surpluses are added to or deducted from the balance brought forward.

(b)   *Realized surpluses*, being the current cost adjustment transferred from the profit and loss account each year.

The difference between the two parts of the current cost reserve is important, because in law a company is allowed to distribute *realized* surpluses.

The significance of current cost profit is that it shows the results for the year after maintaining the *operating capability* of the business, being the fixed assets, stock and monetary working capital required to carry on the company's business at a consistent level.

The problem of 'inflation accounting' continues to be controversial among accountants. Currently the ASC have issued an exposure draft, ED 35, which proposes changes in the presentation of the CCA accounts and in the treatment of the gearing adjustment. Although it is likely that ED 35 will itself be withdrawn in the near future, these aspects of SSAP 16 are likely to be under question in some future exposure draft.

	£000	£000	£000
Retained profits			
As reported at beginning of year			302
Deficit for year			26
Carried forward			276
Current cost reserve	£000	£000	£000
Opening unrealized revaluation surplus			254
Opening realized revaluation surplus			—
			254
Movements on unrealized surpluses:			
Plant		490	
Stock		(2)	
		488	
Movements on realized surpluses:			
Depreciation	58		
COSA	44		
MWCA	28		
	130		
Less Gearing	44		
		86	
Movement in year			574
Carried forward			828
Being:			
Unrealized			742
Realized			86
			828

Figure 9.17   CCA reserve movements

Post-balance sheet events and contingencies

A company's accounts will present a profit and loss account up to, and a balance sheet as at, a specified date, i.e. the balance sheet date. In practice a period of time will elapse between the balance sheet date and the date when the accounts are presented; this period can legally be as long as seven months for a public company and ten months for a private company. The question therefore arises as to whether the accounts should include information on events occurring between the balance sheet date and the date when the accounts are presented. SSAP 17, 'Accounting for Post Balance Sheet Events', considers this issue and divides *post-balance sheet events* into two kinds:

(a) *Adjusting events*, which are events which provide new evidence as to the conditions which existed at the balance sheet date. For example, if the tax rate is changed after the balance sheet date with retrospective effect, then this event will affect tax payable on profits for the year. These events should be reflected in the accounts.

(b) *Non-adjusting events*, which concern conditions which did not exist at the balance sheet date. These should not be reflected in the accounts unless they affect the 'going concern' position. However, material post-balance sheet events which substantially affect the company's position should be reported in a note to the accounts.

A contingency is a condition which exists at the balance sheet date where the outcome is dependent on some uncertain future occurrence. An example might be the outcome of a lawsuit. SSAP 18, 'Accounting for Contingencies', addresses the question of the way in which such items should be reported in the accounts. Basically the requirements of SSAP 18 are that the treatment depends on the probability of the contingency arising.

Contingent losses should be provided for in full where it is probable that they will occur; otherwise they should be disclosed and explained in the accounts unless the risk is 'remote'. Contingent gains should never be provided for in the accounts and should only be disclosed if they are 'probably' going to materialize.

The different accounting treatments for gains and losses is an illustration of the application of the 'prudence' concept.

Conclusion

Some of the problems we have looked at, such as the difficulty in fairly reporting the position of groups of companies, have well-established and generally accepted solutions. Other problems, such as inflation accounting, are still not the subject of general agreement.

Questions

9.1 Anglo Ltd is a well-established private company which, over a number of years, built up a large balance of liquid resources surplus to operating requirements. The decision was taken, late in 1982, to use these resources to diversify the company's activities, and substantial shareholdings were subsequently acquired in Bangle Ltd and Carmen plc. The latter acquisition caused Anglo to arrange for a bank overdraft secured on its freehold property.

The following information is provided in respect of the three companies:

(i)   Summary of balances at 31 December 1983:

	Anglo £000	Bangle £000	Carmen £000
Assets:			
Goodwill at cost	—	—	104
Freehold property at cost less depreciation	200	180	700
Plant and equipment at cost less depreciation	756	107	1113
Investments: Bangle Ltd (180 000 shares)	440	—	—
Carmen plc (500 000 shares)	760	—	—
Current assets	521	351	976
	2677	638	2893
Share capital, reserves and liabilities:			
Issued share capital (£1 ordinary shares)	1000	200	2000
Retained profit at 1 January 1983	950	210	128
Net profit for 1983	247	90	236
Bank overdraft	374	—	—
Other current liabilities	106	138	529
	2677	638	2893

(ii)   The shares in Carmen were purchased on 1 January 1983 and in Bangle on 31 December 1983.

(iii) Following the share acquisition, directors were appointed to the boards of both Bangle and Carmen to take an active part in their financial and operating decisions.

(iv)   The freehold property of Bangle possessed a fair value of £300 000 on 31 December; there were no other significant differences between the fair values and book values of the assets of Bangle and Carmen at the acquisition dates.

(v)   Anglos's freehold property was recently valued at £230 000. This valuation is not to be written into the books.

Required:

A consolidated balance sheet of the group at 31 December 1983, not necessarily in a form for publication but complying, so far as the information permits, with the requirements of SSAPs 1 and 14.

(AIB)

9.2   The summarized balance sheets of Belmont plc and Tredegar plc (both public limited companies) as at 31 December 1981 were as follows:

	Belmont £000	Tredegar £000
Issues share capital (£1 ordinary shares)	1000	400
Reserves at 1 January 1981	750	120
12% debentures	—	100
Trade creditors and accruals	461	190
Bank overdraft (North Bank)	103	—
Profit before depreciation for 1981	308	150
Provision for depreciation of plant and machinery, 1 January 1981	426	240
	3048	1200

Plant and machinery at cost	1420	600
Investment in Tredegar:		
Debenture stock at cost (nominal value £60 000)	60	—
Stocks	1041	340
Trade debtors and prepayments	527	203
Bank balance (South Bank)	—	57
	3048	1200

Belmont purchased the debentures in Tredegar when they were first issued some years ago.

On 1 January 1981 Belmont purchased, by way of a share exchange, 300 000 £1 ordinary shares in Tredegar. The shares of Belmont were valued, at 1 January 1981, at £3.00 each and the terms of the acquisition were that the vendor shareholders of Tredegar would receive two shares in Belmont for every three shares held in Tredegar. In arriving at the purchase price of the shares in Tredegar, the plant machinery of that company were revalued at £500 000. No records were made of the transactions and valuations referred to in this paragraph before preparing the balance sheets set out above.

On 31 March 1981, Tredegar paid a dividend of £60 000 in respect of 1980. Belmont's share of this dividend, £45 000, has been credited to the profit and loss account balance reported in the balance sheet shown above.

Depreciation is to be charged at the rate of 10 per cent for 1981. In the case of Belmont the charge is to be based on the original cost of plant and machinery whereas, in the case of Tredegar, the charge is to be based on the revalued figure of £500 000.

Required:

(a)   The consolidated balance sheet of Belmont plc and its subsidiary company as at 31 December 1981. The consolidated balance sheet should be presented in vertical format and prepared in accordance with normal accounting practice.
(b)   A clear explanation for your treatment of the dividend paid by Tredegar plc to Belmont plc.

Notes:
Ignore taxation.
No dividends were paid or proposed by either of the companies for 1981.
9.3   The summarized accounts for Tisch plc for 1981, prepared on the historical cost basis.

Profit and Loss Account, year ended 31 December 1981

	£000
Operating profit	355
Less Interest payable	60
Net profit before taxation	295
Less Corporation tax	150
Net profit after taxation	145
Add Retained profit at 1 January 1981	180
Retained profit at 31 December 1981	325

Balance Sheet at 31 December 1981

1980 £000		£000	£000
1000	Fixed assets at cost		1000
250	*Less* Depreciation		375
750			625
	Current assets:		
600	Stock (December purchases)	900	
30	Cash	50	
630		950	
	Less Current liability:		
100	Corporation tax payable	150	
530	Net current assets		800
1280			1425
	Financed by:		
700	Share capital (£1 ordinary shares)		700
180	Reserves		325
880			1025
400	15% debenture		400
1280			1425

The directors intended to published supplementary accounts based on the provisions contained in SSAP 16, 'Current Cost Accounting'.

The following additional information is provided:

(1) Sales, purchases and other expenses accrue evenly during the year.
(2) The company purchases and sells all goods on an immediate cash basis.
(3) The fixed assets were purchased on 1 January 1979 and are being depreciated on the straight-line basis over a period of eight years assuming a nil residual value. The depreciation charge in the 1981 accounts was, accordingly, £125 000.
(4) The following price indices are provided for the company's stock and fixed assets:

	Stock	Fixed assets
1 January 1979	*	100
Average for December 1980	130	*
31 December 1980	132	120
Average for 1981	136	124
Average for December 1981	144	*
31 December 1981	145	132

*Indices not provided.

(5) The company's stock turn over, on average, once a month.

Required:

The current cost profit and loss account and balance sheet of Tisch plc for 1981 (1980 comparatives need not be given) in accordance, so far as the information permits, with the principles contained in SSAP 16. The profit and loss account should contain a depreciation adjustment, a cost of sales adjustment and a gearing adjustment. The balance sheet should contain a current cost reserve.

Note:
The monetary working capital is not applicable to the affairs of Tisch plc.
All calculations to the nearest £000.

(AIB, 1982)

9.4   The summarized profit and loss account of Holford plc for 1982, prepared under the historical cost convention, was as follows:

Profit and Loss Account for 1982

	£000	£000
Turnover		360 000
Less Opening stock	35 000	
Purchases	200 000	
Closing stock	(50 000)	
Cost of goods sold		185 000
Gross profit		175 000
Less Depreciation	20 000	
Other running costs	126 000	146 000
Operating profit		29 000
Less Interest payable		5 000
Profit on ordinary activities before taxation		24 000
Taxation		10 000
Profit after tax		14 000
Less Dividends		7 000
Retained profit for the year		7 000

The following additional information is provided:

(i)   Relevant indices for stocks are as follows:

Average for October/December 1981	120
At 31 December 1981	124
Average for 1982	135
Average for October/December 1982	142
At 31 December 1982	145

On average the company holds stock for three months.

(ii) All the company's fixed assets were purchased when the company was incorporated in January 1976. Their original cost was £200 000 000 and they are being depreciated over a ten-year period assuming a nil residual value. The original estimate of these assets' lives is still considered appropriate. The following current cost valuations are provided:

	£000
At 1 January 1982	310 000
Average for 1982	330 000
At 31 December 1982	355 000

(iii)   Net borrowings were approximately one-third of net operating assets throughout 1982.

Required:

A summarized profit and loss account for 1982 prepared on the current cost basis in accordance, so far as the information permits, with the principles contained in SSAP 16.

Notes:
All calculations are to be made to the nearest £000.
Ignore the monetary working capital adjustment.

(AIB, 1983)

9.5   On 1 January 1985, Chestnut Ltd, a UK company, acquired the entire share capital of Acorn SA, a company registered and trading in Ruritania, for a purchase consideration of 600 000 crowns. To help finance the purchase, a loan of 300 000 crowns was raised in Ruritania by Chestnut Ltd on 1 January 1985. These were the only foreign currency items recorded in Chestnut's own accounts.

On 1 January 1985, Acorn SA acquired all the plant currently shown in the balance sheet.

During the year to 31 December 1985, exchange rates moved as follows:

1 Jan 85	20 crowns to £1
Average 1985	18 crowns to £1
At date stock acquired	16 crowns to £1
31 Dec 85	15 crowns to £1

The accounts of Acorn for the year to 31 December 1985 showed:

Balance Sheet as at 31 December 1985

	crowns	crowns
Plant—Cost		604 800
—Depreciation		86 400
		518 400
Current assets:		
Stock	129 600	
Cash	43 200	
		172 800
		691 200
Long-term loan		172 800
		518 400
Ordinary share capital		345 600
Retained Profit—At 1 Jan 85	129 600	
For year	43 200	
		172 800
		518 400

Profit and Loss Account for the year ended 31 December 1985

	crowns	crowns
Sales		864 000
Cost of sales		561 600
Gross profit		302 400
Less Depreciation	86 400	
Other expenses	172 800	
		259 200
Retained profit		43 200

Required:

In compliance with SSAP 20:

(a) Translate the accounts of Acorn SA by the closing rate method. Apply the closing rate to profit and loss items.
(b) Translate the accounts of Acorn SA by the temporal method.
(c) Show the exchange differences taken in Chestnut Ltd's own accounts through the profit and loss account and direct to reserves, respectively:

(1) taking a cover approach;
(2) not taking a cover approach.

10 Analysis of financial information

Introduction

The broad objective of this chapter is to introduce some techniques used by those with access to internal accounting data. Specifically, we consider:

(a) Basic cost and management accounting.
(b) Cash budgeting.
(c) Investment appraisal.
(d) Share valuation.
(e) Company liquidations and reconstructions.

Basic cost and management accounting

Principles

Any accounting system is designed to provide economic information that is useful for decision-making purposes. However, there are certain important differences between internal and external reporting principles:

(a) External reports normally consist of a single set of accounts designed for a wide range of potential users, and are prepared in compliance with externally imposed regulations. By contrast, a range of internal reports are designed for specific purposes, and the manner in which they are prepared is normally totally under the control of management.

(b) External reports have a major stewardship role, in demonstrating to shareholders that the directors have properly employed the resources at their disposal; they are also used for a variety of regulatory purposes, such as taxation. Thus it is essential that such accounts should be objective and easily verifiable. By contrast, the internal reporting system is designed purely for decision making, so that economic realism is their prime objective. Thus costs in the internal reporting system should report the 'value' rather than the historical cost. Similarly the 'prudence' concept is inappropriate, and reports should state the position as fairly as possible without bias.

(c) The prime concern of the external reports is with the computation of profit. For internal reports the analysis of individual income and expenditure items is essential to enable managers to make meaningful decisions.

(d) Internal reports are required urgently as soon as transactions have occurred to enable management to respond rapidly and effectively to changes in circumstances. By contrast, external reports place a greater emphasis on precision, at the price of a delay in publication.

Cost analysis

There are a number of ways in which costs can be analysed. They can be regarded as falling under three broad headings:

(a) *Materials*. These are goods purchased either for resale or for use in the manu-facturing processes of the business.
(b) *Labour*. This is the cost of payments to all employees of the business.
(c) *Expenses*. This embraces all costs other than materials and labour.

```
Direct materials
      +
Direct labour      = Prime cost
      +                   +              = Production cost
Direct expenses    Production overheads           +                = Total cost
                                        Other overheads      +          = Selling price
                                                          Profit
```

Figure 10.1   Build up of costs

Costs can also be regarded as relating to any product or service as shown in Fig. 10.1. The build-up here is:

(a) Prime cost is made up of all those costs directly attributable to goods or services produced.
(b) Production cost is made up of prime cost plus 'production overhead', being those costs of production which cannot be directly attributed to units of output.
(c) Total cost consists of production cost plus all other overheads, costs such as finance, distribution and administration.
(d) Profit is the difference between total cost and selling price.

We have used the term *direct* cost above. A direct cost is one that can be directly attri-buted to whatever is being costed. By contrast, *indirect* costs cannot be directly related to *individual* items in this way.

Another important distinction is between fixed and variable costs. *Fixed* costs are those costs which remain unchanged whatever the level of activity; thus all fixed costs must be indirect. *Variable* costs vary in proportion to the level of activity; thus all direct and some indirect costs are variable. Some costs are *semi-variable*, partially fixed and partially increasing or decreasing in step with the level of activity. For practical purposes, accountants have techniques to split such costs into fixed and variable elements.

Absorption costing

Absorption costing is a technique whereby all costs are related to units of output. Some types of cost, such as materials and direct labour, can be related easily. However, the indirect costs are initially allocated to *cost centre*, which must in turn be apportioned to units of output in some way; this is known as cost 'absorption'. Possible bases of overhead absorption include by reference to the cost of materials consumed, the volume of materials consumed, the cost of labour employed or the labour hours employed. As far as possible the overhead absorption basis chosen should reflect the cause of the over-head. For example, supposing a factory produces nuts and bolts in two types of metal, one cheap and one expensive; since most overheads will be the same irrespective of the cost of materials, a cost of materials basis would be inappropriate and misleading.

It is also important to ensure that costs absorbed relate to the stage of production goods have received. Thus goods in stock only include production costs, since other costs relate to the selling stage.

Variable costing

With variable costing we focus on the distinction between fixed and variable costs, introduced above. The total variable costs, whatever stage they relate to, are computed for each unit of output. The difference between selling price and variable cost is then known as *contribution*.

Marginal costing is a valuable tool in making decisions on selling prices. Example 10.1 shows how a business might analyse costs, with advice on potential sales at different price levels.

Example 10.1

Rodney is in business as a manufacturer of specialist screwdrivers. He expects his costs during the year to 31 December 1986 to be:

	£
Variable cost per screwdriver	1.25
Total fixed costs	£30 000

His marketing consultant advises that sales can be achieved at the following prices:

	A	B	C
Price	£2.00	£1.75	£1.50
Sales – number of units	50 000	80 000	130 000

Figure 10.2 shows how a selling price decision might be made. The contribution per unit is worked out and is then multiplied by expected volume of sales to give total contribution. Profit is maximized by maximizing contribution, as we can see when fixed costs are deducted. Thus in our example a price of £1.75 would be chosen.

Contribution per unit:	A	B	C
	£	£	£
Selling price	2.00	1.75	1.50
Variable cost	1.25	1.25	1.25
	0.75	0.50	0.25
Total contribution	37 500	40 000	32 500
Fixed costs	30 000	30 000	30 000
Profit	7 500	10 000	2 500

Figure 10.2   Rodney

Any system of absorption costing involves prediction of the level of output, so that fixed costs can be apportioned to units produced. In our example the fixed cost per screwdriver, at a predicted output of 80 000, would be:

$$\frac{30\,000}{80\,000} = 37.5\text{p}$$

Total cost per screwdriver would therefore be:

$$1.25 + 0.375 = £1.625$$

Now suppose Rodney is offered a special bulk order for 20 000 screwdrivers at £1.40 each, in addition to the 80 000 sales at the normal price. In that case a sale would yield additional contribution of:

$$(1.40 - 1.25) \times 20\,000 = £3000$$

Thus it would be sensible to take on extra business at a selling price less than the cost per unit computed on a total absorption basis.

It is, however, worth noting that in some businesses, pricing is a matter of convention and consumers may resist a more 'rational' structure. For example, it is common in the catering industry to charge for meals by adding a percentage to the cost of the food ingredients. A restaurant owner who had read about costing decided that a more rational basis would be to charge customers a fixed charge to cover overheads and profit, plus a price for each item on the menu reflecting the cost of the ingredients; he soon abandoned the experiment in the face of customer complaints.

Budgets

A budget is a financial plan, being a forecast profit and loss account. To prepare the budget involves securing the cooperation of all departments of the business, normally coordinated by a budget committee. For example, the budget might involve:

(a) The marketing department forecasting sales at various price levels, with related advertising and distribution costs.
(b) The production department advising on costs at various levels of sales, and fixed asset requirements.
(c) The purchasing department advising on costs and possible problems of supply.
(d) The personnel department advising on likely labour costs and potential industrial relations problems.
(e) The accountant working out the financial implications, particularly relating to cash flow.

Because the budget will be distributed widely throughout the organization there are often, in practice, 'political' distortions. For example, if management wish to make a stand against wage claims they may make a prediction in the budget of a low pay rise, knowing that in practice they are likely to have to make some concessions.

A common way of checking actual performance against the budget is *variance analysis* whereby the reasons for departure from the budget are analysed in detail.

Cash budgeting

A *cash budget* is a statement which shows, normally month by month, the effect on the cash resources of a business of the activities planned during a future accounting period. The cash budget is widely recognized as a vital tool in financial planning, enabling management to anticipate cash shortages and to adjust their plans accordingly.

We have already seen that when a business earns profit this is not necessarily represented by cash resources. Indeed, an increase in trading actively designed to increase profit may, in the short term, actually absorb the cash resources of the business in extra working capital required. Thus a cash budget is particularly important for a new or expanding business. Indeed, it is unlikely that any bank would lend on any business proposition unsupported by a cash budget.

The cash budget is normally prepared by considering the cash effects of management's plans for the business; these can be presented either in the form of a forecast profit and loss account or in narrative form. Example 10.2 shows a very simple example of the kind of information on the basis of which we might set out to construct a cash budget.

Example 10.2

Hood is planning to set up in business as a wholesaler, dealing in electrical goods. He believes that in the first half of 1987 he can achieve the following sales:

	£
January	2 000
February	3 000
March	6 000
April	6 000
May	10 000
June	10 000

Sales are expected to remain at £10 000 per month thereafter. Debtors are expected to take two months' credit on average. Gross profit as a percentage of sales will be 30 per cent. The first purchase of goods will take place on 1 January and thereafter goods will be purchased on the last day of the month. Hood intends when ordering goods to hold enough stock to cover the following two months' sales. Until the end of March, suppliers will require payment in cash; thereafter a trading record will have been established and it is expected that one month's credit will be allowed.

In January, Hood will pay £4000 for storage fittings, payable in cash. Wages, payable in cash, are £300 per month. In addition, Hood plans to draw £500 per month for his own use. The fittings will be depreciated by £50 per month.

Hood has already deposited £20 000 in a business bank account.

Figure 10.3 shows how we might construct a cash budget for Hood's first six months trading. In effect we are reversing our traditional accounting role in that we start from forecast accounting information and work back to the related cash transactions. Thus taking our example:

(a) Cash flows related to sales are received when debtors actually pay. Thus cash inflows are shown two months after related sales because we are told that debtors take two months' credit.

(b) Cash outflows to suppliers are generally the most involved part of a cash budget to compute. Figure 10.4 shows how we compute the closing stock at the end of each month given our assumption that it has to cover two months' sales and that the gross profit is 30 per cent (so that cost of sales must be 70 per cent of sales). We can then compute the purchases each month as the balancing figure in the make-up of cost of sales. Finally, we see that for the first three months, suppliers are paid in cash and thereafter one month's credit is taken.

(c) All other cash flows given in our example are straightforward. Note that depreciation does not appear in the cash budget because it does not involve any cash outlay.

Hood – Cash Budget for the six months to 30 June 1987

	Jan £	Feb £	March £	April £	May £	June £
Cash inflows						
Debtors	—	—	2 000	3 000	6 000	6 000
Cash outflows						
Suppliers	7 700	4 200	7 000		7 000	7 000
Fittings	4 000					
Wages	300	300	300	300	300	300
Drawings	500	500	500	500	500	500
	12 500	5 000	7 800	800	7 800	7 800
Net inflow/(outflow)	(12 500)	(5 000)	(5 800)	2 200	(1 800)	(1 800)
Cash b/fwd	20 000	7 500	2 500	(3 300)	(1 100)	(2 900)
Cash c/fwd	7 500	2 500	(3 300)	(1 100)	(2 900)	(4 700)

Figure 10.3

Closing stock at end of each month:

January	70% × (3 000 + 6 000) =	6 300
February	70% × (6 000 + 6 000) =	8 400
March	70% × (6 000 + 10 000) =	11 200
April	70% × (10 000 + 10 000) =	14 000
May	70% × (10 000 + 10 000) =	14 000
June	70% × (10 000 + 10 000) =	14 000

∴ Purchases:

	Jan	Feb	March	April	May	June
Opening stock	—	6 300	8 400	11 200	14 000	14 000
Purchases*	7 700	4 200	7 000	7 000	7 000	7 000
Closing stock	(6 300)	(8 400)	(11 200)	(14 000)	(14 000)	(14 000)
Cost of sales	1 400	2 100	4 200	4 200	7 000	7 000
(70% × sales)						

*Balancing figure

Figure. 10.4   Cash budget – workings

Having prepared our cash budget we can then consider how to deal with any problem of cash shortages. Often it will be apparent from the cash budget that problems can be solved by deferring certain items of expenditure. Sometimes the cash budget shows that a cash shortage will only be temporary, so that it can be used to support a loan application. Sometimes it may be necessary to slow down the planned rate of expansion in order to avoid cash flow problems. Whatever the solution, the cash budget is an essential tool enabling management to smooth out cash flow problems in advance.

When using a cash flow statement it is essential to look closely at the underlying assumptions on which the statement is based. In practice, inexperienced entrepreneurs often make wildly optimistic assumptions about future cash flows; when a professional accountant translates these into a well-presented cash budget they may acquire a spurious air of validity. Any user evaluating a proposal supported by a cash budget should scrutinize the underlying assumptions carefully and question the proposer closely where necessary.

Capital investment appraisal

The basic issues

Capital investment decisions may be regarded as relating to outlays expected to yield cash inflows in future accounting periods.

Examples of such decisions would include:

(a)   Acquisitions of fixed assets.
(b)   Acquisitions of other existing businesses.
(c)   Expenditure relating to major development or marketing of products.
(d)   Investments in other business or government securities.
(e)   Development of new business activities.

When choosing between capital investment opportunities, there is likely to be some limitation on the number of projects which can be invested in, so that we need to identify criteria which will enable us to rank projects in order of preference. Limitations on capital investment can be divided into two broad headings:

(a)   Availability of cash resources. For example, a private individual may be faced with a choice of ways in which an inherited lump sum can be invested. In practice, a business will normally have some flexibility in the amount of money it can raise from the proprietors or from borrowing, but will have to contain its total capital expenditure within certain broad limits.
(b)   Other constraints. A capital investment decision may relate to the choice between different ways of exploiting a single finite resource. For example, a private individual who has inherited a shop might have a choice between renting the shop out or employing a manager to run it; given that the decision relates to this single shop, a choice has to be made between these two approaches.

Whichever kind of limitation arises, we will require a system for choosing between capital investment proposals.

Financial criteria

There are two broad types of financial consideration which will influence the capital investment decision:

(a)   The desirability of recovering the amount of the investment in the project as quickly as possible.
(b)   The desirability of earning as high a return as possible of the investment.

The first of these objectives can be measured by the 'payback' method, the second by the 'accounting rate of return'.

Example 10.3

Tusk Ltd has to choose between three competing capital projects. Cash flows associated with the projects are:

	A	B	C
	£000	£000	£000
Initial outlay	20 000	35 000	8 000
Cash inflows at end of:			
Year 1	11 000	10 000	1 000
Year 2	9 000	12 000	2 000
Year 3	2 000	16 000	3 000
Year 4	1 000	6 000	4 000
Year 5	606	3 653	2 731

Tusk Ltd's cost of capital is 10 per cent.

Payback

The payback method measures the period of time within which cash inflows from a project will cover the amount of the initial investment. If we consider the figures in Example 10.3 Tusk Ltd, we can compare the cumulative cash inflows at the end of each year with the initial outlay as follows:

Project	A	B	C
	£	£	£
Initial outlay	20 000	35 000	8 000
Cumulative inflow at end of:			
Year 1	11 000	10 000	1 000
Year 2	20 000	22 000	3 000
Year 3	22 000	38 000	6 000
Year 4	23 000	44 000	10 000
Year 5	23 606	47 653	12 731

We can see that the payback period for Project A is exactly 2 years, for Project B between 2 and 3 years, and for Project C between 3 and 4 years.

We can then estimate the exact payback period for Projects B and C by assuming that cash inflows are spread evenly over the year during which payback is achieved, so that the payback period will be:

$$\text{Number of years up to the commencement of the year in which payback is achieved} + \frac{\text{Cash inflow required to achieve payback in year}}{\text{Cash inflow for year}}$$

In our example, the payback period will be:

Project B:
$$2 + \frac{13\,000}{16\,000} = 2.8125 \text{ years}$$

Project C:
$$3 + \frac{2\,000}{4000} = 3.5 \text{ years}$$

Accouting rate of return

The accounting rate of return gives the average return on the investment as a percentage of the initial outlay. It may be calculated as:

$$\frac{\text{Total cash inflows} - \text{Total cash outflows}}{\text{Initial outlay}} \times \frac{1}{\text{Number of years of project}}$$

Taking the figures for our example Tusk Ltd:

Proect A:
$$\frac{23\,606 - 20\,000}{20\,000} \times \frac{1}{5} = \;\; 3.6\%$$

Project B:
$$\frac{47\,653 - 35\,000}{35\,000} \times \frac{1}{5} = \;\; 7.2\%$$

Project C:
$$\frac{12\,731 - 8\,000}{8\,000} \times \frac{1}{5} = 11.8\%$$

Some accountants argue that this ratio should be calculated on the basis of the average investment rather than the gross initial investment, so that the initial investment figure used in computing the ratio would be halved.

Discounted cash flow techniques

When applied to our example, the two methods we have used so far give conflicting results, because each method only takes into account one of our financial objectives. The payback method puts the highest ranking on Project A, ignoring the fact that the project only generates very modest cash flows after payback has been achieved. The accounting rate of return gives Project C the highest ranking, ignoring the problem that cash inflows for the project are delayed until later years. What we clearly require is a method for evaluating capital projects which takes into account the total cash inflow but at the same time recognizes that earlier cash inflows have a greater value than later ones. The total we use is the *discount rate*.

  The discount rate is the amount, expressed as a percentage, which would have to be added on to a cash amount in order to compensate us for sacrificing that cash amount for one year. For example, if our discount rate is 10 per cent, then a sum of £1 at the present point in time would be exactly equal in value to a sum of £1.10 (£1 + 10 per cent) receivable in one year's time. Taking our example further, our sum of £1 would also be equal to £1.21 (£1.10 + 10 per cent) in two years' time.

  Using a compound interest formula, we can state that £1 in the present will be equal to a sum in *n* years' time when the discount rate is *r* of:

$$(1 + r)^n$$

We can similarly evaluate the present value of any sum receivable in the future by applying to it the factor:

$$\frac{1}{(1 + r)^n}$$

For example, the factor to be applied to a sum receivable in one year when the discount rate is 10 per cent will be:

$$\frac{1}{1.1} = 0.9091$$

This is known as a present value factor.

With our formula it is possible for us to compute the present value factor for any discount rate any number of years ahead. However, it is more usual to ascertain the present value factor from a table; Fig. 10.5 gives present value factors up to 15 years for discount rates from 1 to 20 per cent.

Years	1	2	3	4	5	6	7	8	9	10	11	12	13	14	15
1%	0.9901	0.9803	0.9706	0.9610	0.9515	0.9420	0.9327	0.9235	0.9143	0.9053	0.8963	0.8874	0.8787	0.8700	0.8613
2%	0.9804	0.9612	0.9423	0.9238	0.9057	0.8880	0.8706	0.8535	0.8368	0.8203	0.8043	0.7885	0.7730	0.7579	0.7430
3%	0.9709	0.9426	0.9151	0.8885	0.8626	0.8375	0.8131	0.7894	0.7664	0.7441	0.7224	0.7014	0.6810	0.6611	0.6419
4%	0.9615	0.9246	0.8890	0.8548	0.8219	0.7903	0.7599	0.7307	0.7026	0.6756	0.6496	0.6246	0.6006	0.5775	0.5553
5%	0.9524	0.9070	0.8638	0.8227	0.7835	0.7462	0.7107	0.6768	0.6446	0.6139	0.5847	0.5568	0.5303	0.5051	0.4810
6%	0.9434	0.8900	0.8396	0.7921	0.7473	0.7050	0.6651	0.6274	0.5919	0.5584	0.5268	0.4970	0.4688	0.4423	0.4173
7%	0.9346	0.8734	0.8163	0.7629	0.7130	0.6663	0.6227	0.5820	0.5439	0.5083	0.4751	0.4440	0.4150	0.3878	0.3624
8%	0.9259	0.8573	0.7938	0.7350	0.6806	0.6302	0.5835	0.5403	0.5002	0.4632	0.4289	0.3971	0.3677	0.3405	0.3152
9%	0.9174	0.8417	0.7722	0.7084	0.6499	0.5963	0.5470	0.5019	0.4604	0.4224	0.3875	0.3555	0.3262	0.2992	0.2745
10%	0.9091	0.8264	0.7513	0.6830	0.6209	0.5645	0.5132	0.4665	0.4241	0.3855	0.3505	0.3186	0.2897	0.2633	0.2394
11%	0.9009	0.8116	0.7312	0.6587	0.5935	0.5346	0.4817	0.4339	0.3909	0.3522	0.3173	0.2858	0.2575	0.2320	0.2090
12%	0.8929	0.7972	0.7118	0.6355	0.5674	0.5066	0.4523	0.4039	0.3606	0.3220	0.2875	0.2567	0.2292	0.2046	0.1827
13%	0.8850	0.7831	0.6931	0.6133	0.5428	0.4803	0.4251	0.3762	0.3329	0.2946	0.2607	0.2307	0.2042	0.1807	0.1599
14%	0.8772	0.7695	0.6750	0.5921	0.5194	0.4556	0.3996	0.3506	0.3075	0.2679	0.2366	0.2076	0.1821	0.1597	0.1401
15%	0.8696	0.7561	0.6575	0.5718	0.4972	0.4323	0.3759	0.3269	0.2843	0.2472	0.2149	0.1869	0.1625	0.1413	0.1229
16%	0.8621	0.7432	0.6407	0.5523	0.4761	0.4104	0.3538	0.3050	0.2630	0.2267	0.1954	0.1685	0.1452	0.1252	0.1079
17%	0.8547	0.7305	0.6244	0.5337	0.4561	0.3898	0.3332	0.2848	0.2434	0.2080	0.1778	0.1520	0.1299	0.1110	0.0949
18%	0.8475	0.7182	0.6086	0.5158	0.4371	0.3704	0.3139	0.2660	0.2255	0.1911	0.1619	0.1372	0.1163	0.0985	0.0835
19%	0.8403	0.7062	0.5934	0.4987	0.4190	0.3521	0.2959	0.2487	0.2090	0.1756	0.1476	0.1240	0.1042	0.0876	0.0736
20%	0.8333	0.6944	0.5787	0.4823	0.4019	0.3349	0.2791	0.2326	0.1938	0.1615	0.1346	0.1122	0.0935	0.0779	0.0649

Figure 10.5 Present value factors

Net present value

The discounted cash flow tool can be used to compute the present value of a future stream of cash flows to give the *net present value* of a project. Thus for our example, Tusk Ltd, where we are told that the 'cost of capital' (which we will use as our discount rate) is 10 per cent, the net present values are laid out in Fig. 10.6.

Assuming a discount rate of 10 per cent Projects B and C would be beneficial, while Project A would yield neither gain nor loss. On this basis, Project B has the highest ranking.

A situation which arises frequently is that a capital investment results in the receipt of a fixed annual sum for a fixed number of years. In order to simplify the calculation of net present value, tables are available which give the factor to be applied to such an annuity to give the present value of the total sums receivable. For example, supposing we wish to ascertain the present value of an amount of £1500 per year receivable at the end of each of the next ten years; we look up the present value for a ten-year annuity at a discount rate of 10 per cent and, given that this factor is 6.1445, then:

$$£1500 \times 6.1445 = £9216.75$$

	Cash flows	Present value factor (per Fig. 10.5)	Present value
Project A	£		£
Year 1	11 000	0.9091	10 000
Year 2	9 000	0.8264	7 438
Year 3	2 000	0.7513	1 503
Year 4	1 000	0.6830	683
Year 5	606	0.6209	376
	23 606		20 000
Initial outlay	(20 000)		(20 000)
	3 606		—
Project B			
Year 1	10 000	0.9091	9 091
Year 2	12 000	0.8264	9 917
Year 3	16 000	0.7513	12 021
Year 4	6 000	0.6830	4 098
Year 5	3 653	0.6209	2 268
	47 653		37 395
Initial outlay	(35 000)		(35 000)
	12 653		2 395
Project C			
Year 1	1 000	0.9091	909
Year 2	2 000	0.8264	1 653
Year 3	3 000	0.7513	2 254
Year 4	4 000	0.6830	2 732
Year 5	2 731	0.6209	1 696
	12 731		9 244
Initial outlay	(8 000)		(8 000)
	4 731		1 244

Figure 10.6   Net present values of three projects at discount rate 10%

Internal rate of return (IRR)

Computation of the net present value is one form of discounted cash flow technique. Another major form is the 'internal rate of return'. This is the discount rate at which the net present value of a project is exactly nil; thus we have already seen that the internal rate of return for Project A is 10 per cent. There is no formula for computing the precise internal rate of return, but the approximate amount can be found as follows:

(a) Compute the net present value of the project by applying any selected discount rate. This will normally have been done in any case on the basis of the company's own cost of capital. In our example Tusk Ltd this has already been done in Fig. 10.6 and by chance we hit upon the IRR. We also learnt that for the other two projects the IRR is in excess of 10 per cent.

(b) Compute the net present value of the project at a different discount rate, trying to estimate a rate which will be close to the IRR. In Fig. 10.7 we can see the effect of applying a discount rate of 15 per cent to Projects B and C. We happen to have hit upon the IRR of Project C, but since Project B has a negative net present value at this discount rate we know that its IRR must exceed 10 per cent and be less than 15 per cent.

(c) Having arrived at the net present value of a project at two different discount rates, it is possible to estimate the IRR of a project by interpolation, as though the relationship between NPV and the discount rate used is linear. Thus for Project B:

$$10\% + \frac{2395}{3859} \times 5\% = 13.1\%$$

It must be emphasized that this estimate is very much an approximation, because the relationship between the net present value of a project and discount rates used is in fact not linear.

	Cash flows	Present value factor (per Fig. 10.5)	Present value
Project B – Rate 15%	£		£
Year 1	10 000	0.8696	8 696
Year 2	12 000	0.7561	9 073
Year 3	16 000	0.6575	10 520
Year 4	6 000	0.5718	3 431
Year 5	3 653	0.4972	1 816
Initial outlay	(35 000)	1	(35 000)
	12 653		(1 464)
Project C – Rate 15%			
Year 1	1 000	0.8696	870
Year 2	2 000	0.7561	1 512
Year 3	3 000	0.6575	1 973
Year 4	4 000	0.5718	2 287
Year 5	2 731	0.4972	1 358
Initial outlay	(8 000)	1	(8 000)
	4 731		—
Project B – Rate 13%			
Year 1	10 000	0.8850	8 850
Year 2	12 000	0.7831	9 397
Year 3	16 000	0.6931	11 090
Year 4	6 000	0.6133	3 680
Year 5	3 653	0.5428	1 983
Initial outlay	(35 000)	1	(35 000)
	12 653		—

Figure 10.7 Net present value of Projects B and C

(d)   To arrive at a more precise internal rate of return figure it is possible to compute the two discount rates nearest to the figure arrived at by interpolation; in Fig. 10.6 we can see that the IRR is in fact 13 per cent for Project C.

It would be possible by following an iterative process, to eventually quantify the IRR precisely, and modern computing techniques make this feasible; however, given that capital investment appraisal is in any case based on estimates of future cash flows it follows that too great a degree of precision in computation of the IRR would be spurious.

Comparison of methods

Our example, Tusk Ltd, illustrates the way in which different methods of investment appraisal can produce different results.

This can be summarized:

	A	B	C
Payback period	2 years	2.8 years	3.5 years
Accounting rate of return	3.6%	7.2%	11.8%
Net present value	—	£2395	£1244
Internal rate of return	10%	13%	15%

Each of the projects is ranked first by at least one method.

Research has shown that all four methods are commonly used in practice and that it is common for companies to use a mixture of capital investment appraisal methods. The relative merits of the two non-DCF methods can be summarized;

(a)   *Payback*
Benefits:

(1)   The method is simple to apply and understand. A number of companies apply payback to small projects while using more sophisticated methods to assess major projects while using more sophisticated methods to assess major projects.
(2)   Because payback is based on the earliest cash inflows, the projected cash flows are easier to estimate, reducing the risk element.
(3)   Payback minimizes the time cash resources are tied up in capital projects, an advantage to companies with liquidity problems.

Disadvantages:

(1)   Ignores the amount and timing of cash flows after the payback period.
(2)   Ignores scrap values or termination costs at end of project.

(b)   *Accounting rate of return*
Benefits:

(1)   Relatively simple to compute and understand, tieing in with the concept of return on capital employed.
(2)   Takes into account all cash flow.
(3)   Takes total time of project into account.

Disadvantages:

Timing of cash flows within total time span ignored.

Discounted cash flow techniques are more complex (and therefore costly) to apply and are less readily understood by non-financial managers. They have the additional difficulty that it is necessary to decide on a 'cost of capital' figure, to be used to decide net present value or as a minimum target for the internal rate of return. However, many companies take the view that the benefits of DCF techniques justify the cost of use, particularly for major projects. In choosing between the two methods:

(a) IRR maximizes the return from cash employed and therefore may be preferred when the factor limiting choice between projects is availability of cash.

(b) NPV maximizes the return from projects in absolute terms and therefore may be preferred when non-financial constraints compel a choice between projects.

(c) A weakness of IRR is that it is unrealistic to expect to be able to re-invest surplus funds at the IRR rate. On the other hand, NPV calculations depend on the validity of the discount rate used.

(d) The IRR is a concept which non-financial managers are likely to comprehend easily, being similar to the concept of return on capital. The concept of NPV is more technically complex.

Inflation

There are two approaches to the application of DCF techniques in times of inflation. Both rest on the assumption that there is a link between the rate of inflation and market rates of interest, and that in turn market rates of interest affect a company's cost of capital and discount rate.

(a) Ignore inflation, predicting future cash flows at present price levels, and use of discount rate based on the 'real' interest rate, excluding that part of market rates of interest regarded as compensating for the inflation level.

(b) Take anticipated levels of inflation into account when predicting cash flows and use a discount rate based on current market rates of interest.

The first method allows all predictions as to inflation to be concentrated on selection of the discount rate. However, the second method is generally preferred because:

(a) It allows for predictions of different price level movement for different types of income and expenditure.

(b) It is more realistic, being based on predictions of what will actually happen.

(c) It is more easily understood by management.

Valuation of a business

Introduction

The only objective measure of the value of any business arises when a transaction takes place at arm's length between a willing buyer and a willing seller. Even this measure is open to challenge. For example, the price per share at which a small block of shares changes hands may be very different to the price at which a large block could be bought or sold. However, the currently quoted stock market share price of a listed company is widely accepted as a fair measure of value, and is used for a variety of purposes.

If often happens that we need some measure of the value of the shares in an unlisted company or unincorporated business. Examples of situations where such a valuation might be required are:

(a)   On a transfer of shares the Inland Revenue might require a valuation for capital gains tax or capital transfer tax purposes.
(b)   The owner of shares might wish to pledge them as security for a loan.
(c)   A vendor or purchaser of shares might wish to estimate value as a guide to their negotiating position.

As we have already seen, the accounting system is not, and cannot be designed to show the 'value' of the business as a whole. In principle, the value of a share will be the total of future cash flows from it, discounted to present value. In practice, there is so much estimation involved in computing the value of a share in this way that alternative methods have to be found. The two broad approaches are:

(a)   Valuation of the individual assets of the business.
(b)   Valuation of the earnings expected from the business.

Individual assets

The simplest way of estimating a share's value is to divide the total figure for equity shown in the balance sheet by the total number of ordinary shares. This 'book value' of each share for Example 10.4 Oldbuck Ltd would be:

$$\frac{\text{Share capital} + \text{Reserves}}{\text{Number of shares}}$$

$$= \frac{£150\,000}{100\,000} = £1.50 \text{ per share}$$

Since the accounts show assets at historical cost rather than current value, this is not a very meaningful figure. Where information on the value of assets is available, then this might be on either of two bases:

(a)   Replacement cost. For our example of Oldbuck Ltd, using the information in note 1, the total value of the business on a replacement cost basis is:

	£000
Property	120
Plant	70
Stock	45
Debtors	39
Cash	4
	278
Less Creditors	35
	243

$$\therefore \text{Value per share } \frac{£243\,000}{100\,000} = £2.43 \text{ per share}$$

(b) Liquidation basis. Here we total the realizable value of assets, deducting the estimated cost of liquidation:

	£000	£000
Property		115
Plant		15
Stock		40
Debtors		39
Cash		4
		213
Less Creditors	35	
Costs	5	40
		173

$\therefore$ Value per share $\dfrac{\text{£173\,000}}{\text{100\,000}} = \text{£1.73 per share}$

Earnings valuation

A common approach to valuing the shares of an unlisted company is to make a comparison with the relationship between share price and earnings in a similar listed company.

We have already introduced, in Chapter 6 above, the ratio of earnings per share is:

$$\frac{\text{Profit after tax}}{\text{Number of ordinary shares}}$$

This can be related to the share price in two ways:

(a) The earnings yield ratio, being:

$$\frac{\text{Earnings per share}}{\text{Share price}}$$

(b) The price earnings ratio (P/E ratio), being:

$$\frac{\text{Share price}}{\text{Earnings per share}}$$

If we are given one of these ratios for a listed company, we can estimate the value of shares in a similar unlisted company as:

$$\text{Earnings per share} \times \frac{100}{\text{Earnings yield \%}} = \text{Value of share}$$

or $\qquad$ Earnings per share $\times$ P/E ratio = Value of share

The earnings of the company to be valued will sometimes be taken as the average of several years rather than simply the most recent year. In computing the earnings, adjustments may be made to correct errors, allow for expected changes in costs or revenues, and to allow for the 'fair value' of the services performed by shareholder directors rather than actual directors' salaries paid.

To take our example Oldbuck Ltd, adjusted earnings will be:

	1983 £000	1984 £000	1985 £000
Profit	20	18	22
Add Excess director's remuneration	1	1	1
	21	19	23

Average is $\dfrac{21 + 19 + 23}{3} = 21$

$\therefore$ Earnings per share $\dfrac{21\,000}{10\,000} = 21\text{p}$

$\therefore$ Value per share is $21\text{p} \times 7 = £1.47$

Shares may also be valued by reference to the dividend yield, being:

$$\frac{\text{Dividend per share}}{\text{Share price}}$$

When the dividend yield for a similar listed company is known, then the share value will be:

$$\text{Dividend per share} \times \frac{1}{\text{Dividend yield}}$$

Thus in our example, where the dividend yield of a similar listed company is 6 per cent, the dividend per share is:

$$\frac{12\,000}{100\,000} = 12\text{p}$$

and the value per share will be:

$$12\text{p} \times \frac{1}{0.06} = £2$$

It is sometimes argued that a listed company's shares will have a greater relative value because they are more easily marketable. Where this view is taken, the computed value may be cut by a pre-determined percentage to reflect the lower value.

Example 10.4

The accounts of Oldbuck Ltd for the year to 31 December 1985 show:

Balance Sheet as at 31 December 1985

	£000	£000
Fixed assets:		
Freehold property		60
Plant		40
		100

Current assets:
Stock	42	
Debtors	39	
Cash	4	
	85	
Less Creditors	35	
Net current assets		50
		150

Share capital – ordinary shares of £1	100
Reserves	50
	150

Appropriation accounts:	1983	1984	1984
	£000	£000	£000
Profit after interest and tax	20	18	22
Dividend	12	12	12
Retained profit	8	6	10

Notes

(1)   Estimates of replacement cost and net realizable value of assets are:

	Replacement cost	NRV
	£000	£000
Property	120	115
Plant	70	15
Stock	45	40

(2)   It is estimated that in a liquidation, debtors would realize their full amount while the cost of liquidation would be £500.

(3)   Profit is shown after director's emoluments of £13 000 per year. The sold director, Mr Oldbuck, is a major shareholder in the company. He estimates that the market value of his services is £12 000 per year.

(4)   Similar listed companies have a P/E ratio of 7 and a dividend yield of 6 per cent.

Comparison of methods

Figure 10.8 shows how each of our valuation methods had produced a different result. None of these methods can be regarded as giving a single, definitive, figure of 'value'. Considering the significance of each in turn:

(a)   *Book value.* The most available figure from the face of the accounts, but not a very meaningful figure. This might be used to suggest an initial idea of the broad price area in which value might fall.

(b)   *Asset replacement cost.* Since the business already possesses the assets, and would not necessarily choose to replace in the same form if deprived of them, this is not directly linked to any choice faced by the business. It may be an indicator of the upper limit of the value of the business, since any purchaser has the choice of setting up in business by acquiring a similar bundle of assets by direct purchase. However, such a purchaser may be willing to pay a premium price for the 'goodwill' of the business.

Book value	£1.50
Asset replacement cost	£2.43
Liquidation basis	£1.73
Earnings yield	£1.47
Dividend yield	£2.00

Figure 10.8   Valuation of one share in Oldbuck Ltd

(c) *Liquidation basis.* This might be regarded as a base price for the business, since the owners have the option of liquidating the business at this value.

(d) *Earnings yield.* Indicates the value of the business as a going concern. However, its real value depends on estimated future earnings rather than actual reported past earnings. Where a large block of shares is being valued, future earnings will be dependent on the consequences of any management changes made under the influence of the new owner.

(e) *Dividend yield.* On this basis value is established by the flow of benefits to the shareholder. This raises the question of whether future dividends are likely to increase or reduce.

An important factor to be taken into account in share valuation is the size of the block of shares to be traded. Thus a controlling block of shares gives the owner control over both the assets and the management policies of the company, so that all these valuation bases may be significant. By contrast, the owner of a small block of shares has no control over how the assets are employed and may find a dividend yield valuation more significant.

Finally, the value of a business, particularly to an owner manager, is likely to reflect non-financial considerations. For example, a business involving a particularly congenial form of work or location may have a greater value in relation to earnings.

Liquidation and reconstruction

Background

When a company is in difficulties a decision may be taken to liquidate it. Such a decision may originate from the shareholders or on the initiative of creditors whose claims on the company have not been met. There are precise rules on the order in which claims on a company should be met out of the available assets, and these are considered in detail below.

Alternatively, some form of reconstruction of the company may be attempted, in the hope of preserving the business. Below we consider the basic principles involved in putting together a reconstruction scheme.

It should be emphasized that both liquidation and company reconstruction involve complex legal procedures which fall outside the scope of this text.

Liquidation

In a liquidation the assets of a company will be realized and applied to meeting the various claims upon the company. Where a loan is secured by a fixed charge, then the proceeds from disposing of the asset which is the subject of the charge will first be applied to repayment of that loan; if the sale proceeds exceed the amount of the loan, then the excess is included in the funds realized from other assets; if the sale proceeds do not cover the whole of the loan, then the balance of the loan is treated as an unsecured creditor unless there is a *specific* agreement that the balance should be secured by a floating charge.

The proceeds of the sale of all the assets not specifically pledged by a fixed charge will be applied in the following order:

(a) Payment of the costs of liquidation.
(b) Payment of preferential creditors. These are defined precisely by law and fall into two broad categories:

(1) All forms of taxation, including rates, but generally restricted to one year's tax due.
(2) Subject to certain limits, various payments due to employees.

(c) Creditors secured by a floating charge. As we have seen in Chapter 5 above, such a charge only *crystallizes* in specified circumstances and, insofar as it involves postponement of any claim until the preferential creditors are satisfied, is clearly inferior as a security to a fixed charge.
(d) Unsecured creditors. These include all other parties who are owed money by the company.
(e) Shareholders. When all claims upon the company have been met, then any remaining funds will be distributed among the shareholders, in the order laid down by the Articles of Association. It should be noted that preference shareholders do *not* enjoy any priority payment in a liquidation unless the Articles make specific provision for this.

Example 10.5 shows a simple case of how a liquidation might arise.

Example 10.5

At 31 December 1986 the balance sheet of Galt Ltd showed:

	£000	£000
Property		400
Plant		360
		760
Current assets:		
Stock	320	
Debtors	400	
	800	
Current liabilities:		
Overdraft (secured by a floating charge)	550	
Creditors	350	
	900	

Net current assets	(100)
	660
Debenture (secured by a fixed charge on the property	300
	360
10% preference shares of £1	100
Ordinary shares of £1	400
Retained profits	(140)
	360

Notes:
(1) Creditors include preferential creditors of £70 000.
(2) Liquidation costs are expected to amount to £30 000.
(3) Assets are expected to realize the following amounts in a liquidation.

	£000
Property	320
Plant	120
Stock	230
Debtors	420

	£000	£000
Assets not specifically pledged:		
Plant		120
Stock		230
Debtors		420
		770
Pledged assets:		
Property	320	
Less Debenture	300	
		20
		790
Less Liquidation costs		30
		760
Less Preferential creditors		70
		690
Less Overdraft		550
		140
Less Unsecured creditors (350 – 70)		280
Deficiency		(140)

Unsecured creditors receive:

$$\frac{£140\,000}{280\,000} = 50\text{p in }£$$

Figure 10.9 Order of realization of the assets of Galt Ltd

The way in which the liquidation of Galt Ltd would be conducted is shown in Fig. 10.9. Taking each stage:

(a)   We total the expected proceeds from all those assets not subject to a fixed charge.
(b)   We find any surplus arising on the asset subject to the fixed charge and add this on to the funds available for distribution.
(c)   We deduct from the funds available each type of claim, in order of legal priority. When we come to a category of claim that cannot be met in full, then that category of creditor will only be paid in the part, normally expressed as a certain number of 'pence in the pound'.

Reconstruction

Sometimes, when a company is in difficulties, an attempt will be made to rescue the business rather than liquidate. Two broad reasons can be identified for this:

(a)   Assets disposed of in a forced sale may have a very low realizable value, so that it may well be financially more attractive to try and put the business on a viable basis.
(b)   Both employees and trade contracts are likely to be anxious to keep the business intact. Major creditors, such as banks, may consider it worthwhile to look favourably on any rescue scheme in order to maintain good public relations.

A rescue of a business is often combined with a *capital reduction scheme* whereby part of the nominal value of share capital is written off. In such a scheme assets are revalued on a realistic basis, with goodwill almost invariably written off. Accumulated deficits on the reserves will also be written off against share capital. Creditors may be persuaded to offer longer payment terms or to accept new ordinary shares in the business. Preference shareholders will suffer a loss of return on their shares in proportion to the amount of their share capital written off, and might be compensated in part by a new issue of ordinary shares. The ordinary shareholders suffer no direct loss when the nominal value of their share capital is written down, but may suffer an indirect loss in that the issue of new ordinary shares to those involved in the scheme involves a dilution of the equity.

We can illustrate how a capital reconstruction scheme might be put together if we refer back to our example Galt Ltd. In that example, we saw that in a liquidation the unsecured creditors would receive only half the amount due to them, while all shareholders would receive nothing; thus all these parties would have an interest in supporting a scheme to keep the company in business.

Let us suppose that all interested parties agree a reconstruction scheme on the following basis:
(a)   The property is to be sold for £410 000 and leased back, the debenture holders being paid out of the proceeds.
(b)   Plant is to be revalued at £250 000, while on a going concern basis the present figures for stock and debtors are regarded as acceptable.
(c)   £50 000 of the overdraft is to be repaid immediately, the remaining amount being converted to a long-term loan secured by a floating charge.
(d)   The preferential creditors are to be repaid immediately, and unsecured creditors are to receive 25 per cent of the amount owing immediately with the remainder payable in 18 months' time.
(e)   The nominal value of each ordinary share and preference share is to be reduced from £1 to 50p. The preference shareholders will receive one ordinary share for every ten preference shares held, and all the ordinary shareholders have agreed to subscribe for one share at nominal value for every two currently held.

		£000	£000
(a)	*Effects*		
	Amount written off shares		250
	Surplus on asset realization		10
			260
	Less		
	New ordinary shares issued to		
	preference shareholders	5	
	Written off plant	110	
	Debit balance on retained profits	140	255
	Surplus		5
(b)	*Bank balance*		
	Raised from share issue		100
	Property sale		410
			510
	Less		
	Debenture redemption	300	
	Bank overdraft	50	
	Secured creditors	70	
	Unsecured creditors	70	490
	Balance carried forward		20
(c)	*Balance Sheet*		
	Plant		250
	Stock		320
	Debtors		480
	Bank		20
			1070
	Preference shares		50
	Ordinary shares		305
	Capital reserve		5
	Bank		500
	Creditors		210
			1070

Figure 10.10   Application of a capital reduction scheme

Figure 10.10 shows how we would compute the effect of these proposals on the balance sheet of Galt Ltd. The stages are:

(a)   All changes in value, or arising on realization, are reflected in a single capital reduction account which effectively sets off all write downs and costs (such as the issue of ordinary shares to preference shareholders) against the write down of share capital. Any surplus on capital reduction will be a *capital* reserve.

(b)   The second stage is to compute the effect of all cash transactions on the bank balance.

(c)   A balance sheet can now be constructed, showing all items at their new amounts. Note that where current liabilities are deferred by agreement these must be shown as long-term liabilities.

Alternatively, a rescue might be effected by the formation of a completely new company to take over the business of the old. Such a company might satisfy some claims on the old company by an issue of shares in the new company.

Conclusion

This has been a wide-ranging chapter, from which the following broad points emerge:

(a)   In management accounting the conventions used differ materially from financial accounting and, in particular, marginal costing is more likely to be relevant to decision making than absorption costing.

(b)   In planning the management of the cash resources of a business, a cash budget is prepared, reversing the accruals basis used in preparing financial accounts.

(c)   A variety of techniques are used to appraise capital investment proposals, the more sophisticated involving discounted cash flow techniques.

(d)   In valuing shares a number of methods can be used to indicate a spread of potential values.

(e)   In a liquidation the assets of a company may be realized at a very different figure from their book amount, and will be distributed in a strict order of priority to those with claims on the business.

Questions

10.1   Discuss the differing requirements of internal and external financial reporting.
(Cert. Dip. in Accounting & Finance, June 1979)

10.2   A project to produce and market a new electric motor is under consideration by the management of New Xmas Products Ltd. The new product proposal anticipates the following:

Selling price (to the retail trade)	£6 per unit
Advertising and promotion costs as percentage of sales	20%
Variable manufacturing costs for materials, labour and overheads	£1.20 per unit
Variable distribution and selling costs as percentage of sales	4%

Fixed production costs to cover depreciation of plant and associated fixed factory costs are estimated at £8000 and will provide capacity to produce 10 000 units per month. Fixed administration costs are forecasts at £7000 per month.

Production will begin in July at the rate of 5000 units per month, although sales volumes are forecast as follows:

	July	*August*	*September*
Units	3000	5000	7000

You are required to:

(a)   Prepare a forecast profit statement for the electric motor for July, August and September on the following costing bases:

(i)   direct (variable costing),
(ii)   absorption of production fixed costs based on expected output;

(b)   prepare a table of stock valuations at the end of July using both bases above, and reconcile your answers with the answers to (a);

(c)   explain which, if either, basis of accounting you find most justifiable, and why.
(Cert. Dip. in Accounting & Finance, June 1982)

10.3   At the beginning of 1981 Deer Ltd was incorporated and manufactures a single product. At the end of the first year's operations the company's accountant prepared a draft profit and loss account which contains the following financial information:

Profit and Loss Account of Deer Ltd for 1981

	£	£
Sales (200 000 units)		600 000
Less Prime cost of units manufactured during 1981 (500 000 units)	800 000	
Deduct closing stock	480 000	
Prime cost of goods sold	320 000	
Fixed costs:		
Factory expenses	200 000	
General expenses	100 000	620 000
Net loss		£20 000

Additional finance is required, and the directors are worried that the company's bank manager is unlikely to regard the financial facts shown above as a satisfactory basis for a further advance. The company's accountant made the following observation and suggestion.

The cause of the poor result for 1981 was the decision to value closing stock on the prime cost basis. An acceptable alternative practice would involve charging factory expenses to the total number of units produced and carrying forward an appropriate proportion of those expenses as part of the closing stock value.

Required:

(a)   A revised profit and loss account, for presentation to the company's bank, valuing closing stock on the total (absorption) cost basis suggested by the company's accountant.
(b)   Assuming that, in 1982, the company again produces 500 000 units but sells 700 000 units, calculate the expected profit using each of the two stock valuation bases. Assume also that, in 1982, sales price per unit and costs incurred will be the same as for 1981.
(c)   Comment briefly on the accountant's suggestion and its likely effect on the bank manager's response to the request for additional finance.

(AIB, April 1982)

10.4   Ken Dowden and his two brothers are the three directors of a small company, Aluminex Ltd, which manufacturers aluminium widgets. The company has banked with you for a number of years and is financially sound. The summarized final accounts for 1982 are set out below:

Summarized Profit and Loss Account for 1982

	£	£
Turnover (100 000 units at £5 each)		500 000
Less Variable costs	300 000	
Depreciation	20 000	
Other fixed costs	120 000	440 000
Net profit		£60 000

Summarized Balance Sheet at 31 December 1982

	£
Fixed assets at cost	200 000
Less Accumulated depreciation	80 000
	120 000
Working capital	200 000
Bank deposit account	25 000
	£345 000
Financed by:	
Share capital	200 000
Retained profits	145 000
	£345 000

It is expected that during 1983 production costs for the existing level of activity will remain unchanged; the selling price is also expected to remain the same. In 1982 the company worked a day shift only and existing plant was used to its full capacity. There is a heavy demand for the company's product and the three directors are planning to increase the level of activity. Ken Dowden's brothers believe that it will be possible to sell another 50 000 widgets, without reducing the sales price, but Ken believes that an increase of 30 000 is a more realistic estimate. Two alternative proposals for increasing the level of output are under consideration:

(1) **Work an evening shift.** This would enable the company to produce additional output of up to 50 000 units. The variable cost per unit would be 50 per cent higher than the rate for the day shift, the depreciation charge would remain unchanged and other fixed costs would increase by £2000.

(2) **Purchase additional plant** costing £120 000, with a capacity of 50 000 units. The plant would be depreciated on the straight-line basis over ten years, assuming a nil residual value. The variable cost per unit and annual depreciation charge on the existing plant would remain unchanged but other fixed costs would increase by £40 000.

Under either alternative, working capital requirements would increase proportionately with the level of activity. The balance on the bank deposit account, in the balance sheet set out above, is surplus to operating requirements and could be used to help to finance the planned expansion of activity. Your bank has been approached to finance any shortfall.

Required:

(a) A summarized profit and loss account for 1983 and a summarized balance sheet at 31 December 1983, under alternative (1), assuming sales of widgets increase to 150 000 units.

(b) A summarized profit and loss account for 1983 and a summarized balance sheet at 31 December 1983, under alternative (2), assuming sales of widgets increase to 150 000 units.

(c) A full discussion of the two alternatives, including an assessment of the effect of the company failing to achieve additional sales of 50 000 units. You should support your discussion with calculations of the break-even point on the additional sales (i.e. the amount of additional sales required to ensure that profits earned in 1983 are equal to those earned in 1982).

Notes:
(1)   Assume that the calculations are being made on 1 January 1983.
(2)   The balance on the bank account or the bank overdraft may be treated as the balancing item in the balance sheets you prepare.
(3)   The forecast accounts should be presented in columnar format.
(4)   Ignore interest payable, if any.

(AIB, September 1983)

10.5   The directors of Carter Ltd have decided to undertake a programme of expansion. They have under consideration two mutually exclusive five-year projects and intend to invest in the project which offers the greater financial gain. Project I requires an initial capital investment of £140 000 and Project II an initial capital investment of £280 000. The annual net cash flows which are expected to arise from the project are as follows:

Year	Project I	Project II
1	£30 000	£100 000
2	£60 000	£90 000
3	£60 000	£90 000
4	£60 000	£90 000
5	£24 155	£53 706

Required:

(a)   Calculations of the net present value of each of the two projects, assuming a 12 per cent cost of capital.
(b)   Calculations of the discounted cash flow yield (internal rate of return) of each of the two projects.
(c)   Compare and comment on the results of your calculations under (a) and (b). You should support your analysis with relevant numerical calculations.

Notes:
 (i)   The capital investment will be undertaken immediately and the annual cash flows may be assumed to arise at the year end.
(ii)   Ignore taxation.

Table of factors for the present value of £1

Year	12%	13%	14%	15%	16%	17%	18%	19%	20%	21%	22%
1	0.893	0.885	0.877	0.870	0.862	0.855	0.847	0.840	0.833	0.826	0.820
2	0.797	0.783	0.769	0.756	0.743	0.731	0.718	0.706	0.694	0.683	0.671
3	0.712	0.693	0.675	0.658	0.641	0.624	0.609	0.593	0.579	0.564	0.551
4	0.636	0.613	0.592	0.572	0.552	0.534	0.516	0.499	0.482	0.467	0.451
5	0.567	0.543	0.519	0.497	0.476	0.456	0.437	0.419	0.402	0.386	0.370

(AIB, April 1981)

10.6   TVR Manufacturers Ltd (TVR) produces television recording equipment. Its chief designer has discovered a method of improving the performance of domestic TVR equipment, and the company has patented the invention.
   TVR has received offers from two other companies:

(1) Shadow Ltd is prepared to purchase the patent outright for £50 000 (payable immediately).

(2) Contrast Ltd seeks an exclusive licence to use the process in exchange for a royalty. TVR estimates that it would receive £15 000 per annum for 7 years after which the patent would be worthless.

TVR is considering other possibilities:

(3) Sub-contracting both processing and marketing to another manufacturer. TVR estimates that its net receipts would be £13 500 per annum for 8 years, at the end of which the patent would be valueless.

(4) Acquiring equipment to undertake the process itself, and to market the product with its general range. It would be necessary to lease premises and equipment, and it is estimated that after meeting all annual outlays, the net receipts would amount to £25 000 per annum for 9 years. It would also be necessary to buy certain items of equipment for £50 000 and to tie up working capital of £30 000. At the end of the 9 years, the equipment will be valueless, but the working capital will no longer be tied up.

TVR's cost of capital is 10 per cent (throughout).

(i) Prepare a numerical analysis of the options available to TVR.
(ii) Discuss the factors to be taken into account by the directors of TVR in their deliberations.

10.7 (a) From the folowing information calculate:
(i) the net present value,
(ii) the payback period.

The Electrogram

Capital outlay	£240 000
Life of project	5 years

Profit forecast

Year	£
1	16 000
2	24 000
3	30 000
4	60 000
5	24 000

The scrap value of the project is £40 000 and will be received at the end of year five.

The company uses the straight-line method of depreciation.

The company's cost of capital is 14 per cent.

Present value tables

Years (n)	Present value of an annuity of 1 $$\frac{1-(1+r)^{-n}}{r}$$ $r = 14$	Present value of 1 at compound interest $(1+r)^{-n}$ $r = 14$
1	0.8772	0.8772
2	1.6467	0.7695
3	2.3216	0.6750

4	2.9137	0.5921
5	3.4331	0.5194
6	3.8887	0.4556

(b)   Although discounted cash flow is widely considered to be a superior method of investment appraisal, the payback method has still been shown to be the most popular method in practice. Suggest reasons why this may be the case.

(CDFA, December 1977)

10.8   The management of Race Ltd are planning their capital investment programme for the forthcoming twelve months. They now have to consider whether to replace a machine, which the company has owned for five years, with a new and more efficient machine. A full examination of the available information reveals the following facts and estimates:

	Old machine	*New machine*
Original cost	£60 000	
Book value	£30 000	
Cost new		£40 000
Estimated useful life from new		5 years
Net profit per annum	£10 000	£18 000

In calculating the above figures for net profit, all operating costs have been deducted. These include depreciation calculated on the straight-line basis, assuming a nil residual value at the end of the estimated useful life.

The company pays corporation tax at 50 per cent on its taxable profits, calculated as follows:

 (i)   For the old machine: net profit before depreciation.
(ii)   For the new machine: net profit before depreciation (except that a 100 per cent first-year allowance will be obtained on the new plant, and it is to be assumed that the allowance will be offset only against the taxable profit arising from this project until exhausted).

Any tax liabilities will be paid exactly twelve months after the end of the accounting period in respect of which they accrue.

Required:

(a)   Calculations of the total future net cash flow arising from each of the above alternatives.
(b)   Calculations of the net present value of each of the above alternatives. You should assume an 11 per cent cost of capital for discounting purposes.
(c)   A comparison of the results obtained under (a) and (b) above.
(d)   A brief report to the management of Race Ltd, advising them on their choice between the two alternatives.

(AIB, September 1979)

10.9   The Striker Light Engineering Company has recently completed its functional budgets. An analysis of the budgets reveals the following situation:

Month (4 weeks) 1979	Sales £	Materials £	Wages £
February	40 000	30 000	10 000

March	50 000	40 000	10 000
April	50 000	40 000	14 000
May	60 000	60 000	14 000
June	50 000	60 000	14 000
July	70 000	50 000	12 000
August	60 000	50 000	12 000
September	70 000	40 000	12 000

Overheads (excluding depreciation):
  Fixed   £5000 per month
  Variable   5% of sales

Notes
(1)   The cash balance on 1 April 1979 will be £150 000.
(2)   The company is at present taking two months' credit from its creditors and extending one month's credit to its customers. Twenty per cent of sales are for cash. Thirty per cent of purchases are for cash on which 2 per cent cash discount is received.
(3)   All overheads are paid one month after they have incurred.
(4)   Wages are paid one week in arrears.
(5)   From 1 June the company will start to supply goods under a special contract. The contract is for additional sales of £20 000 per month for the next six months, payable three months after delivery. The company will be able to supply from existing stocks. Payment of commission of 5 per cent to an agent will be made one month after delivery.
(6)   On 1 July the company will take delivery of a new delivery van. The old van which has been fully depreciated will be traded in against the new van at a value of £500. The price of the van will be £5500 after allowing for the trade-in and is expected to have a six-year life. Payment will be made on delivery.

You are required:
(a)   To prepare the cash budget for the six months ending 30 September 1979.
(b)   To consider the company's cash situation in the light of demands from customers for an extra two months' credit on sales from 1 April 1979.

(CDFA, December 1978)

10.10   Popplewell Ltd is an engineering company and the directors have decided to extend the range of items manufactured by producing a special type of steel pallet suitable for the storage of cylinders or dangerous gases. The summarized accounts of Popplewell Ltd for 1980 are as follows:

Manufacturing, Trading and Profit and Loss Account for 1980

	£	£
Sales		1 160 000
Less Raw materials consumed	305 200	
Manufacturing wages	246 500	
Factory overheads (depreciation £27 000)	238 300	
Cost of goods manufactured	790 000	
Opening stock of finished goods	167 000	
Closing stock of finished goods	(167 000)	
Cost of goods sold		790 000
		370 000

Gross profit (b/d)	370 000
Administration, selling and distribution costs (depreciation £10 000)	277 000
Net profit	£93 000

Balance Sheet at 31 December 1980

	£		£
Share capital	300 000	Fixed assets at cost	
Reserves	223,000	less depreciation	301 000
		Stocks of raw materials	
	523 000	and finished goods	187 000
		Debtors	73 000
Trade creditors	62 000	Bank	24 000
	£585 000		£585 000

It is expected that existing activities will continue at a similar level during the forth-coming year, and for forecasting purposes it is to be assumed that the 1980 results will be exactly repeated. None of the existing plant will require replacement until 1985.

The following plans and forecasts are provided in connection with the plan to manufacture pallets.

(i)   Plant and machinery costing £80 000 will be required and this will be purchased in March and paid for immediately. The plant is expected to have a five-year life and a nil scrap value at the end of that period.

(ii) The raw materials needed to manufacture 150 pallets will be purchased in March and sufficient purchases will be made in each subsequent month to replace quantities consumed. The raw materials cost per pallet is estimated at £50 and one month's credit will be obtained from suppliers.

(iii) Production will commence on 1 April 1981 at the rate of 100 pallets each month and sales are expected to be made at a similar rate commencing 1 May 1981. The selling price of each pallet is to be £130 and one month's credit is to be allowed to customers. No bad debts are expected to arise.

(iv) Direct wages are expected to amount to £30 per pallet, and factory overhead expenses (other than depreciation) relating specifically to this project will commence in March and will be £1900 per month. Both wages and overheads will be paid for during the month the service is provided. There will be no increase in administration, selling and distribution costs.

Required:

(a)   A forecast of cash receipts and cash payments for the new project covering each of the ten months to 31 December 1981.

(b)   A forecast profit statement for the new project for 1981.

(c)   A calculation of the bank balance of Popplewell Ltd at 31 December 1981.

(d)   A brief report, for the company's bank, on the profitability and financial implications of the new project, for which the bank has been asked to provide overdraft facilities if required.

Notes:
(1) It is the company's policy to value finished stock at prime cost, i.e. raw materials and direct labour only, in its management reports.
(2) Ignore work in progress, taxation, dividends and any bank interest payable.
10.11   The directors of Connecticut plc, who own 50 per cent of the company's ordinary shares, have approached the bank requesting a renewal of the overdraft facility of £50 000 for a further twelve months. Connecticut's share quotation was suspended last month because of irregularities concerning the purchase and sale of the company's shares by one of its directors. The director has since resigned and it is expected that the Stock Exchange will resume dealing in the company's shares in the near future.

The following historical cost information has been extracted from previously published acounts:

Balance Sheet at 31 December 1982

	£000	£000
Fixed assets:		
Equipment at cost less depreciation		800
Current assets:		
Stocks	810	
Debtors	580	
	1390	
Current liabilities;		
Trade creditors	316	
Proposed dividends	100	
Bank overdraft	24	
	440	
Net current assets		950
		1750
Capital and reserves:		
Ordinary shares (£1 each)		1000
Reserves		550
		1550
10% preference shares		200
		1750

Profit and Loss Accounts

	1980	1981	1982
Net profit for the year	126	210	240
Less Dividends — ordinary shares	80	80	80
— preference shares	20	20	20
Retained profit for the year	26	110	140

The following additional information is provided:

(1) Depreciation of £60 000 per year has been charged on the equipment during each of the last three years. The equipment is old and in need of replacement; annual

depreciation based on current replacement cost would be in the region of £76 000.

(2)   On investigation, the stock in the balance sheet shown above was found to be overvalued by £14 000.

(3)   The profit for 1980 was arrived at after deducting an exceptional loss of £56 000 arising from the liquidation of a major customer.

(4)   It is estimated that the equipment and stocks possess respective liquidation values of £240 000 and £600 000. The debtors would be collected in full and liquidation costs would amount to £52 000.

(5)   A recent article in the financial press estimated a dividend yield of 12 per cent and an earnings yield of 20 per cent for other companies in Connecticut's industry.

Required:

(a)   A table, completed in the following form, showing valuations for the entire ordinary share capital of Connecticut plc.

	Valuation
(1) Earnings yield basis (based on average earnings for the last three years, after making appropriate adjustments)	
(2) Liquidation (break-up basis)	
(3) Dividend yield basis	

(b)   Comments on the significance of the above-mentioned valuations, paying particular attention to the request for a renewal of the overdraft facility.

Notes:

(1)   Assume that you are making the valuations at 31 December 1982.

(2)   Ignore taxation.

(AIB, April 1983)

10.12   The following is the summarized balance sheet of Allerton Ltd at 31 March 1984:

	£000		£000
Issued share capital, £1 shares	400	Freehold building at cost less depreciation	40
Profit and loss account	80	Plant and equipment at cost less depreciation	504
	480		544
12% debentures repayable 1990	400		
Sundry creditors	205	Stock	420
Bank overdraft	195	Debtors	316
	1280		1280

The bank overdraft is secured by a fixed charge on the freehold building; the debentures, all held by Shipley plc, are secured by a floating charge over the remaining assets of Allerton.

Allerton has been trading unprofitably for over two years and is now finding it impossible to meet its financial obligations. A meeting of creditors has been called to examine its affairs, and the following proposals are put forward for consideration:

(1)   Piecemeal liquidation of the company. It is estimated that the company's assets, sold individually, would realize the following amounts:

	£000
Freehold building	70
Plant and equipment	20
Stocks	290
Debtors	250

Liquidation costs are estimated at £10 000 and sundry creditors, in the above balance sheet, include preferential creditors of £30 000.

(2)   Sale of company as a going concern. Shipley would purchase the shares for a token sum and pay immediately the preferential creditors, in full, and the other sundry creditors and the bank 20p in the £ on account of the amounts shown as due to them in the balance sheet. Seventy-five per cent of the balances then remaining outstanding would be repaid after one year but would not attract interest during the interim period.

Assume that:

(1)   the current rate of interest on all forms of borrowing is 12 per cent;
(2)   the £195 000 overdraft in the balance sheet included interest to date;
(3)   the calculations are being made on 1 April 1984;
(4)   piecemeal liquidation, if selected, would occur immediately; alternatively the company could be sold to Shipley at once.

Required:

(a)   Calculations showing the amount which would be received by the bank under each proposal.
(b)   A brief explanation of the relative merits of the two proposals from the bank's point of view.

(AIB, May 1984)

10.13   Arches Limited has incurred trading losses during each of its last three accounting periods and is now in severe financial difficulty. The company's balance sheet at 31 March 1980 is as follows:

Balance sheet

	£		£
Ordinary shares (£1 each)	200 000	Fixed assets at cost	
Profit and loss account	(30 000)	less depreciation	239 000
	170 000		
12% debenture stock	100 000	Goodwill	37 000
Bank overdraft (secured)	67 000	Stock	90 000
Trade creditors	93 000	Trade debtors	64 000
	430 000		430 000

A reorganization of the company's activities during March 1980 resulted in a transfer of resources from loss-making to profitable product lines. A meeting of all parties involved is held on 2 April 1980 to consider a scheme of reconstruction under the Companies Acts. The proposal made by the directors is that a new company called Arches (1980) Limited be formed to take over the assets, liabilities and business activities of Arches

Limited. It is estimated that the annual trading profits of Arches (1980) Limited, for the foreseeable future, will be £43 500 before charging debenture interest (see below). After debenture interest has been deducted, 50 per cent of the balance remaining is to be paid out as dividends.

Arches (1980) Limited would take over the fixed assets at their depreciated replacement cost, estimated at £156 000; stock, trade debtors, trade creditors and the bank overdraft would be transferred as the figures appearing in the above balance sheet.

Arches (1980) Limited would issue 20p ordinary shares and 15 per cent debenture stock as follows:

(1)   The existing debenture holders of Arches Limited would receive £10 of 15 per cent debenture stock for every £20 of 12 per cent debenture stock presently held. They would also receive the number of 20p ordinary shares which causes the dividend plus debenture interest receivable from Arches (1980) Limited to be equal to the amount of debenture interest previously received from Arches Limited.

(2)   The issued share capital of Arches (1980) Limited would consist of 500 000 ordinary shares of 20p each. After the issue of ordinary shares referred to above, the balance of the 500 000 shares would be issued on a pro-rata basis in exchange for the ordinary shares held in Arches Limited.

If the reconstruction proposal is accepted, the existing ordinary shareholders of Arches Limited have agreed to subscribe in cash for an additional 400 000 ordinary shares of 20p each at par. The proceeds would be used primarily to repay the bank overdraft.

Required:

The opening balance sheet of Arches (1980) Limited assuming the proposed reconstruction is adopted and put into effect. The balance sheet should show clearly the number of ordinary shares issued to the debenture stock holders of Arches Limited and the number of shares issued to the ordinary shareholders of Arches Limited, distinguishing those paid for in cash.

Notes:
(1)   Ignore taxation and any arrears or accruals of dividends or interest.
(2)   Assume that no changes have occurred since the balance sheet date.

(AIB, April 1980)

10.14   The following is the summarized balance sheet of Lowdown Ltd at 15 September 1978:

	£		£
Issued share capital	50 000	Leasehold property less depreciation	40 000
Revenue reserves	64 000	Equipment, less depreciation	38 000
Debentures	32 000	Stocks	70 000
Bank loan	30 000	Debtors	72 000
Creditors	49 000	Cash	5 000
	£225 000		£225 000

The debentures, which are held by one of the company's directors, are secured by a floating charge over the company's assets and are payable between 1992 and 1995.

The bank loan is secured by a charge over the leasehold property. Lowdown Ltd is a publishing company and has recently lost a court case for publishing a libel in a book produced by the company. The company now owes damages and legal costs totalling £53 000, which do not appear in the balance sheet shown above. Consequently, a meeting of creditors has been called to consider the company's affairs. Two proposals are to be considered at the meeting:

(a) Immediate liquidation of the company
In these circumstances the company's assets would realize the following amounts:

Leasehold property	£20 000
Equipment	£12 000
Stocks	£18 000
Debtors	£65 000
Cash	£5 000

Estimated liquidation costs would be £16 000.

Preferential creditors for £12 000 are included among creditors in the balance sheet.

The damages and legal costs of the libel action can be assumed to rank as unsecured creditors.

(b) Takeover by Jackal Press
Jackal Press would be prepared to acquire the shares of Lowdown Ltd for a token sum. Jackal Press would provide funds for continuing the operations of Lowdown Ltd and preferential creditors would be immediately paid in full. But all other liabilities (including those to the debenture holders and the bank) would be subject to a moratorium of one year. At the end of the year, 85 pence in the £ would be paid on those liabilities irrespective of their nature, and in exchange the holders of those liabilities would be required to waive all claims (including security) and interest.

Jackal Press offers undoubted financial guarantees to back its proposals. Assume that:

(1) the current rate of interest on all forms of borrowing is 12 per cent;
(2) the debentures and bank loan in the balance sheet include interest to date;
(3) the proposal adopted would be put into effect immediately;
(4) no changes have occurred since the balance sheet date.

Required;

(a) Calculations showing the amounts which would be received by the bank and unsecured creditors under both proposals.
(b) Brief comments on the relative merits of the proposals from the bank's viewpoint.

(AIB, September 1978)

10.15   One of your bank's customers, Jeremiah, has deposited 6000 shares in Eastgate Ltd as security for a personal bank overdraft on which £2460 is at present outstanding. You have heard that, at a meeting between the directors and creditors of Eastgate Ltd held on 20 April 1981, it was decided to liquidate that company. Certain facts and estimates were examined by the meeting. These included:

(1) Balance Sheet of Eastgate Ltd at 19 April 1981:

	£	£		£	£
Share capital (£1 shares)		100 000	Goodwill at cost		22 000
Reserves at 31 December 1980	70 000		Freehold property at cost		45 000
Loss for 1981 to date	68 000		Plant and machinery at cost less depreciation		48 000
		2 000			115 000
		102 000	Quoted investments (market value £16 000)		12 000
12% debenture		50 000	Current assets:		
Current liabilities:			Stock	108 000	
Creditors	209 000		Debtors	194 000	302 000
Bank overdraft	68 000				
		277 000			
		£429 000			£429 000

(2)   The following asset values were considered to be relevant in a liquidation:

	£
Plant and machinery	10 000
Stock	47 000
Debtors	160 000

There was significant disagreement regarding the likely value of the freehold property. The majority accepted a valuation of £60 000 recently obtained from a firm of surveyors. A minority argued that, in view of the development potential in the area where this property was located, a sale figure of £150 000 was likely to be much nearer the mark.

(3)   Eastgate's Ltd's bank holds a fixed charge on the freehold property as security for the overdraft.

(4)   Of the £209 000 creditors, £57 000 were estimated as being preferential.

(5)   The debenture is secured by a floating charge over the assets of Eastgate Ltd other than the freehold property. There are no arrears of debenture interest.

(6)   Liquidation expenses are estimated at £6000.

Required:

(a)   Calculations of the amounts which would be received by each of the providers of finance, assuming that the majority view regarding the value of the freeholds is correct and that the other information proves accurate. You should show clearly the order of priority for repayment.

(b)   An indication of the effect of the findings under (a) if the minority view regarding the value of the freeholds proves to be correct.

Note: Ignore taxation.

(AIB, April 1981)

10.16   Kester, Wang, Pollins and Fraser carry on business in partnership as Kester & Co. They are all in their late fifties or early sixties and decide to sell the firm and retire. They believe that there are several firms who would be willing to take over their business assets and assume responsibility for paying their trade creditors but, before entering into negotiations, they wish to have some idea of the value of the firm. They approach you for advice.

The balance sheet of the firm, prepared on the historical cost basis as at 30 June 1984, is as follows:

Balance Sheet, 30 June 1984

	£000	£000
Fixed assets at cost less depreciation		350
Current assets;		
Stocks at the lower of cost and net realizable value	210	
Debtors, net of provision for bad debts	145	
	355	
Current liabilities:		
Trade creditors	105	
Bank overdraft	75	
	180	
Net current assets		175
		525

	Capital account £000	Current account £000	
Kester	150	10	160
Wang	100	15	115
Pollins	100	50	150
Fraser	100	—	100
			525

The following details have been extracted from the profit and loss accounts for the last three years.

Profit and Loss Account extracts, year to 30 June

	1982 £000	1983 £000	1984 £000
Interest charged on bank overdraft	4	8	10
Depreciation charged	50	50	50
Net profit	125	150	145

In the course of discussions, the partners make the following comments:

Kester: 'The balance sheet has been prepared by a reputable firm of accountants and is based on objective facts. I think that we should value the business at what it shows.'

Wang: 'The fixed assets were purchased three years ago and the policy of writing them off by ten equal annual instalments is proving to be realistic. The balance sheet value is, however, out of date. It would cost £490 000 to replace the fixed assets with items of a similar age and condition. In addition, raw material costs have recently risen quite rapidly and it would cost £250 000 to replace the stocks held at 30 June. These facts should be taken into account in arriving at the valuation.'

Pollins: 'The business exists to earn profits and should be valued as a whole. I am told that companies in our line of business have a price/earnings ratio of 8:1. I think that we should apply this ratio to our average net profit as shown in the accounts for the last three years, after taking account of our drawings which averaged £100 000 per annum.'

Fraser: 'On the open market we could, in a quick sale, get £295 000 for our fixed assets and £220 000 for our stocks. This is what I think is important.'

Required:

(a) Valuations of the firm on each of the bases suggested by the four partners. For the purpose of your calculations, assume that the buyer is to accept responsibility for paying the trade creditors but will not take over the bank overdraft.

(b) In the context of this question, comment briefly on the merits, if any, of each valuation.

(c) Prepare an earnings yield valuation based on average 'maintainable profits' for the last three years and assess the merits of this basis. For the purpose of this valuation, you should take account of the fact that £60 000 per annum is adequate remuneration for the services provided by the four partners. In addition, enquiries reveal that the opening stock for the year to 30 June 1982 was overvalued by £32 000.

Notes:

(1) Assume that you are making the valuations on 30 June 1984.
(2) Ignore taxation.

(AIB, September 1984)

10.17   A colleague of yours has recently been considering leaving his position as sales manager of a medium-sized pharmaceutical business and purchasing a small chemical company, the summarized accounts of which appear below.

Balance Sheet at 31 December 1983

	£ million	£ million
Fixed assets		8.2
Current assets	10.2	
Creditors: amounts falling due within 1 year	7.8	
Net current assets		2.4
Total assets less current liabilities		10.6
Creditors: amounts falling due after more than 1 year:		
Long-term loans		4.2
		6.4
Capital and reserves:		
Called up share capital—4 million 25p ordinary shares		1.0
Share premium account		2.0
Reserves		3.4
		6.4

Profit and Loss Account year ended 31 December 1983

	£ million
Turnover	20.3

Profit on ordinary activities before taxtation	2.2
Taxation on profit on ordinary activities	1.0
Profit on ordinary activities after taxation	1.2
Dividends (net)	0.7
Retained profit for the financial year	0.5

You ascertain that the gross dividend yield for a similar company is 7 per cent and its price earnings ratio is 8 times. Advanced corporation tax is 3/7th of the net dividend.

Required:

(a) Calculate the share price on the basis of:

(1) dividend yield,
(2) price earnings ratio, and
(3) net assets.

(b) Comment on the use of each of these methods in company valuation.

(Cert. Dip. F.A., June 1984)

11 The interpretation of accounts

Objectives

The basic objective of this chapter is to consider how we set about analysing a set of accounts, with particular emphasis on ratio analysis techniques. Specifically, we consider:

(a) The nature, uses and limitations of ratio analysis.
(b) Accounting ratios used to example the liquidity position.
(c) Ratios used to examine the gearing position.
(d) Ratios used to consider the performance of a business.
(e) The way in which a ratio analysis exercise is conducted, drawing together the various accounting ratios.
(f) Other ratios are also considered.

Ratios – uses and limitations

A ratio expresses the relationship between two figures, normally as a proportion or percentage. This can be a very powerful tool in the interpretation of a set of accounts. Let us imagine, for example, that we are told that our company last year achieved sales of £10 000 000 and employed 250 people. Either of these two pieces of data in isolation is meaningless, but taken together we can identify sales per employee as:

$$\frac{\text{Sales}}{\text{Number of employees}} = \frac{£10\ 000\ 000}{250} = £40\ 000$$

By computing a ratio we enjoy the following benefits:

(a) We can compare aspects of businesses of different size. Thus if we know of a company in the same line of business with sales of £50 000 000 and 1000 employees, we can identify their sales per employee as:

$$\frac{50\ 000\ 000}{1000} = £50\ 000$$

Thus we can see that our company generates a lower level of activity per employee than our competitor.
(b) A ratio can express the relationship between two accounting figures or, as in our example, can relate a piece of accounting data to a piece of non-accounting data, thus broadening the view given by the accounts.
(c) The computation of a small number of key ratios enables the analyst to assess rapidly the substantial amount of detail contained in a set of published accounts.

(d)   Some ratios are designed to give a simple picture of the manner in which actual transactions occur. The 'number of days debtors', considered below, is an example of such a ratio.

(e)   Where industrial average ratios are published, computation of a company's own ratios becomes possible.

(f)   By use of ratios, confidential information can be shared on an anonymous basis. For example, a professional accounting body might arrange an inter-firm comparison exercise whereby each firm in an area reports, in confidence, average profit earned per partner. A list of such ratios can then be published without stating which ratio relates to which firm.

When we have computed a ratio which expresses some aspect of the position of a business we need to find some way of comparing that ratio. Comparison may be made with:

(a)   Preceding years of the same business. This can be especially useful in identifying trends.

(b)   Other companies in the same industry. Most ratios will not be comparable with other companies in different industries because the trading structure of each industry will be different. For example, we would expect a hairdresser to have far lower sales per employee than a retail food store, because a large part of the costs of the latter consist of bought-in goods.

(c)   Similar operating divisions within the same organization. It is important to be aware that national or even regional variations in trading practices can distort such a comparison.

(d)   Target ratios laid down for the guidance of management. For example, in large enterprises divisional managers may be required to achieve a specified rate of return on assets employed.

(e)   Industrial average ratios, obtained from published data or from some form of inter-firm comparison exercise.

An inter-firm comparison exercise involves a number of firms each agreeing to submit data to an independent organizer who will collate and summarize it in order to offer a useful collection of statistics. The organizer must be independent of all parties involved, in order to avoid the risk of breach of confidentiality, and aware of the significant issues in the business, in order to collect and publish relevant data. Such exercises will often be organized by a trade association or professional body. Because data is collected on a confidential basis, far more detail is available than can be derived from normal published accounts. It is important that data is published in such a way as to preserve confidentiality for participants.

The value of ratio analysis is restricted by the inherent limitations of published accounts for decision making. As we have seen, historical cost accounts do not necessarily present an economically realistic picture of profit or asset values. Variations in accounting policies may make the accounts of different companies unsuitable for comparison. Moreover, the accounting entity may not represent the business entity with which a user is concerned. For example, employees considering the accounts of a large company may not be able to identify information relating to the specific unit of the business in which they are employed. The balance sheet of a business represents a snapshot at one point in time and, particularly in a seasonal business, may not be typical of the position through the year.

Finally, the amount of information disclosed, particularly by small companies, may be very limited.

Ratios themselves must also be used with caution. It is important to be aware of the significance of individual amounts in isolation as well as considering relationships expressed by ratios. Some terms used in ratio analysis have several meanings, such as 'return on capital employed' (discussed below), and it is necessary to avoid ambiguity when presenting such ratios.

These limitations do not invalidate ratio analysis as a technique in the use of accounts. They do mean that ratios should be analysed with caution and with an awareness of potential alternative interpretations.

Example 11.1 presents a simple set of accounts which will be used to illustrate the computation of ratios.

Example 11.1

Pioneer Ltd – Profit and Loss Account for the year ended 31 December 1986

	1986		1985	
	£000	£000	£000	£000
Turnover		720		600
Cost of sales		432		348
Gross profit		288		252
Distribution costs	72		54	
Administration expenses	66		60	
		138		114
Operating profit		150		138
Interest payable		45		45
Profit before taxation		105		93
Taxation		42		37
Profit after taxation		63		56
Dividends (proposed)		30		25
Retained profit		33		31

Balance Sheet as at 31 December 1986

Fixed assets (note 1)		1155		1118
Current assets:				
Stock	115		82	
Debtors (note 2)	99		70	
Bank	6		46	
	220		198	
Creditors (note 3)	125		99	
Net current assets		95		99
		1250		1217
12% debentures (repayable 1988)		375		375
		875		842

Ordinary shares of £1	500	500
Retained profits	375	342
	875	842

Notes

	1986	1985
	£000	£000
1. Trade purchases were:	144	116

2. Fixed assets:

Cost	Land & buildings	Plant	Total
	£000	£000	£000
Bfwd	700	1000	1700
Additions	—	164	164
Disposals	—	10	10
C/fwd	700	1154	1854
Depreciation			
B/fwd	85	497	582
Charge for year	15	110	125
Disposals in year	—	8	8
C/fwd	100	599	699
NBV 31 Dec 86	600	555	1155
NBV 31 Dec 85	615	503	1118

(The plant was sold at a profit of £5000)

3. *Debtors*	1986	1985
	£000	£000
Trade debtors	80	61
Prepayments	10	9
	99	70

4. *Creditors*	1986	1985
	£000	£000
Trade creditors	45	30
Taxation	42	37
Proposed dividend	30	25
Accruals	8	7
	125	99

Analysis of the liquidity position

Under this heading we consider accounting ratios used to assess a company's ability to meet its liabilities as they fall due. Some authors distinguish between 'liquidity', being short-term financial strength, and 'solvency', being longer-term financial strength; other authors treat the two terms as interchangeable.

The normal starting point for an analysis of the liquidity position is to look at the relationship between those assets which will be turned into cash in the short term and those liabilities which have to be paid in the short term.

Two ratios used for this purpose are:

(a)   The *current ratio*, computed as:

$$\frac{\text{Current assets}}{\text{Current liabilities}}$$

For our example, Pioneer Ltd, this will be computed as:

1986	1985
$\frac{220}{125} = 1.8$	$\frac{198}{99} = 2$

(b)   The *liquidity ratio*, also known as the quick asset ratio or *acid test*. This is most commonly computed as:

$$\frac{\text{Current assets} - \text{Stock}}{\text{Current liabilities}}$$

For our example, Pioneer Ltd, this will be computed as:

1986	1985
$\frac{220 - 115}{125} = 0.8$	$\frac{198 - 82}{99} = 1.2$

The thinking underlying the composition of the liquidity ratio is that stock is the least liquid of current assets, and that most current liabilities will have to be met before stock is likely to convert into cash.

In most kinds of business the liquidity ratio is likely to give earlier warning of financial problems than the current ratio. For example, a retrospective study of a company which had suffered financial difficulties found that an analysis of the balance sheet immediately prior to the liquidity crisis showed an *increase* in the current ratio and a *decrease* in the liquidity ratio. The reason in this case was that the company had had difficulty selling goods and, in order to go on using the labour force and production facilities, had carried on producing goods for stock. Thus the current ratio was boosted by the greatly increased stock level, while the falling liquidity ratio indicated the imminent problem arising from the fall in cash flow from debtors.

In some kinds of business, where stock turns over rapidly, the current ratio will be more relevant than the liquidity ratio; an example would be a retail food store, where we would expect stock to be sold for cash before most current liabilities have to be met.

There is no 'correct' level for the current ratio or the liquidity ratio, because the desirable position depends on the type of business. For example, we would expect a car manufacturer to have a high current ratio because of the amount of stock involved in the manufacturing process and the sale of goods on credit to garages. By contrast, a retail butcher selling on cash terms and with only a modest amount of stock at any one time might be expected to have a very low current ratio.

A complicating factor in the computation of both the current ratio and the liquidity ratio is that the bank overdraft will be shown as a current liability, but may in practice be regularly renewed and so effectively constitute a form of long-term loan. Where there is evidence that this situation has arisen, it may be appropriate to recompute these two ratios with the overdraft excluded from current liabilities. Note that where such a situation arises it may still be appropriate to observe that the business is vulnerable to the bank deciding to withdraw the overdraft facility.

When the relationship between current assets and current liabilities has been considered, the liquidity position can be investigated further by considering individual current assets and current liabilities in detail.

Those current assets and liabilities which form part of the operating cycle of the business are influenced by two factors:

(a)   Any increase in the activity of the business creates a related increased working capital requirement. Thus for our example Pioneer Ltd, the turnover has increased by:

$$\frac{720 - 600}{600} = 20\%$$

Thus we would expect a 20 per cent increase in the amount of funds tied up in working capital.

(b)   Management may tighten or relax working capital, so that the amount of each working capital item may correspondingly decrease or increase in relation to the level of activity.

There are a number of ways in which 'working capital activity ratios' can be computed. Taking each of the three main working capital items in turn:

(a)   *Stock*. This can be examined by the *stock turnover ratio*, computed as:

$$\frac{\text{Cost of sales}}{\text{Stock}}$$

For our example Pioneer Ltd, this ratio would be:

$$
\begin{array}{cc}
1986 & 1985 \\
\dfrac{432}{115} = 3.8 & \dfrac{348}{82} = 4.2
\end{array}
$$

This gives an impression of the number of times stock 'turns over' in the year, assuming reasonably consistent stock and sales levels throughout the year. Making the same assumptions, we can also express the same relationship as the *number of days stock* as:

$$\frac{\text{Stock}}{\text{Cost of sales}} \times 365$$

For Pioneer Ltd, this ratio will be:

$$
\begin{array}{cc}
1986 & 1985 \\
115/432 \times 365 = 97 \text{ days} & 82/348 \times 365 = 86 \text{ days}
\end{array}
$$

When the cost of sales figure is not available, then the relationship between the level of stock and the level of activity can be expressed as:

$$\frac{\text{Turnover}}{\text{Stock}}$$

This is confusing because the term 'stock turnover ratio' can have two meanings, one relating to cost of sales being the number of times stock 'turns over', the other expressing the relationship between stock and turnover. The former approach is to be preferred because stock is shown in the accounts at cost, and by relating this to cost of sales we are relating 'like to like'.

(b) *Debtors.* In this case we would normally compute the *number of days debtors*, being

$$\frac{\text{Trade debtors}}{\text{Sales}} \times 365$$

For our example, the ratios will be:

1986	1985
$\frac{89}{720} \times 365 = 45$ days	$\frac{61}{600} \times 365 = 37$ days

Note that to ascertain trade debtors it was necessary to go to the notes to the accounts.

(c) *Creditors.* In this case we would prefer to compute the *number of days creditors*, being:

$$\frac{\text{Trade creditors}}{\text{Purchases}} \times 365$$

For our example, the ratio will be:

1986	1985
$\frac{45}{144} \times 365 = 114$ days	$\frac{30}{116} \times 365 = 94$ days

Frequently information on trade purchases will not be available from the accounts. In such a case some impression of the relationship between creditors and the level of activity can be given by the *creditors' turnover ratio*, being:

$$\frac{\text{Turnover}}{\text{Creditors}}$$

Each of these working capital activity ratios may be computed either by relation to year end balance sheet figures, as in this case, or by reference to average balance sheet figures for the year. Each of our working capital activity ratios has expressed the relationship between an individual working capital item and the level of activity. In addition, where we have been able to assume a reasonable even level of sales and stock, some of our ratios have given a physical picture of the business; for example, the 'number of days debtors' gives a picture of the length of trade credit given to customers. However, this assumpton will not necessarily apply invariably. For example:

(a) A business with a highly seasonal trade may present a very distorted picture at the balance sheet date. Thus a toy wholesaler might show high trade debtors and low stock at 31 December.

(b) A change in the trading pattern near the end of the accounting year might distort the ratios. Thus a special successful sales drive in the last month of the year might lead to abnormally high trade debtors.

(c) Special circumstances might distort the trading pattern. For example, a strike at a major supplier near the year end might cause a drop in stock levels.

Non-working capital items may also affect the liquidity position. Example of such items include tax liabilities, and long-term loans becoming repayable on maturity. Such items have to be considered individually, being identifiable but not explicable by ratio analysis techniques.

Pioneer Ltd – Statement of Source and Application of Funds for the year ended 31 December 1986

	1986	
	£000	£000
Source of funds:		
Profit before tax		105
Adjustments for items not involving the movement of funds:		
Depreciation		125
(Gain)/loss on fixed asset disposal		(5)
		225
Funds from other sources:		
Sale of fixed assets		7
		232
Applications:		
Fixed asset purchase	164	
Taxation	37	
Dividends	25	
		226
		6
Increase/(decrease) in working capital:		
Increase in stock	33	
Increase in trade debtors	28	
Increase in prepayments	1	
Increase in trade creditors	(15)	
Increase in accruals	(1)	
	46	
Decrease in net liquid funds	(40)	
		6

Figure 11.1

The prepartion of a funds statement, explained in Chapter 8 above, is another useful tool in the analysis of the liquidity position. The funds statement for Pioneer Ltd is shown in Fig. 11.1, and readers interested in revising this topic might like to confirm the figures by preparing such a statement from those given in Example 11.1. The preparation of such a statement may sometimes be incomplete, as for example when detailed information on fixed asset movements is not available, but even if imperfect may still be useful.

Management of the liquidity position involves a compromise. On the one hand, the higher the current assets the lower the risk of financial difficulties. On the other hand, the lower the funds tied up in working capital the more profitably those funds can be used elsewhere in the business.

Analysis of the financial structure

The concept and significance of 'gearing' has already been considered in detail in

Chapter 5 above. Gearing can be considered in relation to either long-term funds employed or in relation to total funds employed, and can be measured either:

(a) On a 'capital' basis, which compares the amount derived from borrowing with the amount derived from equity.

(b) On an 'income' basis, which compares interest payments with total profit.

Thus 'capital' based gearing ratios might be measured as:

$$\frac{\text{Borrowings}}{\text{Equity plus borrowings}}$$

For our example Pioneer Ltd, this ratio will be computed:

Long-term

1986	1985
$\dfrac{375}{875 + 375} = 30\%$	$\dfrac{375}{842 + 375} = 31\%$

Total

$$\frac{375 + 125}{875 + 375 + 125} = 36\% \qquad \frac{375 + 99}{842 + 375 + 99} = 36\%$$

Some authorities prefer to express this relationship more simply, as:

Borrowings:Equity

In this form the ratio is often known as the *Debt:Equity ratio*, in which case 'debt' generally refers to *total* borrowings.

The most commonly used income-based gearing ratio is the 'interest cover' ratio, measured as:

$$\frac{\text{Profit before tax} + \text{Interest}}{\text{Interest}}$$

In practice, the ratio is normally computed by reference to both long-term and short-term interest taken together. For our example, the ratio will be:

1986	1985
$\dfrac{150}{45} = 3.3$	$\dfrac{138}{45} = 3.1$

A special problem that arises in computing the gearing ratios relates to the treatment of preference shares. As we have already considered in Chapter 5 above, these have a somewhat ambiguous character. In law they are a form of share capital, while since their claim on the profits of the business is fixed they can be regarded as in substance akin to borrowing. We may have difficulty, therefore, in deciding how to classify preference share capital and preference dividend in preparing our gearing ratios.

In practice, it is normal to classify the preference shares as a form of share borrowing in computing capital-based gearing ratios, and this makes sense as showing the proportion of non-equity finance. However, a borrower assessing the degree of risk involved in lending to a company might classify preference shares as part of share capital since, in the event of liquidation, no payment is made to preference shareholders unless the creditors have been paid in full.

In computing the interest cover ratio preference dividends would not normally be included in the interest charge. This also makes sense since no form of dividend is payable unless it can be covered from profit, whereas there is a legal obligation to pay interest whatever the profit level. However, a *fixed charge cover ratio* might also usefully be computed.

We have already seen, in Chapter 5 above, that a *degree of capital gearing* ratio can be computed, showing the factor to be applied to any fluctuation in operating profit to find the fluctuation in profit attributable to shareholders. This ratio is computed as:

$$\frac{\text{Profit before tax} + \text{Interest}}{\text{Profit before tax}}$$

For Pioneer Ltd, the ratios will be:

1986	1985
$\frac{150}{105} = 1.4$	$\frac{138}{93} = 1.5$

As with our ratios relating to liquidity, there is no single desirable level of gearing; the appropriate level will depend on the type of business under consideration. The balance to be achieved in gearing policy is:

(a)   On the one hand, as long as the return earned on resources financed by borrowed funds exceeds related interest charges, then increased gearing yields a benefit to shareholders.

(b)   On the other hand, increased gearing involves increased risk.

Analysis of performance

A business employs resources in order to earn profits, so that it seems reasonable to embark on any examination of business performance by considering what level of profit has been earned in relation to the resources employed in the business. This can be done by computing the *Return on Capital Employed* (ROCE), often known as the *primary ratio*, and calculated as:

$$\frac{\text{Return}}{\text{Capital}}$$

There are a number of ways in which 'return' and 'capital' can be defined, including:

(a)   After tax return on equity, computed as:

$$\frac{\text{Profit after tax}}{\text{Equity}}$$

For our example, Pioneer Ltd, this ratio will show:

1986	1985
$\frac{63}{875} = 7.2\%$	$\frac{56}{842} = 6.7\%$

(b)   Pre-tax return on equity, computed as:

$$\frac{\text{Profit before tax}}{\text{Equity}}$$

In our example, the ratio shows:

1986	1985
$\dfrac{105}{875} = 12\%$	$\dfrac{93}{842} = 11\%$

(c)   Pre-tax return on long-term funds employed, computed as:

$$\frac{\text{Profit before tax} + \text{Long-term interest}}{\text{Equity} + \text{Long-term liabilities}}$$

Interest is added back because it represents the return belonging to long-term finance in the same way as profit is the return belonging to equity.

For our example, the ratio shows:

1986	1985
$\dfrac{150}{875 + 375} = 12\%$	$\dfrac{138}{842 + 375} = 11.3\%$

(d)   Pre-tax return on total funds employed, being:

$$\frac{\text{Profit before tax} + \text{All interest}}{\text{Equity} + \text{All liabilities}}$$

For our example, that is:

1986	1985
$\dfrac{150}{875 + 375 + 125} = 10.9\%$	$\dfrac{138}{842 + 375 + 99} = 10.5\%$

Each of these ratios looks at the performance of the busines from a different aspect.

The after-tax return on equity shows what has been achieved on behalf of the owners of the business. From the shareholders' point of view, this is obviously a highly significant ratio! However, the case for looking at the pre-tax return on equity is that the tax charge needs to be considered separately when analysing a company's position, being influenced by a number of special factors such as the tax rate, changes in tax law, tax planning and the accounting policy on deferred taxation.

ROCE ratio	Difference explained by:
After-tax return on equity	
↑	Company's tax position
Pre-tax return on equity	
↑	Company's long-term gearing position
Return on long-term funds	
↑	Company's total gearing position
Return on total funds	

Figure 11.2

The pre-tax return on equity may differ from the return on both long-term and total funds because of the impact of gearing. We have already seen how the significance of gearing can be assessed by the use of ratios.

The ratios of return on long-term and on total funds both attempt to show what the management have achieved with the resources they control. The return on total funds has the advantage of showing what has been achieved with the total resources at management's disposal, but can be somewhat erratic as an indicator because short-term liabilities can be subject to fluctuation or even manipulation. Figure 11.2 shows how the variations between our different versions of the ROCE ratio can be explained.

In order to take our analysis of company performance further, we can analyse any version of the primary ratio into the two secondary ratios, being:

(a) *Net profit percentage,* computed as:

$$\frac{\text{Return}}{\text{Turnover}}$$

This shows the profit achieved in relation to the level of activity.

(b) *Asset turnover,* computed as:

$$\frac{\text{Turnover}}{\text{Capital}}$$

This shows the level of activity achieved in relation to the resources employed by the business.

We can see how these two ratios relate to the primary ratio by considering the simple equation:

$$\frac{\text{Return}}{\text{Capital}} = \frac{\text{Return}}{\text{Turnover}} \times \frac{\text{Turnover}}{\text{Capital}}$$

In principle, these secondary ratios can be computed in relation to any version of the primary ratio. However, in practice, it is only sensible to compute them in relation to the return on either long-term or total funds, since we have seen that these two ratios constitute the best evidence of the company's trading achievement.

In the case of Pioneer Ltd, we would probably consider the return on total funds as our best guide to management achievement since there is no evidence of undue fluctuation in the current liabilities. On this basis we would compute the secondary ratios as:

	1986	*1985*
Net profit (%)	$\frac{150}{720} = 20.8\%$	$\frac{138}{600} = 23\%$
Asset turnover	$\frac{720}{875 + 375 + 125} = 0.52$	$\frac{600}{842 + 375 + 99} = 0.46$

Each of these ratios can then be analysed in more detail. The asset turnover can be analysed by computing the relationship between each type of asset and the turnover. Thus for our example the fixed asset turnover would be computed as:

1986	*1985*
$\frac{720}{1155} = 0.62$	$\frac{600}{1118} = 0.54$

We have already seen, when considering the measures of liquidity, that for working capital items alternative measures of activity might be used.

The analysis of the net profit percentage is more complex, and normally takes place in two stages. First, the *gross profit percentage* is computed, being:

$$\frac{\text{Gross profit}}{\text{Sales}}$$

For our example, the ratio will be:

1986	1985
$\dfrac{288}{720} = 40\%$	$\dfrac{252}{600} = 42\%$

Even a modest change in the gross profit percentage can have a significant impact on the profitability of a business and would be fully investigated. Possible explanations for a change in gross profit percentage include:

(a)   A deliberate change in pricing policy. For example, management may decide to cut prices in the hope of compensating for lost profit with increased trade.

(b)   When a number of different sales lines are marketed at different profit margins, then a change in sales mix will change the overall gross profit percentage.

(c)   A change in the cost of goods purchased. Sometimes, in particular, management may respond to a sharp change in purchase price by maintaining gross profit on each item sold in absolute rather than proportional terms, so that gross profit as a proportion of selling price is correspondingly changed.

(b)   Stock may have been consumed or destroyed other than in the course of trade, e.g. flood damage, fire, pilfering. Computation of the gross profit percentage is a useful management tool for identifying such situations.

(e)   Clearance of old stock may have involved sales below the normal gross profit margin.

(f)   There may have been some error in the preparation of the accounts. In particular, an error in the computation of closing stock will distort gross profit in both the current and following accounting periods.

When making comparisons between companies it is important to bear in mind that there might be some inconsistency in the decision as to which expenses constitute part of cost of sales.

Following examination of the gross profit percentage, the second stage in examination of the net profit percentage is to examine the expenses deducted from gross profit to arrive at net profit. The amount of detail in which such an examination can be made will depend on how much detail has been disclosed in the accounts. There are two broad ways of making such an examination:

(a)   Express each expense as a proportion of sales. For our example, these proportions are:

	1986	1985
Administration expenses	$\dfrac{66}{720} = 9.2\%$	$\dfrac{60}{600} = 10\%$

Distribution costs $\qquad\dfrac{72}{720} = 10\%\qquad\qquad\dfrac{54}{600} = 9\%$

(b) Identify the percentage increase or decrease in each type of expenditure. For Pioneer Ltd, this will be:

Administration expenses $\qquad\dfrac{66 - 60}{60} = 10\%$

Distribution costs $\qquad\qquad\dfrac{72 - 54}{54} = 33\tfrac{1}{3}\%$

The first method is more appropriate for variable costs, the second for fixed costs; but, of course, expenses are not analysed for us in this way in the accounts.

When computing the primary ratio, and the other performance ratios that follow therefrom, a number of adjustments might be made in order to identify the trading position:

(a) When comparing two companies which have different accounting policies, adjustments might be made to apply the same policies to both companies.

(b) When a company owns investments the income from them may be excluded from 'return' and the balance sheet value of them excluded from 'capital'.

(c) When comparing a company that owns premises or plant with one that rents property or hires plant, the view might be taken that the first company is carrying on what amounts to a separate trade of hiring out property or plant to itself. In such a case the two sets of accounts can be made comparable by adjusting one of the company's accounts so that either:

(1) The first company excludes the plant or premises from 'capital' and deducts a notional rental charge from 'return'.

(2) The second company adds back the actual rental charge to 'return' and adds a notional value of the rented asset to 'capital'.

(d) A sole trader's or partnership's profit figure combines a return on capital element with remuneration for the services of the proprietor(s). Thus to show return on capital employed it is necessary to deduct a notional remuneration figure for the proprietors.

(e) Where the directors of a limited company are also major shareholders, the directors' remuneration figure may significantly over or under state the real value of their services. In such a case an appropriate adjustment to profit must be made in defining 'return'.

We have already alluded to the fundamental deficiencies of financial accounts for decision making. These deficiencies are particularly significant in the computation of performance ratios, since both the profit figure and the capital employed figure are not necessarily economically realistic.

Drawing the ratios together

So far we have defined individual ratios and discussed their significance. We will now consider how an interpretation of accounts excercise is conducted.

The stages of such an exercise might occur in the following sequence:

(a)   Consider the specific problem under review and decide whether any specific aspect of the business needs to be concentrated on.

(b)   Examine the accounts for any conspicuous changes, e.g. dramatic shift in cash balance. Scrutiny of the funds statement is useful at this stage.

(c)   On the basis of the first two stages, compute some half a dozen key ratios which highlight the company's position.

(d)   In the light of the ratios computed, consider which aspects of the position of the business require further investigation and compute relevant ratios.

(e)   Summarize the key points emerging, noting interrelationships between these points.

(f)   Present a report in simple language. Show the ratios computed in a separate appendix so as to avoid cluttering the report with technical detail.

Let us imagine that we have been asked to review the accounts of our example Pioneer Ltd and comment on any trends emerging. Following each stage in turn:

(a)   In this case we have not been told of any particular issue to be considered. Therefore we will review all aspects of the company's position.

(b)   On glancing through the accounts in Example 11.1 and the funds statement in Fig. 11.1 we might note, in particular, the growth in sales and the substantial cash outflow. Thus our attention is drawn particularly to both performance and liquidity.

Initial computation	1986	1985
Current ratio	1.8	2
Acid test	0.8	1.2
Sales increase	20%	
Total gearing	36%	36%
Return on equity (after tax)	7.2%	6.7%
Return on total funds	10.9%	10.5%
Net profit	20.8%	23%
Total asset turnover	0.52	0.46
Further investigation		
Days stock	97	86
Days debtors	45	37
Days creditors	114	94
Gross profit	40%	42%
Admin expenses: sales	9.2%	10%
Distribution costs: sales	10%	9%
Increase in:		
Admin. costs	10%	
Distribution costs	33.33%	
Fixed asset turnover	0.62	0.54

Figure 11.3   Pioneer Ltd – Summary of Ratios

(c)   Figure 11.3 shows the selection of ratios we might compute initially. Each of these ratios has already been explained above. The sales increase ratio is computed because of the observation we made from glacing through the accounts, while the other ratios represent a fairly basic collection for an initial broad review of a company.

(d)   The fall in the current ratio and the acid test suggest that further investigation of working capital management may be appropriate. A slight increase in return on capital results from a drop in net profit percentage being compensated for by improved asset turnover, so that close examination of the secondary ratios is also useful. The additional ratios we might consider are listed under 'further investigation' in Fig. 11.3.

(e)   Key points emerging might include:

(1)   The drop in the current ratio, and sharper drop in the acid test, suggest that the company may face liquidity problems. This is reflected in the sharp fall in the bank balance revealed in the funds statement.

(2)   We would expect some strain on liquid resources since the company has increased turnover by 20 per cent without raising any new finance, relying entirely on internally generated funds.

(3)   The strain on liquidity arising from expansion has been exacerbated by a relaxation of working capital control, as indicated by increased stock and debtors.

(4)   The company appears to have tried to finance expansion partly by taking extended trade credit, the payment period rising from 94 to 114 days. This is dangerous in terms of supplier goodwill.

(5)   Asset turnover has improved overall because of fuller use of fixed assets, and despite relaxed stock and debtor control.

(6)   The fall in net profit percentage is mainly attributable to the fall in profit margin on sales. Distribution costs have risen in relation to sales. Administration costs, which we would expect to be fixed rather than variable, have risen less than the rate of increase in sales.

(7)   Some of these changes may have resulted from a deliberate management policy to boost turnover. Thus the cut in gross profit percentage may indicate a price cut to attract new business. Increased days debtors may indicate favourable credit terms to attract business. Increased days stock may be designed to reduce the risk of running out of individual stock items. Increased distribution costs may indicate sales to a wider geographical area.

(f)   When composing our report the above conclusions would be put into a suitable format, e.g. letter or report. If asked for advice, we might reasonably suggest that any further expansion be financed from new long-term sources of finance.

Note how we can strengthen our analysis by looking at the funds statement and the ratios *together*.

Other ratios

We have already considered how the earnings per share ratio is computed in Chapter 6 above. The significance of the earnings per share figure is that it relates the profit after-tax figure in the accounts to the individual share held. This can then be linked to the share price by computing the *Price/Earnings (P/E) ratio*, being:

$$\frac{\text{Share price}}{\text{Earnings per share}}$$

This ratio is commonly quoted in the financial press and gives some indication of the market's confidence in the 'quality' of earnings. A high ratio indicates a belief that earnings will rise, a low ratio indicates a belief that earnings will fall.

Another ratio of interest to investors is the *dividend per share*, computed as:

$$\frac{\text{Ordinary dividend for year}}{\text{Number of ordinary shares}}$$

From this we can compute the *dividend yield ratio*, being

$$\frac{\text{Dividend per share}}{\text{Share price}}$$

This ratio indicates the return yielded on a share in the form of dividends. In addition, shareholders will also hope to earn a return by virtue of the share price rising, so that a low dividend yield indicates market belief that the share price will perform well.

Another ratio based on earnings per share is dividend cover, computed as:

$$\frac{\text{Earnings per share}}{\text{Dividends per share}}$$

	1986		1985	
Fixed assets		132		133
Current assets:				
Stock	13		10	
Debtors	11		8	
Bank	1		5	
	25		23	
Creditors	14	11	12	11
Net current assets		143		144
Debentures		43		44
		100		100

Figure 11.4   Pioneer Ltd – common size statements

Another tool used to examine a set of accounts is the *common size statement*, illustrated for our example Pioneer Ltd in Fig. 11.4. This expresses each figure in an accounting statement as a percentage of one common figure. In our example, each balance sheet figure has been expressed as a percentage of the equity, e.g. fixed assets as:

$$\frac{1986}{\frac{1155}{875}} = 132\%$$

If computed over a number of years, such a statement enables us to identify changes in the composition of the balance sheet.

Another tool for looking at the accounts is the trend statement, in which each figure in an accounting statement is expressed as a percentage of the same figure for a 'base' year. Assuming 1985 as the base year, a trend statement for Pioneer Ltd is shown in Fig. 11.5.

Given a trend statement, it is possible to go back and compute the percentage movement on each item in each year as:

$$\frac{\text{Current year's trend figure} - \text{Previous year's trend figure}}{\text{Previous year's trend figure}}$$

	1985	1986
Sales	100	120
Cost of sales	100	124
Gross profit	100	114
Distribution costs	100	133
Administration costs	100	110
Operating profit	100	109
Interest	100	100
Net profit	100	113
Taxation	100	113
Dividends	100	120
Retained profit	100	106

Figure 11.5   Pioneer Ltd – trend statement

Thus a company's trend statement for sales might show:

Year	1	2	3	4
	100	120	132	171.6
Increase in year (%)		20	10	30
Computed:		$\frac{120-100}{100}$	$\frac{132-120}{120}$	$\frac{17.6-132}{132}$

Accounting ratios can also be used 'in reverse', as it were, to construct a predicted set of accounts based on a single predicted variable. Such a *financial model* assumes a consistent set of relationships, such as a constant gross profit percentage. To verify the usefulness of such a model, we would have to consider the validity of both the predicted variable and the assumed ratios.

Conclusion

In this chapter we have considered a wide range of interpretation techniques. Perhaps the most important point to remember is that ratio analysis is a tool for interpretation, not an objective in itself. Ratios should be examined in conjunction with the funds statement, the accounts themselves and any outside information on the business we possess.

Questions

11.1   The following information is provided in respect of three companies, of which one is a steel manufacturer, another is a grocery store chain and the third a finance company. Extracts from the accounts of each of these companies are reproduced below:

Profit and loss account extracts

	Company A £000	Company B £000	Company C £000
Turnover/revenue	3029	1556	206
Net profit	45	67	43

Summarized balance sheets

	Company A £000	Company B £000	Company C £000
Fixed assets at book value	257	1094	6
Stock	236	241	—
Debtors	9	201	1347
Other assets	66	286	413
	568	1822	1766
Shareholders' equity	320	1200	410
Long-term liabilities	64	321	578
Current liabilities	184	301	778
	568	1822	1766

Required:

(a)   Calculate the following accounting ratios for each of the three companies:

(1)   net profit percentage;
(2)   total asset turnover;
(3)   rate of return on gross assets;
(4)   liquidity ratio (assume that the 'other assets' are non-current for the purpose of this calculation).

(b)   Indicate which company you believe is the steel manufacturer, which is the grocery store chain and which is the finance company.

Briefly explain your choice using clues obtained from calculating the accounting ratios and from examining the accounting information provided.

(AIB, September 1984)

11.2   The following balance sheet, profit and loss account and statement of source and application of funds are those of a group of manufacturing companies. Also shown are some statistics prepared by the appropriate trade association.

Balance Sheet as at 31 October

	1982 £000	£000	1983 £000	£000
Fixed assets:				
Tangible assets				
Cost	540		680	
Depreciation	120		188	
Net book amount		420		492
Current assets:				
Stock	300		356	
Trade debtors	200		300	
Cash	4	504	5	661
Total assets		924		1153
Capital and reserves:				
Share capital paid up		200		300
Share premium account		100		200

Profit and loss account		246		275
Shareholders' funds		546		775
Creditors due after more than one year:				
Debenture, 1995		200		150
Creditors due within one year:				
Trade creditors	150		175	
Taxation	15		30	
Bank overdraft	13	178	23	228
		924		1153

Profit and Loss Account year ended 31 October

	1982	1983
	£000	£000
Sales turnover	826	1043
Cost of sales, after charging depreciation £54 000		
and £68 000	(734)	(896)
Gross profit	92	147
Interest payable		
Debenture interest paid £20 000 and £15 000		
Bank interest paid £2000 and £3000	(22)	(18)
Profit before tax	70	129
Tax	(15)	(30)
Profit for the financial year	55	99
Dividend paid	(35)	(70)
Surplus transferred to reserves	20	29

Statement of Source and Application of Funds year ended 31 October

	1982	1983
	£000	£000
Cash flow from operations	124	197
Shares issued	—	200
	124	397
Fixed assets purchased	—	(140)
Debentures repaid	—	(50)
Dividends paid	(35)	(70)
Tax paid	—	(15)
Change in working capital	89	122
Analysis of change in working capital:		
Increase in stock	60	56
Increase in debtors	30	100
Increase in cash	(5)	1
(Increase) in creditors	(20)	(25)
(Increase) in overdraft	24	(10)
	89	122

Statistics prepared by the Trade Association: industry averages

		1982	1983
1	Return on all assets employed (%)	12	14
2	Return on shareholders funds (%)	15	16
3	Return on long-term funds (%)	14	15
4	Profit margin (%)	9	10
5	Sales turnover ratio (tims)	1.5	1.5
6	Fixed assets ratio (%)	30	40
7	Debt equity ratio	0.4:1	0.45:1
8	Current ratio	2:1	2.1:1
9	Liquid ratio (sometimes called acid ratio)	0.9:1	1.1:1
10	Debtors (days sales)	70	75

You are required to:

(a) Calculate the corresponding statistics for the company for 1983 from the financial statements provided in respect of 31 October 1982 and 1983 and the years ended on those dates (to two significant figures).

(b) Comment on the performance of the company, with appropriate statistics from the viewpoint of:

(1) the management,
(2) the shareholders,
(3) the debenture holders, and
(4) the trade creditors.

(Cert. Dip. in Accounting & Finance, June 1984)

11.3   Greywell plc and Kendall plc trade in the same industry but in different geographical locations. The following data are taken from the 1982 annual accounts:

	Greywell	Kendall
	£000	£000
Turnover	40 000	60 000
Total operating expenses	36 000	55 000
Average total assets during 1982	30 000	25 000

Required:

(a)   Calculate the rate of return on total assets (profit as a percentage of total assets) for each company.

(b)   Analyse the rate of return in part (a) into the net profit percentage and the ratio of turnover of total assets.

(c)   Comment on the relative performance of the two companies insofar as the information permits. Indicate what additional information you would require to decide which company is the better proposition from the viewpoint of:

(1)   potential shareholders; and
(2)   potential loan creditors.

Note: Ignore taxation.

(AIB, September 1983)

11.4   **Rufus Ltd** has requested you to carry out an analysis of the results of 1986 as shown in the following financial statements and to compare the results obtained with the industrial averages in order to identify possible areas of difference in management policy.

Income Statement for the year ended 31 December 1986

	£	£
Sales		690 000
Cost of goods sold:		
Materials	260 000	
Labour	165 000	
Heat, light and power	25 000	
Indirect labour	40 000	
Depreciation	15 000	505 000
Gross profit		185 000
Selling expenses	70 000	
General and administrative expenses	70 000	140 000
Operating profit		45 000
Interest		8 800
Net profit before tax		36 200
Taxation (40%)		14 480
Net profit after tax		£21 720

Balance Sheet as at 31 December 1986

	£	£
Fixed assets		
Plant and machinery		250 000
Less Depreciation		100 000
		150 000
Current assets		
Stock	200 000	
Debtors	70 000	
Cash	55 000	
	325 000	
Less Creditors	95 000	230 000
		380 000
11% debentures		80 000
		300 000
Represented by		
Ordinary share capital		200 000
Undistributed profits		100 000
		300 000

Industrial average ratios

Current ratio	5.7
Acid test	2.3
Total borrowings: total funds	25%
Interest cover	6.5
Stock turnover	4.5
Days debtors	40
Return on total assets made up of	10%
Asset turnover	2
Net profit (%)	5%
Pretax return on equity	11.3%

You are required to:

(a) Compute these ratios for Rufus Ltd.

(b) Briefly comment on these ratios.

11.5 Detailed below are the summarized accounts of Goodtrade plc. One of your friends, a shareholder of Goodtrade plc, is totally confused by what he sees as conflicting information given in these accounts. (See Exhibits I and II.) The chairman of Goodtrade, in his chairman's report, praises the company for doubling the 1982 profits—a fact borne out by the profit and loss account. Yet when your friend scrutinized the balance sheet he saw that the bank overdraft had substantially increased and that the cash balances that the company had held had virtually disappeared. Furthermore, in September 1982 the company asked each shareholder to buy 3 £1 shares for every 8 that they held at a price of £2.50 each.

You are required to:

(a) explain to your friend how these apparently conflicting results have occurred:

(b) briefly assess Goodtrade plc's performance during 1983.

Exhibit I
Goodtrade plc
Balance Sheet as at 31 March 1983

1982 Comparatives		Cost	£000s Acc. Depn	Net
	Fixed assets			
	Tangible assets:			
8 005	Land/buildings	9 245	430	8 815
7 104	Plant/machinery	13 430	4 866	8 564
516	Motor vehicles etc.	613	227	386
15 625		23 288	5 523	17 765
3 780	Investments at cost			4 520
	Current assets			
13 345	Stocks	22 040		
11 240	Debtors	19 600		
920	Cash balances	30		
25 505			41 670	

	Less: Creditors—Amounts falling due within one year		
9 840	Trade creditors	18 260	
1 330	Accrued expenses	2 630	
770	Taxation	1 620	
5 170	Bank overdraft	9 710	
17 110			32 220
8 395	Net current assets		9 450
27 800	Total assets less current liabilities		31 735
	Less: Creditors—Amounts falling due after one year		
8 250	14% debentures 1991/4	8 250	
7 200	Long-term bank loan	5 150	13 400
12 350			18 335
	Capital and reserves		
4 000	Called-up share capital		5 500
500	Share premium account		2 750
450	Revaluation reserve		1 450
4 675	General reserve		5 675
2 725	Profit and loss account		2 960
12 350			18 335

Exhibit II
Goodtrade plc
Profit and Loss Account for the year ended 31 March 1983

1982 Comparatives			
62 410	Turnover		97 340
52 310	Cost of sales		81 100
10 100	Gross profit		16 240
5 255	Distribution costs	8 310	
3 450	Administration costs	4 970	13 280
8 705			
1 395	Operating profit (note 2)		2 960
345	Income from other fixed asset investments		560
1 740	Profit before taxation		3 520
770	Tax on profit on ordinary activities		1 620
970	Profit on ordinary activities after taxation		1 900
225	Dividends		665
745	Retained profit for the year (note 1)		1 235

Notes:
(1) £1m (1982 £0.5m) was transferred from the profit and loss account to the general reserves in the year ended 31 March 1983.
(2) Operating profit is after charging:

	Comparatives (£000)	Accounts (£000)
Depreciation	1120	1960
Loan interest	1310	1230
Directors:		
Fees	94	120
Other emoluments	361	462
Auditors' remuneration	110	135

When looking through the accounts you note that:

(a) Goodtrade plc revalued the land and buildings during the year, increasing the value by £1m.

(b) No fixed assets were sold during the year.

(c) The market value of investments were:

$$31 \text{ March } 1982 \quad £3\,640\,000$$
$$31 \text{ March } 1983 \quad £4\,740\,000$$

(d) During the year £3.1m was spent upon new plant and machinery. No other fixed assets were purchased.

(Cert. Dip. in Finance & Accounting, June 1983)

11.6 The following information has been extracted from the published accounts of two companies during 1982.

		Company Gamma	Delta
(A)	Profit before interest and tax as % sales turnover	16.0	5.9
(B)	Profit before interest and tax as % capital employed	11.6	14.5
(C)	Equity as % capital employed	54.0	32.3
(D)	Profit after tax as % equity	5.0	10.8
(E)	Earnings per £1 ordinary share (pence)	60.0	12.5

You are required to:

(a) Calculate the following for Company Gamma given that capital employed of Company Gamma used as the basis for the above statistics was £18 000 000:

(1) profit before interest and tax,
(2) sales turnover,
(3) profit after interest and tax,
(4) total shareholders' funds,
(5) number of issued ordinary shares, and
(6) retained profits and other reserves.

(b) Explain and examine the relationship between ratios (A) and (B) above.

(c) Explain and examine the relationship between ratios (B) and (D) above.

(d) Does the higher earnings per share of Company Gamma indicate that it is 4.8 times more efficient than Company Delta? Give your reasons.

(e) Consider if the relationship shown in ratio (B) above is a good indicator of effective company management.

(Cert. Dip. in Finance & Accounting, December 1983)

11.7 Your employer's finance department has recently developed a computer model to assist in the prediction of profits, balance sheets and cash flow. By entering the sales forecast and the values of various parameters the model will print data about profit, and an outline balance sheet. The parameters are as follows:

Gross profit % sales	60
Selling expenses as % sales	15
Fixed costs, excluding interest	£12 000
Tax rate on profits	40%
Pre-tax return on capital employed	20%
Debt:equity ratio	1:2
Interest rate % on debt	10
Ratio of fixed to net current assets	1:1
Current ratio	3
Ordinary dividend pay out (%)	25

The first trial of the model will use sales of £80 000.

You are required to:

(a) Prepare a profit statement based upon the above factors which show:

(1) net profit before interest and tax;
(2) earnings available for distribution;
(3) ordinary dividends.

(b) Determine the book value of long-term debt and the current liabilities.
(c) Explain how you would check the validity of the model as a mechanism for prediction.

(Cert. Dip. in Accounting & Finance, June 1982)

11.8 Mitchell owns 98 per cent of the issued share capital of Sentinel Ltd and is also the company's managing director. The remaining 2 per cent of the share capital is held by members of Mitchell's family.

The summarized balance sheets of Sentinel Ltd at 31 December 1979 and 31 December 1980 (unaudited) were as follows:

	1979	1980		1979	1980
	£000	£000		£000	£000
Ordinary shares £1 each	1200	1200	Goodwill	260	260
Profit and loss account	400	780	Freehold at cost	420	420
Bank overdraft	—	180	Plant and machinery at cost		
Trade creditors	280	840	less depreciation	60	20
			Motor vehicles at cost		
			less depreciation	—	120
			Stocks: Raw materials	260	220
			Work in progress	60	40
			Finished goods	400	1140
			Debtors and prepayments	300	780
			Cash at bank	120	—
	1880	3000		1880	3000

The following additional information is available:

(1)   Extracts from manufacturing, trading and profit and loss accounts:

	1979	1980
	£000	£000
Sales	4640	7740
Net profit	200	380
Depreciation: Plant and machinery	40	40
Motor vehicles	—	20
Cost of materials consumed	2400	5200

(2)   It is the company's policy to give cash discounts for prompt payments. *An analysis of debtors* at 31 December produces the following figures:

	1979	1980
	£000	£000
Botterill Ltd	20	22
Norton Ltd	180	620
Newbould Ltd	35	34
Parker Ltd	27	31
Other customers	38	53
20 per cent deposit on purchase of additional freehold property	—	20
	300	780

(3)   *Analysis of sales*

		1979	1980
		£000	£000
1 January to 30 June:	Botterill Ltd	224	240
	Norton Ltd	—	2480
	Newbould Ltd	275	290
	Parker Ltd	306	300
	Other customers	1155	1270
1 July to 31 December:	Botterill Ltd	207	210
	Norton Ltd	580	1240
	Newbould Ltd	281	296
	Parker Ltd	240	250
	Other customers	1372	1164
		4640	7740

(4)   No sales have been made to Norton Ltd since 1 September 1980.
(5)   The vehicles purchased in 1980 cost £140 000 and are used for delivering goods to customers.
(6)   The market value of the freehold property shown in the balance sheet is £600 000.

Mitchell is satisfied with the company's record during 1980, but considers that further growth is going to be hindered by a lack of finance with which to fund stocks and debtors. He takes the view that further growth is possible and the lack of finance could be overcome by increasing the bank overdraft. Accordingly, he approaches the company's bank with a request that the overdraft limit be raised from £200 000 to £400 000.

Required:

A report for the company's bank on the progress, position and prospects of Sentinel Ltd. Your report should give a reasoned conclusion on whether the request for additional overdraft facilities should be granted.

(AIB, April 1981)

11.9   Fast Developments Ltd is a rapidly expanding company, which during the last eighteen months has trebled its turnover. The majority of this increase in the company's sales is due to the successful penetration of a number of export markets. The internal monthly accounts have shown that profits have continually advanced. Throughout this period the net profit percentage has declined from 9.1 per cent of sales in October 1981 to 5.4 per cent of sales in March 1983. It was expected that profitability would have to be sacrificed in order to achieve an increase in turnover. What was not anticipated was either the size of the increase in sales nor the amount of the reduction in profitability.

However, as the actual profits are well ahead of the plan the Board of Fast Development Ltd are not unduly worried. The one major concern of the Board is the ever increasing bank overdraft—which has now reached the limit agreed with the bank. Furthermore, the company's gearing is quite high and there is no real scope for reducing it. What is worrying the Board even more is that there are plans to double the turnover next year even though the company's margins will have to be trimmed even further.

Below is a summary of the financial data for Fast Developments Ltd for the last three years.

Would you be happy about the company's future prospects?

Ignore taxation.

Fast Developments Ltd
Summary of financial data from past accounts

		£000	
Years ended 31 March	*1981*	*1982*	*1983*
Sales	90.0	170.0	460.0
Gross profit	19.8	34.4	69.2
Net profit	6.4	17.5	28.1
Dividends	—	9.0	15.0
Equity capital	28.0	36.5	49.6
Long-term loans	16.2	31.1	53.0
Fixed assets	30.0	42.3	64.7
Current ratio	2.7	2.6	1.6
Liquid ratio	1.5	1.6	0.8

(Cert. Dip. in Accounting & Finance, June 1983)

11.10   The following data reflects the accounts of three companies in a segment of the cosmetics industry.

(1)   *Balance sheets at 31 December 1980—Current cost basis*

	Schwarz	Weiss	Blau
	£m	£m	£m
Fixed assets (net)	2.9	3.3	1.5
Stocks	0.6	1.5	0.8
Debtors and prepayments	0.8	2.9	0.3

Bank balances (overdraft)	(1.3)	0.2	(0.2)
Creditors	0.7	1.7	1.9
Ordinary shares £1, fully paid	1.4	0.7	0.4
Preference shares 10% fully paid	—	1.0	—
Debentures 15%	—	2.0	—
Retained profit (including current cost reserve)	0.9	2.5	0.1

(2) *Profit for year ended 31 December 1980—Current cost basis*

	£m	£m	£m
Sales	5.0	13.0	4.0
Profit before interest and tax	1.1	3.0	0.1
Debenture interest	—	0.3	—
Bank interest—net paid	0.5	—	—
Gearing adjustment (negligible)	—	—	—
Taxation (rebate)	0.2	0.4	(0.2)
Dividends—Preference	—	0.1	—
Ordinary	0.4	0.8	0.5

(3) *Market share—Sales volume (%)*   15   39   12

Schwarz and Weiss are independent public companies and Blau is a wholly owned division of a vertically integrated multi-national.

You are required to:

(a) Compute the following four ratios using the information from Schwarz's accounts:

(1) Return on capital employed.
(2) Current ratio.
(3) Debt:equity ratio.
(4) Debtor turnover.

(b) For each ratio comment briefly on any computational problems and limitations in using this ratio and identify the 'key area of performance' to which it relates.
(c) Explain and illustrate any limitations in using the ratios from (a) in performance comparison between Schwarz, and Weiss and Blau.

(Cert. Dip. in Accounting & Finance, June 1981)

11.11   Discuss the return on capital employed yardstick for assessing performance. How does it apply in the case of a business such as an advertising agency or an architectural partnership?

(Cert. Dip. in Accounting & Finance, June 1978)

11.12   Following a retail trade association meeting you have been asked to draft a report on the advantages, disadvantages and the problems associated with the establishment of an inter-firm comparison scheme within the association.

(Cert. Dip. in Accounting & Finance, June 1979)

Additional questions

The following is a selection of questions drawing on topics from several chapters of this book. Note that references to 'The Companies Acts 1948–81' may be taken as referring to the Companies Act 1985.

AQ.1   The final accounts of Milford Ltd are in the course of preparation, and it is intended to publish them in accordance with the formats prescribed by the Companies Act 1981. The draft profit and loss account and balance sheet, both of which comply with format 1, are set out below.

Profit and Loss Account for the year ended 31 December 1982

	£	£
Turnover		862 150
Less Cost of sales		484 500
Gross profit		377 650
Less Distribution costs	25 000	
Administration expenses	185 700	210 700
Operating profit		166 950
Less Interest payable		12 000
Profit on ordinary activities before taxation		154 950
Tax on profit on ordinary activities		77 000
Profit on ordinary activities after taxation		77 950
Retained profit as at 1 January 1982		96 800
Retained profit as at 31 December 1982		£174 750

Balance Sheet as at 31 December 1982

	£	£
Fixed assets:		
Intangible assets: Development costs	24 100	
Goodwill	33 000	57 100
Tangible assets: Land and buildings	85 000	
Plant and machinery	126 600	211 600
		268 700
Current assets:		
Stocks	139 400	
Debtors	91 200	
Cash at bank and in hand	14 000	
	244 600	

Creditors: amounts falling due within one year:		
Trade creditors	57 100	
Current corporation tax	77 000	
	134 100	
Net current assets		110 500
Total assets less current liabilities		379 200
Creditors: amount falling due after more than one year:		
12% debenture		100 000
		£279 200
Capital and reserves:		
Called-up share capital		100 000
Share premium account		4 450
Profit and loss account		174 750
		£279 200

The following additional information is provided:

(1)   Development costs £24 100 are made up of:

	£
Research costs	15 000
Development expenditure	9 100
	£24 100

The development expenditure relates to a separately identifiable project which will undoubtedly produce a significant improvement in the quality of one of the company's product lines.

(2)   The figure for goodwill is stated at cost, and arose as the result of purchasing the business of a former competitor on 1 January 1982. It is thought that the goodwill possesses an economic life of five years.

(3)   Stock is valued at 'total' cost in the balance sheet set out above. Stock was valued at 'prime' cost, £75 000, for the purpose of the 1981 accounts, and this amount was used when computing the cost of sales figure appearing in the profit and loss account. The corresponding total cost valuation of stock at 31 December 1981 is £98 300 made up as follows:

	£
Prime cost	75 000
Production overheads	23 300
	£98 300

(4)   It has recently come to light that an invoice for £4900, received from a supplier, has been erroneously omitted from the books. The goods referred to in the invoice were included in the physical stock-take.

(5)   The company's land and buildings are stated in the balance sheet at cost less depreciation. They were professionally revalued at £120 000 on 1 January 1982. It has now been decided to use this figure for the purpose of the accounts. Administration expenses include a depreciation charge of £2000 which should be revised to £3500 to take account of the revaluation.

Required

(a) The profit and loss account of Milford Ltd 1982 and the balance sheet at 31 December 1982 redrafted, as necessary, to take account of the additional information. The revised accounts should comply, so far as the information permits, with the requirements of the Companies Act 1981 and Statement of Standard Accounting Practice.

(b) A calculation of the profit available for distribution according to the requirements of the Companies Act 1980.

Notes:

Show all adjustments clearly.

Assume that the adjustments you make do not alter tax payable.

(AIB, April 1983)

AQ.2 A recent conference of businessmen listened to a lecture on 'Accounting Policies' and were surprised to discover the extent to which the level of reported profit depends on the accounting procedures chosen for the purpose of valuing assets and liabilities. One of the participants suggested that this was a good reason for adopting a prudent approach when measuring profit, and there was some support for this view, though others argued that it was important to adopt a realistic approach rather than a pessimistic approach when preparing company accounts.

Required:

Indicate which accounting policy is likely to produce the more conservative figure for reported profit in each of the circumstances listed below. You should explain your choice.

(a) Using first in—first out (FIFO) *or* last in—first out (LIFO) as the basis for valuing stock, assuming prices are rising and there is no change in the volume of stock held.

(b) Using marginal *or* total cost as the basis for valuing stock, assuming prices are stable and the volume of stock held is increasing.

(c) Using marginal *or* total cost as the basis for valuing stock at the end of the first year of a company's operations.

(d) Applying the lower of cost and net realizable value rule to separate items of stock and work-in-progress *or* to groups of similar items.

(e) Using the reducing balance *or* straight-line method of depreciation during the early years of a particular asset's life.

(f) Valuing freehold property at historical cost less depreciation *or* current cost less depreciation when prices are rising.

(AIB, September 1983)

AQ.3 The accountant of Wiley Ltd has prepared the following estimated balance sheet as at 31 December 1982 for the company's directors.

Estimated Balance Sheet as at 31 December 1982

	£	£		£
Ordinary share capital			Freehold property at cost	600 000
(£1 shares)		500 000	*Less* Depreciation	100 000
				500 000

	£	£		£
Reserves at 1 January			Stock valued at	
1982	250 000		marginal cost	590 000
Add Net profit for 1982	50 000		Trade debtors	160 000
		300 000		
		800 000		
Loan repayable 1985		250 000		
Trade creditors		140 000		
Bank overdraft		60 000		
		£1 250 000		£1 250 000

The directors are disappointed with the estimated net profit for 1982 and the estimated financial position as at 31 December 1982 displayed in the balance sheet shown above. The following suggestions are made for consideration by the company's accountant.

(1) A bonus (capitalization) issue of shares to existing shareholders on the basis of one additional £1 share for every two shares held at present.

(2) Increase the depreciation charged on the freehold buildings from £20 000 to £30 000.

(3) Arrange for a loan of £100 000, also repayable in 1985, to be made to the company on 31 December 1982.

(4) Value stock at total cost, £680 000, for the purpose of the accounts. The 1981 accounts included stock at marginal cost of £400 000 and the corresponding figure for total cost at that date was £470 000.

(5) Offer cash discount for prompt payment in respect of future sales. If this course is followed it is estimated that sales will be unaffected, but discounts of £3000 will be allowed during the period October—December 1982 and trade debtors at the year end will amount to £120 000.

Required:

Taking each course of action separately, a statement showing the following:

(a) net profit for 1982;

(b) bank overdraft (or balance) at 31 December 1982;

(c) working capital at 31 December 1982; and

(d) liquidity ratio, defined as the ratio of trade debtors + bank balance (if any) to current liabilities at 31 December 1982.

Consider each course of action separately and present your answer in a table as shown below:

Course of action	Net profit £	Bank overdraft (or balance) £	Working capital £	Liquidity ratio
(1)				
(2)				
(3)				
(4)				
(5)				

Notes:

Ignore taxation.

Assume that no course of action will alter the amount of bank interest payable.

(AIB, September 1982)

AQ.4 The accounts of Hatfield Ltd for the year ended 30 June 1984 are being prepared for publication. The following information is provided:

A. **Stock**

Groups of similar items	Marginal cost	Total cost	Net realizable value
	£	£	£
Group A	16 000	25 000	36 000
Group B	9 000	12 000	4 000
Group C	63 000	71 000	94 000
Group D	46 000	51 000	67 000

B. **Long-term contract work in progress**

The company has one long-term contract in respect of which costs incurred to 30 June 1984 amount to £51 000. Estimates suggest that, on completion, the contract will show a total profit of £30 000. Architects have certified the contract to be 60 per cent complete on 30 June 1984.

C. **Tangible fixed assets**

These include:

(1) Freehold land and a building purchased on 1 July 1973 for £380 000 (including £80 000 for the land). The building has been depreciated at the rate of 4 per cent per annum on cost for each of the ten years to 30 June 1983. The property was professionally revalued at £800 000 (including land £200 000) on 1 July 1983 and the directors have decided to write this figure into the books. It is now estimated that the building has a remaining useful life of 20 years and a residual value of £100 000 at the end of that period.

(2) A machine which was shown in the 1983 accounts at cost, £100 000 less accumulated depreciation, £30 000. The machine has been depreciated on the straight-line basis assuming a zero residual value after ten years. The directors now believe that the reducing balance method will provide users of accounts with a fairer presentation of the financial results and position of the company. The directors consider a depreciation rate of 30 per cent to be appropriate. They do not expect any change in the useful life of the machine.

D. **Research and development expenditure**

Expenditure incurred during the year is as follows:

Research expenditure	£1500
Development expenditure	£5000

The expenditure has been incurred in an attempt to develop a new product line. The directors are not entirely confident that a new product line will eventually materialize but a minority are fairly hopeful.

Required:

For each of the items A—D, calculations of the balances for inclusion in accounts prepared in accordance with the Companies Acts 1948—81 and relevant Statements of Standard Accounting Practice. It is not necessary to give the exact location of each item in the balance sheet and profit and loss account, but the balances should be suitably described. In respect of balance sheet items it should be made clear whether the balance is an asset or a liability and, in respect of profit and loss account items, whether the balance is a revenue or an expense. You may, if necessary, explain the treatment you have adopted.

Notes:
(1) For the purpose of your calculations, treat each item in isolation.
(2) Comparative figures for the previous year are not required.

(AIB, September 1984)

AQ.5   The following balances have been extracted from the books of Malham Ltd, a trading company, as at 31 March 1984:

	£000
Issued share capital: 800 000 ordinary shares of £1 each	800
Bank loan	140
Retained profit at 1 April 1983	573
Net profit for the year to 31 March 1984	229
Freehold properties at cost	780
Fixtures and fittings at cost	217
Accumulated depreciation on fixtures and fittings at 31 March 1984	76
Creditors	206
Trade debtors	391
Prepaid expenses	13
Stocks at cost	464
Balance of cash at bank	75
Cash in hand	24
Goodwill at cost	60

The following additional information is provided:

(1) The freehold properties, purchased in 1965, were revalued at £1 050 000 on 31 March 1984. The valuation was made by Collins and Co., a firm of chartered surveyors, and the directors have decided to use this figure for the purpose of the accounts.

(2) The company purchased fixtures and fittings costing £67 000 during the year to 31 March 1984. The depreciation charge for the year amounted to £22 000. There were no sales of fixed assets.

(3) The figure for creditors includes advance payments of £15 000 from a customer who was not supplied with the goods ordered until 5 April 1984.

(4) The following information is provided in respect of groups of similar items of stocks:

Group	Cost £000	Net realizable value £000
W	127	186
X	35	7

Y	209	352
Z	93	184

(5) The goodwill arose on the purchase of the business assets of Tarn Ltd, a small private company, on 1 April 1983. The goodwill is believed to have a useful economic life of five years.

(6) A bank loan of £160 000 was raised to help to finance the acquisition of Tarn's business assets. The loan carries interest at a fixed rate of 12 per cent and is repayable by eight equal annual instalments. The first instalment was paid on 31 March 1984 together with interest accrued to that date.

(7) The directors propose to recommend to the annual general meeting the payment of a dividend of eight pence per ordinary share.

Required:

The balance sheet of Malham Ltd at 31 March 1984 together with relevant notes complying with the minimum requirements of the Companies Acts 1948–81 so far as the information permits.

Notes:

(1) The main headings contained in balance sheet format 1 are reproduced below.

(2) Ignore depreciation of freehold properties and taxation.

(3) Show your calculation of the profit and loss account balance for inclusion in the balance sheet.

Companies Act 1981. Balance Sheet Format 1
A. Called-up share capital not paid
B. Fixed assets
(1) Intangible assets
(2) Tangible assets
(3) Investments
C. Current assets
(1) Stocks
(2) Debtors
(3) Investments
(4) Cash at bank and in hand
D. Prepayments and accrued income
E. Creditors: amounts falling due within one year
F. Net current assets (liabilities)
G. Total assets less current liabilities
H. Creditors; amounts falling due after more than one year
I. Provisions for liabilities and charge
J. Accruals and deferred income
K. Capital and reserves
(1) Called-up share capital
(2) Share premium account
(3) Revaluation reserve
(4) Other reserves
(5) Profit and loss account

(AIB, May 1984)

Appendix A Specimen accounts

Grog plc—Profit and Loss Account for the year ended 31 December 1985

	1985		*1984*	
	£000	£000	£000	£000
Turnover		13 200		12 000
Cost of sales		8 052		7 080
Gross profit		5 148		4 920
Distribution costs	1 056		960	
Administration costs	756		720	
		1 812		1 680
Operating profit		3 336		3 240
Other income		135		274
		3 471		3 514
Interest		400		480
Profit before taxation		3 071		3 034
Taxation		1 298		1 476
Profit after taxation		1 773		1 558
Extraordinary items		700		—
Profit after taxation and extraordinary items		2 473		1 558
Dividend		800		600
Retained profit for year		1 673		958
Retained profit b/fwd		2 056		1 098
Retained profit c/fwd		3 729		2 056
Earnings per share		£1.61		£1.42

Grog plc—Balance Sheet as at 31 December 1985

	1985		*1984*	
	£000	£000	£000	£000
Fixed assets:				
Tangible assets		9 974		9 055
Investments		1 030		2 500
		11 004		11 555

Current assets:		
Stock	1 364	1 062
Debtors	1 627	1 360
Cash at bank and in hand	765	10
	3 756	2 432
Current liabilities:		
Creditors	2 569	3 305
Net current assets	1 187	(873)
	12 191	10 682
Deferred taxation	1 962	2 126
Loans	4 000	4 000
	5 962	6 126
	6 229	4 556
Share capital	1 100	1 000
Share premium	400	500
Revaluation reserve	1 000	1 000
Retained profits	3 729	2 056
	6 229	4 556

Notes to the accounts:

(1) *Accounting policies*

(a) Stocks and work in progress are stated at the lower of cost and net realizable value. Cost includes direct materials and labour plus attributable overheads based on the normal levels of activity.

(b) Depreciation is provided on all fixed assets at rates calculated to write off the cost or valuation, less estimated residual value, of each asset evenly over its expected useful life.

Estimated lives of the assets are:

	Years
Freehold buildings	50
Plant and machinery	10
Motor vehicles	5

(c) Deferred taxation is provided under the liability method, to the extent that it is probable that a liability will arise.

(Plus others as appropriate.)

2. *Operating profit*

Operating profit is stated after charging:

	1985	1984
	£000	£000
Depreciation	1361	1136
Hire of plant and machinery	360	330
Auditors' remuneration and crediting	28	19
Profit on sale of vehicles	52	18

3. *Directors' emoluments*

	1985	*1984*
	£000	£000
Fees	14	11
Other emoluments	110	101
	124	112
Chairman's emoluments	£28 900	£26 700
Highest paid director	£35 000	£32 500
Others:		
£10 001 to £15 000	1	2
£20 001 to £25 000	2	1

4. *Employees*

	1985	*1984*
The average weekly number of employees was:	190	195
Staff costs were:	£000	£000
Wages and salaries	1945	1738
Social security costs	140	120
Pension costs	125	117
	2210	1975

No employees received emoluments in excess of £30 000.

5. *Other income*

Other income was derived from:

	1985	*1984*
	£000	£000
Listed investments	—	154
Unlisted investments	135	120
	135	274

6. *Interest*

	1985	1984
Interest paid	£000	£000
On bank loans and overdrafts wholly repayable within five years	—	80
On other loans	400	400
	400	400

7. *Taxation*

The taxation charge which is based upon profits of the year is made up as follows:

	1985	1984
	£000	£000
Corporation tax at 41%		
(1984 46%)	1400	1410
Deferred taxation	(79)	81
Taxation over-provided in previous		
years	(23)	(15)
	1298	1476

8. *Extraordinary items*

	£000
Profit on disposal of long-term	
investment	1000
Less Related taxation	300
	700

9. *Dividends*

	1985	1984
	£000	£000
Interim paid	330	300
Final proposed	470	300
	800	600

10. *Earnings per share*

The calculations of earnings per share is based on earnings of £1 773 000 (1984 £1 558 000) and on 1 100 000 ordinary shares, being the weighted average number of shares in issue during the year (1984 1 100 00).

11. *Tangible fixed assets*

Cost/valuation	Freehold Land	Freehold Buildings	Plant	Vehicles	Plant
	£000	£000	£000	£000	£000
At 1 Jan 85	1 450	550	9 500	930	12 430
Additions	—	—	1 700	620	2 320
Disposals	—	—	—	400	400
At 31 Dec 85	1 450	550	11 200	1 150	14 350
Accumulated depreciation					
At 1 Jan 85	—	55	2 850	470	3 375
Provision for year	—	11	1 120	230	1 361
Disposals for year	—	—	—	360	360
At 31 Dec 85	—	66	3 970	340	4 376
Net book value:					
31 Dec 85	1 450	484	7 230	810	9 974
31 Dec 84	1 450	495	6 650	460	9 055

12. *Fixed asset investments*

	Listed companies	*Other*	*Total*
	£000	£000	£000
Cost 1 Jan 85	1500	1000	2500
Additions	—	30	30
Disposals	1500	—	1500
Cost 31 Dec 85	—	1030	1030

The market value of the Stock Exchange listed shares as at 1 January 1985 was £2 200 000 and the liability to capital gains tax on a sale at that price would have been £210 000.

The company holds more than 10 per cent of the equity, and no other share or loan capital, of the following companies:

Name of company	*Country of registration*	*Holding*	*Proportion held*
Main Ltd	England	Ordinary shares	15%
Brace Ltd	Scotland	Ordinary shares	10%

13. *Stocks*

	1985	*1984*
The main categories of stock are:	£000	£000
Raw materials	320	310
Work in progress	170	165
Finished goods	874	587
	1364	1062

14. *Debtors*

	1985	*1984*
Amounts falling due within one year:	£000	£000
Trade debtors	1507	1250
Prepayments	120	110
	1627	1360

15. *Creditors*

	£000	£000
Amounts falling due within one year:		
Current instalment due on loan	—	1000
Trade creditors	336	320
Current corporation tax	1601	1539
Other taxes and social security costs	125	122
Proposed dividend	470	300
Accruals	37	24
	2569	3305

16. *Deferred taxation*
Deferred taxation provided in the accounts, and the potential amounts are:

	Provision		Potential	
	1985	1984	1985	1984
	£000	£000	£000	£000
Accelerated capital allowances	2408	2489	2408	2489
Short-term differences	25	23	25	23
Tax on revaluation surplus	—	—	300	300
	2433	2512	2733	2812
Less ACT recoverable	471	386	471	386
	1962	2126	2262	2426

17. *Loans*

	1985	1984
Not wholly repayable within 5 years	4000	4000
Wholly repayable within 5 years	—	1000
	4000	5000
Less Amounts due within 1 year	—	1000
	4000	4000

The loan not wholly repayable within five years is a 10 per cent secured debenture repayable by ten annual instalments of £400 000 commencing on 1 January 1987.

18. *Share capital*

	1985	1984
	£000	£000
Authorised		
Ordinary shares of £1 each	2000	2000
Issued and fully paid		
Ordinary shares of £1 each	1100	1000

19. *Reserves*

	£000
Share premium	
At 1 Jan 85	500
Less Bonus issue on 30 June 85	100
At 31 Dec 85	400
Retained profits	
At 1 Jan 85	2056
Retained profit for year	1673
At 31 Dec 85	3729

Appendix B Summary of the disclosure requirements of the Companies Act 1985

This is not a comprehensive list of the disclosure requirements, but covers major items. In some cases requirements are referred to but not fully described, e.g. 'Certain information is required when . . .'.

Balance sheet notes

Share capital

(a) Total authorized amount.
(b) Number and nominal value of each class of allotted share.
(c) Details of any redeemable shares.
(d) Details of any shares allotted in year.
(e) Details of any share options.

Debentures

(a) Reasons for, nature of, and amount raised from, any issue in year.
(b) Details of redeemed debentures available for reissue and debentures held for the company by a nominee.

Fixed assets

(a) For each heading cost or value, and accumulated depreciation at beginning and end of year, with an analysis of movements in year.
(b) For assets, other than listed investments shown at a valuation, year and amounts of valuation. Also, in year revalued, names or qualifications of valuer and basis of valuation.
(c) Freehold, long leasehold (over 50 years) and short leasehold (under 50 years) property must be distinguished in the analysis of fixed assets.
(d) Development costs may only be capitalized in special circumstances, with the reasons and the amortization period disclosed.
(e) The amortization period for goodwill must be shown.

Investments

(a) Total listed investments, split between those listed on a recognized Stock Exchange and others.
(b) The market value of listed investments, and their Stock Exchange value if that is lower.

(c)   Detailed information concerning investments amounting to more than 10 per cent of the share capital of the investee or more than 10 per cent of the assets of the investee.
(d)   Certain information extracted from the accounts of companies where more than 20 per cent of the share capital is held.

Reserves and provisions

(a)   Details of movements during the year on all reserves and provisions shown in the balance sheet.
(b)   Tax implications of movements on revaluation reserves.
(c)   Amount of any provisions for tax other than deferred tax.

Creditors

(a)   For loans over one year there must be identified:

(1)   Total loans repayable by instalments, any of which fall due after more than 5 years, and details of the total falling due after more than 5 years.
(2)   Total loans not repayable by instalments and falling due after more than 5 years.

Repayment terms and interest rates should be shown for each such loan.
(b)   The part of each type of liability which is secured, and the nature of the security.
(c)   Details of the proposed dividend, and any arrears of cumulative dividends.

Stocks

The difference between balance sheet value and replacement cost, if material.

Loans to directors

Extensive details of loans to directors, and loans to employees to buy shares.

Commitments

(a)   Details of all contingent liabilities.
(b)   Authorized capital expenditure, distinguishing that contracted for and that not contracted for.
(c)   Details of pension commitments not provided for.
(d)   Details of commitments on behalf of other group companies.

Profit and loss account notes

Items to be disclosed

(a)   Interest on:

(1)   Bank loans, overdrafts and other loans repayable within five years.
(2)   Other loans.

(b)   Income from listed investments.

(c)   Rental income if 'substantial'.
(d)   Costs of hiring plant.
(e)   Audit fee including expenses.
(f)   Depreciation charge.
(g)   Directors' remuneration, split into:

(1)   Fees.
(2)   Other emoluments.
(3)   Pensions.
(4)   Compensation for loss of office.

(h)   For directors:

(1)   Emoluments of chairman.
(2)   Emoluments of highest paid director (if other than chairman).
(3)   Number of directors in each £5000 band of remuneration.

(j)   Average number of employees in each category of business.
(k)   Total of:

(1)   Wages and salaries.
(2)   Social security costs.
(3)   Pension costs.

(l)   Number of employees (other than directors) earning over £20 000 p.a., in rising bands of £5000.

Turnover

(a)   For each class of business:

(1)   Turnover.
(2)   Related pre-tax profit.

(b)   Turnover split by geographical market.

Taxation

(a)   Basis for computing UK tax.
(b)   Details of any special circumstances affecting the tax charge.
(c)   The following, split between tax on ordinary activities and tax on extraordinary items:

(1)   UK corporation tax.
(2)   Effect of double tax relief.
(3)   UK income tax.
(4)   Foreign tax.

Appendix C   Marks & Spencer plc accounts

Included below are the accounts of Marks & Spencer plc, giving readers a useful insight into how a major company prepares published accounts in practice.

The following points might usefully be noted in relation to individual chapters.

Chapter 2

The basic accounting equation in the Marks & Spencer balance sheet is in the form:

$$\text{Assets} - \text{Liabilities} = \text{Equity}$$

Chapter 3

The audit report, prepared by one of the leading firms of chartered accountants, is on the final page of the accounts. Note that this report differs slightly from that shown as an example in the chapter, because:

(a)   The report was prepared prior to the 1985 Companies Act.
(b)   The report does not allude to the accounting convention under which the accounts were prepared. This may be because the matter is covered by the first accounting policy note.

Chapter 4

Fixed assets are fully explained in Notes 9, 10 and 11, together with the accounting policy note on depreciaton.

The accounting policy on stock tells us that cost has been computed as selling price less gross profit margin; in practice this is a common way of estimating the cost of stock in the retail trade.

Chapter 5

Notes 18 and 19 together explain the total movements in the equity during the year.

Chapter 6

Note 6 to the accounts explains the computation of the earnings per share figure.

Note how the profit and loss account uses a 'type of operation' format for expenses.

Chapter 7

Notes 4 and 17 together explain the tax position. In a company with such consistent profitability and dividend payments as this there is no problem in treating ACT recoverable as an asset.

Chapter 8

The funds statement presented by Marks & Spencer is in a rather different format to that in Chapter 8, focussing on the movement from opening to closing cash balances. This may be because the company wishes to highlight its strong liquidity position.

Chapter 9

The accounting policies notes explain foreign currency translation and consolidation practices fully. Note 20 gives full disclosure in relation to commitments and contingencies.

ACCOUNTING POLICIES

Basis of accounting
The financial statements are drawn up on the historical cost basis of accounting, modified to include the valuation of the United Kingdom properties at 31 March 1982.

Basis of consolidation
The Group financial statements incorporate the financial statements of:–

(i) The retailing activities of Marks and Spencer p.l.c. and its wholly-owned subsidiaries to 31 March.

(ii) The partly-owned Canadian subsidiary to 31 January. The directors consider that if the Canadian subsidiary prepared financial statements to 31 March, it would unduly delay the presentation of consolidated financial statements to the members of Marks and Spencer p.l.c.

(iii) The financial activities of the Group's wholly-owned subsidiaries to 31 March. In order to reflect the different nature of the business of the financial activities and so present fairly the Group's state of affairs, the assets and liabilities of such activities are shown as a net investment in the Group balance sheet and are analysed separately in note 11 on pages 33 and 34.

Deferred taxation
Deferred taxation is provided on the liability method, unless there is reasonable probability that a liability will not crystallise in the foreseeable future. It is provided on the excess of capital allowances over depreciation in respect of assets leased to third parties and on items of income and expenditure included in the profit and loss account in different years from those in which they are assessed for taxation purposes.

Depreciation
Depreciation is provided to write off the cost or valuation of tangible fixed assets by equal annual instalments at the following rates:–

Freehold and leasehold land over 99 years – Nil
Leasehold land 50–99 years – 1%

Freehold and leasehold buildings over 50 years – 1%
Leasehold land and buildings under 50 years – Over the remaining period of the lease
Fixtures, fittings and equipment – 10% or 20% according to the estimated life of the asset.

Foreign currencies
The financial statements of overseas subsidiaries are translated into sterling at the rates of exchange ruling at 31 March. Exchange differences arising between the translation into sterling of the net assets of these subsidiaries at rates ruling at the beginning and end of the year are dealt with through reserves.

The cost of the Company's investment in overseas subsidiaries is translated at the rate ruling at the date of investment.

All other foreign currency assets and liabilities of the Company and its United Kingdom subsidiaries are translated into sterling at the rate ruling at 31 March, except in those instances where forward cover has been arranged in which case this forward rate is used. Any exchange differences are dealt with through the profit and loss account.

Transactions during the year between the Company and its subsidiaries, customers and suppliers are translated into sterling at the rate of exchange ruling on the date of the transaction. All profits and losses on exchange realised during the year are dealt with through the profit and loss account.

Pension contributions
The Group operates pension schemes for the benefit of all its employees. The funds of the schemes are administered by Trustees and are separate from the Group. Independent actuaries complete valuations at least every 3 years and, in accordance with their recommendations, annual contributions are paid to the schemes so as to secure the benefits set out in the rules and the periodic augmentation of current pensions. The cost of these is charged against profits when the contributions are made. When the contributions are

not sufficient, the capital cost of such augmentation is charged against the profits of the Group for the year in which the increases are granted.

Repairs and renewals
Expenditure on repairs, renewals and minor items of equipment is written off in the year in which it is incurred.

Stocks
Stocks which consist of goods for resale are valued at the lower of cost and net realisable value. Cost is computed by deducting the gross profit margin from the selling value of stock. When computing net realisable value an allowance is made for future markdowns.

Leases
For finance leases where the Group is the lessor, gross earnings are allocated to accounting periods such that the profit after tax represents a constant rate of return on the net cash investment in the lease during the period of the lease.

The net investment in finance leases which represents total lease payments receivable net of finance charges allocated to future periods, has been included under debtors in the net assets of financial activities. This presentation has been adopted for the first time in this financial year to comply with Statement of Standard Accounting Practice No 21. Comparative figures have been re-stated on the new basis.

Trading results in the United Kingdom
The trading results in the United Kingdom include transactions at stores up to and including the nearest Saturday to 31 March. All other transactions are included up to 31 March in each year.

CONSOLIDATED PROFIT AND LOSS ACCOUNT
FOR THE YEAR ENDED 31 MARCH 1985

	Notes	1985 £m	1984 £m
Turnover	1	3,213·0	2,868·4
Cost of sales		2,292·5	2,059·4
Gross profit		920·5	809·0
Other expenses	2	617·1	529·7
Profit on ordinary activities before taxation	3	303·4	279·3
Tax on profit on ordinary activities	4	120·3	111·1
Profit on ordinary activities after taxation		183·1	168·2
Minority interests		2·0	1·8
Profit for the financial year	5	181·1	166·4
Dividends			
Preference shares		·1	·1
Ordinary shares:–			
Interim of 1·08p per share		28·5	27·0
Final of 2·32p per share		61·2	55·3
		89·8	82·4
Undistributed surplus		91·3	84·0
Earnings per share	6	6·9p	6·3p

BALANCE SHEETS
AT 31 MARCH 1985

	Notes	The Group 1985 £m	The Group 1984 £m	The Company 1985 £m	The Company 1984 £m
Fixed assets					
Tangible assets:	9				
Land and buildings		1,178·4	1,115·7	1,121·5	1,061·4
Fixtures, fittings and equipment		167·1	136·8	147·8	118·3
Assets in course of construction		17·3	33·2	17·1	33·0
		1,362·8	1,285·7	1,286·4	1,212·7
Investments	10	—	—	64·3	69·2
Net assets of financial activities	11	10·7	8·0	—	—
		1,373·5	1,293·7	1,350·7	1,281·9
Current assets					
Stocks		229·7	194·1	185·2	157·5
Debtors	12	67·4	61·9	100·0	92·1
Investments	13	108·3	58·4	102·0	57·9
Cash at bank and in hand	14	83·8	73·4	16·6	10·5
		489·2	387·8	403·8	318·0
Current liabilities					
Creditors: amounts falling due within one year	15	477·3	396·4	402·5	337·1
Net current assets/(liabilities) (excluding financial activities)		11·9	(8·6)	1·3	(19·1)
Total assets less current liabilities		1,385·4	1,285·1	1,352·0	1,262·8
Creditors: amounts falling due after more than one year	16	49·3	49·5	45·0	45·0
Net assets		1,336·1	1,235·6	1,307·0	1,217·8
Capital and reserves					
Called up share capital	18	661·3	330·5	661·3	330·5
Share premium account		·3	15·9	·3	15·9
Revaluation reserve		82·9	391·2	86·7	395·6
Profit and loss account		580·8	489·2	558·7	475·8
Shareholders' funds	19	1,325·3	1,226·8	1,307·0	1,217·8
Minority interests		10·8	8·8	—	—
Total capital employed		1,336·1	1,235·6	1,307·0	1,217·8

Approved by the Board
7 May 1985

THE LORD RAYNER
Chairman

W B HOWARD
*Deputy Chairman and
Joint Managing Director*

CONSOLIDATED SOURCE AND APPLICATION OF FUNDS
FOR THE YEAR ENDED 31 MARCH 1985

	1985 £m	1984 £m
Cash and short-term funds at 1 April 1984	95·2	83·5
Source of funds		
Arising from trading		
Profit on ordinary activities before taxation	303·4	279·3
Depreciation	44·3	34·7
Sales of fixed assets	2·4	4·5
	350·1	318·5
From other sources		
Shares issued under employees' share schemes	6·4	4·8
	451·7	406·8
Application of funds		
Payment of dividends	83·9	69·8
Payment of taxation	94·1	71·2
Purchase of fixed assets	121·8	120·4
Miscellaneous	1·2	(·9)
	301·0	260·5
Increase/(decrease) in working capital		
Stock	35·6	30·8
Debtors	·6	(8·8)
Creditors under one year (excluding taxation and dividends)	(18·7)	(1·9)
Group relief payable	24·0	(9·1)
Creditors over one year	·2	1·5
Net assets of financial activities (see below)	7·9	38·6
	49·6	51·1
	350·6	311·6
Cash and short-term funds at 31 March 1985	101·1	95·2

Cash and short-term funds comprise cash at bank and in hand and current asset investments less bank loans and overdrafts.

Movement on net assets of financial activities		
Purchase of assets for finance leasing	28·6	76·8
Capital repayments on leases	(13·9)	(5·5)
	14·7	71·3
Increase in trade debtors	4·2	·9
(Decrease)/increase in group relief receivable	(24·0)	9·1
Decrease/(increase) in bank loans and overdrafts	9·4	(38·7)
Increase/(decrease) in other working capital	3·6	(4·0)
Net movement	7·9	38·6

NOTES TO THE FINANCIAL STATEMENTS

1 Turnover

a Retailing

Turnover represents goods sold to customers outside the Group, less returns and sales taxes.

b Financial activities

Financial activities comprise the operation of the Marks and Spencer Chargecard together with leasing and insurance. Turnover represents the interest and other income attributable to these activities.

In previous years, the amount of income attributable to financial activities was insignificant in the context of the Group financial statements and was included under the category of 'other income'. In preparing the financial statements for the current year, the income in respect of such services for last year has been reclassified.

c Analysis of turnover – by activity and geographical market.

(i) Retailing

	1985 £m	1984 £m
United Kingdom stores	2,900·2	2,596·7
Overseas stores:–		
Europe	80·9	74·4
Canada	175·0	150·2
	255·9	224·6
Export sales outside the Group:–		
Europe	19·5	18·3
America	4·8	3·2
Africa	7·6	5·2
Far East	6·3	6·5
	38·2	33·2
	3,194·3	2,854·5
(ii) Financial activities	18·7	13·9
	3,213·0	2,868·4

The turnover attributable to financial activities arises wholly within the United Kingdom and the Channel Islands.

NOTES TO THE FINANCIAL STATEMENTS
CONTINUED

2 Other expenses	1985 £m	1984 £m
Other expenses comprise:–		
Staff costs (see also note 7)	382·3	332·9
Occupancy costs	79·9	70·0
Other costs	88·3	77·8
including – Auditors' remuneration of £·3 million (last year £·3 million) – Hire of plant and machinery of £2·0 million (last year £1·2 million)		
	550·5	480·7
Repairs, renewals and maintenance of properties, fixtures, fittings and equipment	29·3	24·7
Depreciation of tangible fixed assets	44·3	34·7
	624·1	540·1
Less: Other income (see below)	12·8	15·6
	611·3	524·5
Interest payable (see below)	5·8	5·2
	617·1	529·7

The directors consider that the nature of the business is such that the analysis of expenses shown above is more informative than that set out in the Companies Act 1981.

Other income comprises:–		
Bank and other interest	1·2	·7
Profit on sales of tangible fixed assets	·3	—
Income from current asset investments:		
listed	1·1	·9
unlisted	7·5	9·8
Profit on sales of current asset investments	·6	1·6
Miscellaneous	2·1	2·6
	12·8	15·6

Interest payable comprises:–		
Debenture stocks repayable in more than 5 years	3·2	3·2
Bank loans and overdrafts	2·1	1·5
Other loans repayable in more than 5 years	·5	·5
	5·8	5·2

Included in the trading results of the financial activities:–		
Bank and other interest receivable	8·0	6·7
Interest payable on bank loans and overdrafts	13·0	10·5
Income from finance leases	10·4	6·5
Income from listed current asset investments	·3	·3
(Loss)/profit on sales of current asset investments	(·3)	·4

3 Profit on ordinary activities before taxation		1985 £m	1984 £m
	This arises as follows:–		
	United Kingdom	288·7	265·3
	Europe	7·1	6·7
	Canada	7·6	7·3
		303·4	279·3
	and can be analysed between:–		
	Retailing	299·4	275·0
	Financial activities	4·0	4·3
		303·4	279·3

4 Tax on profit on ordinary activities			
	The taxation charge comprises:–		
	United Kingdom corporation tax at 45% (last year 50%)		
	Current	111·9	74·7
	Deferred	2·8	31·5
	Overseas taxation	5·6	4·9
		120·3	111·1

a The current charge for United Kingdom corporation tax has been reduced by £17·3 million (last year £56·4 million) in respect of the excess of all capital allowances over depreciation.

b Under the terms of the agreements between the Group and the lessees of leased assets, certain benefits accruing to the Group, as a result of the changes in the rates of corporation tax announced in the 1984 Finance Act, give rise to reductions in the amounts receivable from lessees by a similar amount. The current year's deferred tax charge relating to leased assets, calculated at 45%, exceeds future tax liabilities in respect of these assets by £3·0 million (last year £8·8 million) which has been transferred from the deferred tax account to reduce the net investment in finance leases.

5 Profit for the financial year

As permitted by Section 149 (5) of the Companies Act 1948, the profit and loss account of the parent company is not presented as part of these financial statements.
The consolidated profit of £181·1 million (last year £166·4 million) includes £172·5 million (last year £156·3 million) which is dealt with in the financial statements of the parent company.

6 Earnings per share

The calculation of earnings per ordinary share is based on earnings of £181·0 million (last year £166·3 million) after deducting preference dividends, and on 2,638,129,288 ordinary shares (last year 2,632,081,522), being the weighted average of shares in issue during the year ended 31 March 1985, as adjusted for the one for one scrip issue in July 1984. At 31 March 1985, directors and senior executives held unexercised options in respect of 6,534,851 ordinary shares (last year 7,327,620). There were options outstanding under the Savings-Related Share Option Scheme in respect of 25,466,721 shares (last year 18,472,026). If all outstanding options had been exercised, the diluted earnings per share would not have been materially different.

NOTES TO THE FINANCIAL STATEMENTS
CONTINUED

---

7 Directors and employees

a The number of directors and employees of the Company performing their duties mainly within the United Kingdom whose emoluments (excluding pension contributions) were within the following ranges, are:-

Gross Emoluments £	Directors 1985	1984	Employees 1985	1984
175,001–180,000	1	—	—	—
155,001–160,000	—	1	—	—
130,001–135,000	1	—	—	—
125,001–130,000	2	—	—	—
120,001–125,000	1	2	—	—
115,001–120,000	—	2	—	—
105,001–110,000	—	1	—	—
95,001–100,000	2	—	—	—
90,001– 95,000	3	—	—	—
85,001– 90,000	1	4	—	—
80,001– 85,000	—	2	—	—
75,001– 80,000	2	1	—	—
65,001– 70,000	3	3	—	—
60,001– 65,000	—	1	1	—
55,001– 60,000	1	—	2	1
50,001– 55,000	1	2	6	2
45,001– 50,000	—	—	13	5
40,001– 45,000	2	—	36	18
35,001– 40,000	—	—	45	44
30,001– 35,000	—	—	107	60
25,001– 30,000	1	—		
20,001– 25,000	1	—		
15,001– 20,000	—	2		

Included in the above is The Lord Rayner's remuneration as Chairman from 5 July 1984 of £137,709 and Lord Sieff's remuneration as Chairman prior to 5 July 1984 of £32,337; these both include overseas remuneration. Last year the remuneration of Lord Sieff as Chairman was £123,004.

This year The Lord Rayner is the highest paid director with remuneration of £178,952 including overseas remuneration. Last year the highest paid director's remuneration was £158,508, including overseas remuneration.

Total directors' emoluments, including pension scheme contributions, were £2·1 million (last year £1·9 million). Payments to directors after leaving service amounted to £0·4 million (last year £ nil).

---

b The average weekly number of employees of the Group during the year was:-

		1985	1984
U.K. Stores:	Management and supervisory categories	6,076	5,799
	Other	44,029	41,446
U.K. Head Office:	Management and supervisory categories	1,978	1,925
	Other	1,880	1,736
Overseas:		6,289	5,985
		60,252	56,891

If the number of part-time hours worked was converted on the basis of a full working week, the equivalent average number of full-time employees would have been 41,026 (last year 39,043).

The aggregate remuneration and associated costs of Group employees were:–

	1985	1984
	£m	£m
Wages and salaries	**300·3**	261·5
Social security costs	**23·0**	21·3
Pension costs	**37·9**	33·1
Allocation to Employees' Profit Sharing Schemes	**6·5**	5·8
Staff welfare and other personnel costs	**14·6**	11·2
	382·3	332·9

8   Share schemes

a   Profit Sharing:–
The Trustees of the United Kingdom Employees' Profit Sharing Scheme have been allocated £6·5 million (last year £5·8 million) with which to subscribe for ordinary shares in the Company. The price of each share is 141p, being the average middle market price for the 20 dealing days immediately preceding the announcement of the results for the year ended 31 March 1985.

b   United Kingdom Senior Staff Share Option Schemes:–
Under the terms of the schemes, during the 28 days following the announcement of the Company's results, the Board may offer options to purchase ordinary shares in the Company to directors and to senior executives at the higher of the nominal value of the shares and the average middle market price for the 3 dealing days immediately preceding the date of the offer. Although options may be granted under both the 1977 and 1984 schemes, the maximum option value that can be exercised is limited to 4 times earnings less the value of all options previously exercised. Outstanding options granted under these schemes are as follows:–

Options granted	No. of Shares (as adjusted for scrip issue in July 1984)			
(1977 Scheme)	*This year*	*Last year*	*Option price*	*Option dates*
May 1978	123,540	1,506,740	36·675p	May 1981–May 1985
May 1979	325,202	551,726	61·175p	May 1982–May 1986
May 1980	836,478	1,237,120	44·425p	May 1983–May 1987
May 1981	1,011,450	1,286,082	68·325p	May 1984–May 1988
May 1982	901,418	1,007,552	75·375p	May 1985–May 1989
May 1983	1,717,666	1,738,400	107·475p	May 1986–May 1990
May 1984	336,648	—	127·625p	May 1987–May 1991
(1984 Scheme)				
October 1984	3,642,451	—	115·667p	Oct 1987–Oct 1994

c   United Kingdom Employees' Savings-Related Share Option Scheme:–
Under the terms of the scheme the Board may offer options to purchase ordinary shares in the Company once in each financial year to those employees who enter into an Inland Revenue approved Save As You Earn (SAYE) savings contract. The price at which options may be offered is 90% of the middle market price for the 3 dealing days immediately preceding the date of offer. The options may normally be exercised during the period of 6 months after the completion of the SAYE contract, either 5 or 7 years after entering the scheme.
Outstanding options granted under this scheme are as follows:–

Options granted	No. of Shares (as adjusted for scrip issue in July 1984)		
	This year	*Last year*	*Option price*
January 1982	11,540,242	11,944,998	49·0p
January 1983	3,260,482	3,402,886	88·5p
January 1984	3,016,844	3,124,142	93·5p
January 1985	7,649,153	—	103·0p

NOTES TO THE FINANCIAL STATEMENTS
CONTINUED

8   Share schemes continued

d   Subsidiary company's option and stock purchase schemes:–
Certain directors of the Company who are also directors of Marks & Spencer Canada Inc. participate in the following schemes:–

(i)   The Canadian Stock Option Scheme, under which options to purchase new common shares in Marks & Spencer Canada Inc. may be offered to directors and to senior executives of that company, at 90% of the middle market price on the day options are granted. The options may be exercised at the rate of 20% per annum on a cumulative basis.

Outstanding options granted under this scheme are as follows:–

	No. of Shares			
Options granted	*This year*	*Last year*	*Option price*	*Option dates*
June 1979	30,000	38,000	C$4·165	June 1980–June 1989

(as adjusted for a one for one sub-division in June 1984—see note 22)

(ii)   The Canadian Stock Purchase Scheme, under which new common shares in Marks & Spencer Canada Inc. may be offered to directors of that company at the middle market price on the offer date. Under this arrangement interest-free loans are granted to purchase the shares. In June 1979 Mr A S Orton, an alternate director of the Company, was granted an interest-free loan of C$139,000 to subscribe for 15,000 shares at C$9·25 each. This loan, which is repayable by June 1987, amounted to C$83,250 at 31 March 1985 (last year C$83,250).

9   Fixed assets – tangible assets   **a**   The Group

	Freehold	Long leasehold	Short leasehold	Total	Fixtures, fittings & equipment	Assets in the course of construction	Total fixed assets
	£m	£m	£m	£m	£m	£m	£m
Cost or valuation							
At 1 April 1984	712·8	385·6	40·6	1,139·0	207·6	33·2	1,379·8
Additions	7·1	7·3	6·4	20·8	63·2	37·8	121·8
Transfers from assets in the course of construction	20·4	25·7	7·6	53·7	—	(53·7)	—
Disposals	(1·8)	(·1)	(·5)	(2·4)	(11·0)	—	(13·4)
Differences on exchange	(·1)	(·1)	1·8	1·6	1·6	—	3·2
At 31 March 1985	738·4	418·4	55·9	1,212·7	261·4	17·3	1,491·4
At valuation	615·3	347·9	13·2	976·4	—	—	976·4
At cost	123·1	70·5	42·7	236·3	261·4	17·3	515·0
	738·4	418·4	55·9	1,212·7	261·4	17·3	1,491·4
Accumulated depreciation							
At 1 April 1984	9·8	6·1	7·4	23·3	70·8	—	94·1
Depreciation for the year	4·8	3·0	3·0	10·8	33·5	—	44·3
Disposals	—	—	(·4)	(·4)	(10·6)	—	(11·0)
Differences on exchange	—	—	·6	·6	·6	—	1·2
At 31 March 1985	14·6	9·1	10·6	34·3	94·3	—	128·6
Net book value							
At 31 March 1985	723·8	409·3	45·3	1,178·4	167·1	17·3	1,362·8
At 31 March 1984	703·0	379·5	33·2	1,115·7	136·8	33·2	1,285·7

b The Company

| | Land and buildings | | | Fixtures, fittings & equipment | Assets in the course of construction | Total fixed assets |
	Freehold	Long leasehold	Short leasehold	Total			
	£m	£m	£m	£m	£m	£m	£m
Cost or valuation							
At 1 April 1984	679·9	375·5	20·7	1,076·1	175·9	33·0	1,285·0
Additions	7·0	7·3	2·6	16·9	59·6	37·8	114·3
Transfers from assets in the course of construction	20·4	25·7	7·6	53·7	—	(53·7)	—
Disposals	(1·8)	—	(·2)	(2·0)	(10·7)	—	(12·7)
At 31 March 1985	705·5	408·5	30·7	1,144·7	224·8	17·1	1,386·6
At valuation	615·3	347·9	13·2	976·4	—	—	976·4
At cost	90·2	60·6	17·5	168·3	224·8	17·1	410·2
	705·5	408·5	30·7	1,144·7	224·8	17·1	1,386·6
Accumulated depreciation							
At 1 April 1984	8·4	5·0	1·3	14·7	57·6	—	72·3
Depreciation for the year	4·5	2·8	1·3	8·6	29·8	—	38·4
Disposals	—	—	(·1)	(·1)	(10·4)	—	(10·5)
At 31 March 1985	12·9	7·8	2·5	23·2	77·0	—	100·2
Net book value							
At 31 March 1985	**692·6**	**400·7**	**28·2**	**1,121·5**	**147·8**	**17·1**	**1,286·4**
At 31 March 1984	671·5	370·5	19·4	1,061·4	118·3	33·0	1,212·7

(i)   If the Company's land and buildings had not been valued at 31 March 1982 they would have been included at the following amounts:–

	1985 £m	1984 £m
At valuation at 31 March 1975	362·4	364·9
At cost	408·0	337·5
At 31 March 1985	770·4	702·4
Accumulated depreciation	41·7	35·5
	728·7	666·9

The Company also valued its land and buildings in 1955 and in 1964. In the opinion of the directors unreasonable expense would be incurred in obtaining the original costs of the assets valued in those years and in 1975.

(ii)   For fixtures, fittings and equipment detailed records of cost and depreciation are not maintained. The cost figures represent reasonable estimates of the sums involved.

NOTES TO THE FINANCIAL STATEMENTS
CONTINUED

10 Fixed assets – investments

These investments comprise unlisted investments in and loans to subsidiaries.

	The Company	
	1985	1984
	£m	£m
a At cost at 31 March:–		
Shares in subsidiaries	43·3	40·5
Loans	21·0	28·7
	64·3	69·2

During the year a long term loan to Marks and Spencer (France) S.A. of £5·7 million was repaid and the funds utilised in paying up the uncalled balance of the share capital of M&S Participations (France) S.A.

b Cost movement:–	
Disposals	(2·9)
Transfer to current assets	(2·0)
	(4·9)

c   The Company's principal subsidiaries are set out below. A schedule of interests in all subsidiaries is filed with the Annual Return.

	Principal activity	Country of Incorporation and Operation	Proportion of ordinary shares held by:	
			The Company	A Subsidiary
St. Michael Financial Services Limited	Finance	England	100%	—
St. Michael Finance Limited	Finance	England	100%	—
Marks and Spencer (Nederland) B.V.	Holding Company	The Netherlands	100%	—
Marks & Spencer Canada Inc.	Chain Store	Canada	—	53·7%
Marks and Spencer (France) S.A.	Chain Store	France	—	100%
Marks and Spencer (Ireland) Limited	Chain Store	Ireland	—	100%
S.A. Marks and Spencer (Belgium) N.V.	Chain Store	Belgium	—	100%
M. S. Insurance Limited	Insurance	Guernsey	—	100%
St. Michael Leasing Limited	Leasing	England	—	100%

The Company also owns all the participating preference shares in Marks & Spencer Canada Inc. (giving it a total interest of 57·2% in the equity) and in Marks and Spencer (Ireland) Limited.

11 Net assets of financial activities		1985 £m	1984 £m
Current assets			
Debtors (see a below)		111·0	131·3
Listed investments – market value £4·0 million (last year £3·4 million)		4·0	3·6
Cash at bank and in hand		4·2	·2
		119·2	135·1
Current liabilities			
Creditors: amounts falling due within one year (see b below)		72·1	80·4
Net current assets		47·1	54·7
Creditors: amounts falling due after more than one year (see c below)		2·2	4·1
Provision for liabilities and charges:– Deferred taxation (see f on page 34)		34·2	42·6
Net assets		10·7	8·0

a Debtors

Amounts falling due within one year:–

	1985	1984
Trade debtors	3·0	·9
Net investment in finance leases	19·7	13·8
Group relief receivable in respect of financial activities	1·9	25·9
Other debtors	1·8	3·5
Prepayments and accrued income	·3	·2
	26·7	44·3

Amounts falling due after more than one year:–

	1985	1984
Net investment in finance leases	82·2	87·0
Trade debtors	2·1	—
	111·0	131·3

b Creditors: amounts falling due within one year:–

	1985	1984
Bank loans and overdrafts	50·3	57·8
Bills of exchange payable	—	8·8
Other creditors	6·6	·2
Accruals and deferred income	15·2	13·6
	72·1	80·4

c Creditors: amounts falling due after more than one year

Bank and other loans:–

	1985	1984
Repayable between one and two years	1·2	3·7
Repayable between two and five years	1·0	·4
	2·2	4·1

	1985	1984
d Total rentals receivable during the year in respect of finance leases	23·3	11·8
e Assets acquired during the year for finance leasing	28·6	76·8

NOTES TO THE FINANCIAL STATEMENTS
CONTINUED

11 Net assets of financial activities continued

		1985 £m	1984 £m
f	The provision for deferred taxation arises on:–		
	The excess of capital allowances over depreciation on assets leased to third parties	47·8	57·4
	Transfer to assets leased to third parties	13·6	14·8
		34·2	42·6

The increase in the provision for deferred taxation of £5·2 million (last year £34·9 million) is represented by a transfer from the profit and loss account. As a result of the 1984 Finance Act the deferred tax provisions relating to leased assets exceed future tax liabilities in respect of these assets by £13·6 million (last year £14·8 million). Accordingly, in order to reflect the terms of the lease agreements, as explained in note 4 on page 27, £13·6 million has been transferred from deferred tax accounts to reduce the net investment in finance leases.

12 Debtors

	The Group		The Company	
	1985 £m	1984 £m	1985 £m	1984 £m
Amounts falling due within one year:–				
Trade debtors	17·8	16·0	16·5	14·4
Amounts owed by Group companies	—	—	35·9	33·2
Other debtors	5·8	5·3	5·0	4·7
Prepayments and accrued income	11·2	14·1	9·6	12·7
	34·8	35·4	67·0	65·0
Amounts falling due after more than one year:–				
Advance corporation tax (see note 17)	23·3	18·4	24·7	19·9
Other debtors	9·3	8·1	8·3	7·2
	32·6	26·5	33·0	27·1
	67·4	61·9	100·0	92·1

Trade debtors include advances to suppliers of £9·4 million (last year £8·7 million) against bills of exchange drawn on the Company in respect of merchandise to be delivered during April and May 1985.

Other debtors include loans to employees, the majority of which are connected with house purchases. Among these are loans made to directors (see note 21(b) and (c)) and a loan to an officer of the Company, the balance of which amounted to £17,480 at 31 March 1985 (last year £19,688).

13 Current assets – investments		_The Group_		_The Company_	
		1985	1984	1985	1984
		£m	£m	£m	£m
	Investments listed on a recognised stock exchange:–				
	Government securities	25·3	20·3	19·0	19·8
	Certificates of tax deposit	83·0	38·1	83·0	38·1
		108·3	58·4	102·0	57·9
	Aggregate market value of listed investments	25·7	20·8	19·3	20·3

14 Cash at bank and in hand	Cash at bank includes short-term deposits with banks and other financial institutions.				

15 Creditors:					
amounts falling due within one year:–	Bank loans and overdrafts	91·0	36·6	—	—
	Trade creditors	99·1	82·1	90·9	73·8
	Bills of exchange payable	16·2	15·2	16·2	15·2
	Amounts owed to Group companies	—	—	43·8	·2
	Group relief payable in respect of financial activities	1·9	25·9	1·9	25·9
	Taxation	127·8	101·9	121·1	97·3
	Social security and other taxes	12·1	13·0	10·2	10·6
	Other creditors	49·6	48·6	42·6	43·6
	Accruals and deferred income	18·4	17·8	14·6	15·2
	Proposed final dividend	61·2	55·3	61·2	55·3
		477·3	396·4	402·5	337·1

16 Creditors:					
amounts falling due after more than one year:–	Repayable between two and five years:–				
	Bank and other loans	1·7	1·0	—	—
	Repayable in five years or more:–				
	Debenture loans – secured				
	5½% – 1985/1990	5·0	5·0	5·0	5·0
	6½% – 1989/1994	10·0	10·0	10·0	10·0
	7½% – 1993/1998	15·0	15·0	15·0	15·0
	7¾% – 1995/2000	15·0	15·0	15·0	15·0
	Bank and other loans	2·6	3·5	—	—
		49·3	49·5	45·0	45·0

Debenture loans comprise first mortgage debenture stocks which are secured on certain freehold and leasehold properties of the Company. The Company is entitled to redeem the whole or any part of each stock at par, at any time between the two years shown above.

NOTES TO THE FINANCIAL STATEMENTS
CONTINUED

17 Deferred taxation

	The Group		The Company	
	1985 £m	1984 £m	1985 £m	1984 £m
Deferred taxation provision arising on short-term timing differences	2·9	5·3	1·5	3·8
This provision has been offset by advance corporation tax recoverable on the proposed final dividend, of	26·2	23·7	26·2	23·7
Shown as: Advance corporation tax (see note 12)	23·3	18·4	24·7	19·9

The movement in the Group's provision for deferred taxation of £2·4 million (last year £3·4 million) is represented by a credit to the profit and loss account.

18 Called up share capital

	The Company	
	1985 £m	1984 £m
Authorised:–		
2,800,000,000 ordinary shares of 25p each	700·0	375·0
350,000 7% cumulative preference shares of £1 each	·4	·4
1,000,000 4·9% cumulative preference shares of £1 each	1·0	1·0
	701·4	376·4
Allotted, called up and fully paid:–		
2,639,666,750 ordinary shares of 25p each (last year 1,316,535,382)	659·9	329·1
350,000 7% cumulative preference shares of £1 each	·4	·4
1,000,000 4·9% cumulative preference shares of £1 each	1·0	1·0
	661·3	330·5

a   At the Annual General Meeting on 5 July 1984 the authorised capital of the Company was increased by £325 million by the creation of 1,300,000,000 additional ordinary shares of 25p. At the same meeting an ordinary resolution was passed approving a one for one scrip issue which resulted in 1,318,911,755 ordinary shares being issued on 27 July 1984 as a capitalisation of reserves.

b   4,219,613 ordinary shares having a nominal value of £1·1 million were allotted during the year under the terms of the Company's share schemes which are described in note 8. The aggregate consideration received was £6·4 million. Contingent rights to the allotment of shares are also described in note 8 on pages 29 and 30.

19 Shareholders' funds

	The Group 1985 £m	The Group 1984 £m	The Company 1985 £m	The Company 1984 £m
Called up share capital (see note 18)	661·3	330·5	661·3	330·5
Reserves				
Share premium account:–				
At 1 April	15·9	11·8	15·9	11·8
Movement during the year	5·3	4·1	5·3	4·1
Less capitalised on scrip issue (see note 18)	(20·9)	—	(20·9)	—
At 31 March	·3	15·9	·3	15·9
Revaluation reserve:–				
At 1 April	391·2	393·0	395·6	395·6
Less capitalised on scrip issue (see note 18)	(308·9)	—	(308·9)	—
Exchange movement	·6	(1·8)	—	—
At 31 March	82·9	391·2	86·7	395·6
Profit and loss account:–				
At 1 April	489·2	405·4	475·8	401·6
Undistributed surplus for the year	91·3	84·0	82·9	74·2
Exchange movement	·3	(·2)	—	—
At 31 March	580·8	489·2	558·7	475·8
Shareholders' funds	1,325·3	1,226·8	1,307·0	1,217·8

20 Commitments and contingent liabilities

	The Group 1985	The Group 1984	The Company 1985	The Company 1984
a Commitments in respect of properties in the course of development	78·6	73·9	76·5	72·5
b Capital expenditure on leased assets contracted but not provided in the financial statements	—	19·5	—	—
c Capital expenditure authorised by the directors but not yet contracted	155·4	115·0	151·9	112·8
d Deferred taxation not provided on the excess of capital allowances over depreciation on tangible assets other than those leased to third parties	109·6	93·3	106·7	93·0
e Guarantees by the Company of the bank borrowings of subsidiaries	—	—	4·3	4·2
f Other guarantees by the Company	10·2	12·6	10·2	12·6

g   If revalued properties were to be sold at the values included in the balance sheet the liability to U.K. taxation would be about £105 million. In the opinion of the directors, since these properties are retained for use in the business, the likelihood of any taxation liability arising is remote and it has been quantified only to comply with the provisions of Statement of Standard Accounting Practice No. 15.

NOTES TO THE FINANCIAL STATEMENTS
CONTINUED

20 Commitments and contingent liabilities continued

h The Group pension schemes for its employees have all been professionally valued within the past 3 years. These valuations indicated there were sufficient assets in the funds to secure the benefits of existing pensioners and to provide paid-up pensions to present employees on the basis of present salaries and credited periods of service and to cover the capital cost of augmentation to date of pensions in payment.

i Commitments under operating leases

At 31 March annual commitments under non-cancellable operating leases were as follows:–

	The Group		The Company	
	Land and buildings £m	Other £m	Land and buildings £m	Other £m
Expiring within one year	·3	1·3	—	·9
Expiring between two and five years	7·0	2·9	·3	2·8
Expiring in five years or more	14·9	—	9·3	—
	22·2	4·2	9·6	3·7

21 Transactions with directors

a During the year the Company was the lessee of a property which was sub-let to The Lord Rayner at a rent equal to its annual value for rating purposes at the date of the sub-letting, as shown below. The Lord Rayner surrendered his sub-lease in June 1984.

Property Cost (nearest £'000)	Company's Tenure	Acquired From: Date of Acquisition	Length of sub-lease to director	Annual Rental Payable £
121,000	Leasehold to 2013	Open Market 23 June 1978	7 years from 28 November 1978	2,650

The property cost shown above is the purchase price paid for the property, excluding acquisition costs, with the addition of the cost of subsequent capital expenditure.

In the opinion of Gerald Eve & Co., who have been consulted by the Board, it is not possible to attribute a market value to the Lease at the time it was granted by reason, *inter alia*, of the restrictions thereon. Since the value of the arrangement is not capable of being expressed as a specific sum of money, it is a requirement of Section 65(5) of the Companies Act 1980 that the value is deemed to exceed £50,000, regardless of its actual value.

b Interest-free house purchase loans were made by the Company to the following, prior to their appointments as directors. These loans were made under the employees' loan scheme and are being repaid by equal monthly instalments:

Director	Date of loan	Balance outstanding at year end	
		This year	Last year
Mr N L Colne	1980	**£8,280**	£9,720
Mr D G Trangmar	1979–1982	**£10,160**	£11,960

c An interest-free loan to Mr Orton of C$83,250 (last year C$83,250) was outstanding in respect of the Canadian Stock Purchase Scheme – see note 8(d)(ii) on page 30.

22 Directors' interests in shares and debentures

The beneficial interests of the directors and their families in the shares of the Company and its subsidiaries, together with their interests as trustees of both charitable and other trusts, are shown. Further information regarding share options is given in note 8 on pages 29 and 30.

Interests in the Company
Ordinary shares – beneficial and family interests

	At 31 March 1985		At 1 April 1984 or date of appointment if later (as adjusted by scrip issue)	
	Shares	**Options**	Shares	Options
Lord Sieff of Brimpton	821,836	157,528	876,836	263,016
The Lord Rayner	36,472	362,729	32,128	297,370
W B Howard	25,276	350,644	21,568	292,720
R Greenbury	20,458	179,800	16,900	129,562
H N Lewis	34,976	230,658	37,532	244,080
N L Colne	11,628	264,679	9,524	327,936
A E Frost	15,042	129,096	13,376	122,828
J A Lusher	19,706	92,827	17,946	146,610
J K Oates	4,000	242,074	4,000	—
S J Sacher	655,076	214,934	752,412	179,488
J J Salisse	29,216	158,710	27,066	280,386
The Hon David Sieff	329,652	165,714	386,928	162,014
C V Silver	18,306	239,912	15,582	204,466
A K P Smith	17,630	255,982	14,586	295,656
P H Spriddell	25,179	211,700	22,780	234,286
D R Susman	54,232	—	208,404	—
D G Trangmar	11,210	98,728	9,446	363,172
B J Lynch	26,346	60,316	23,744	76,486
A S Orton	6,124	214,042	5,166	153,524

Ordinary shares – trustee interests

	At 31 March 1985		At 1 April 1984 (as adjusted by scrip issue)	
	Charitable Trusts	**Other Trusts**	Charitable Trusts	Other Trusts
	Shares	**Shares**	Shares	Shares
Lord Sieff of Brimpton	875,000	396,312	972,000	396,312
S J Sacher	1,282,536	241,348	1,457,536	558,596
The Hon David Sieff	110,000	302,652	126,000	380,652
D R Susman	825,984	—	875,984	—

The reduction in the shareholdings of certain directors arises mainly from such reasons as distributions to beneficiaries of trusts or estates or the coming of age of children.

Because of joint trusteeships the above holdings have been duplicated by a total of 340,664 shares (last year 416,664 shares).

NOTES TO THE FINANCIAL STATEMENTS
CONTINUED

22 Directors' interests in shares and debentures continued

Preference shares and debentures
At 31 March 1985 N L Colne owned 500 4·9% preference shares (last year 500 shares). None of the other directors had an interest in any preference shares or in the debentures of the Company.

Interests in subsidiaries
Marks & Spencer Canada Inc. – common shares

	At 31 March 1985		At 1 April 1984	
	Beneficial and Family Interests		Beneficial and Family Interests	
	Shares	**Options**	Shares	Options
Lord Sieff of Brimpton	**18,000**	**30,000**	13,816	30,000
The Lord Rayner	**500**	**—**	3,138	8,000
A S Orton	**18,012**	**—**	18,012	—

On 5 June 1984 the authorised and issued share capital of Marks & Spencer Canada Inc. was sub-divided on a one for one basis. The beneficial and family interests at 1 April 1984 have therefore been adjusted to reflect this sub-division.

Save as set out above, none of the directors had any interests in any other subsidiaries at the beginning or end of the year.

There have not been any changes in the directors' interests in shares and debentures of, or in share options granted by, the Company and its subsidiaries between the end of the financial year and the date of these financial statements.

REPORT OF THE AUDITORS
TO THE MEMBERS OF MARKS AND SPENCER p.l.c.

We have audited the financial statements on pages 21 to 40 in accordance with approved Auditing Standards.

In our opinion the financial statements give a true and fair view of the state of affairs of the Company and the Group at 31 March 1985 and of the profit and source and application of funds of the Group for the year then ended and comply with the Companies Acts 1948 to 1981.

Deloitte Haskins & Sells
Chartered Accountants.

London.

7 May 1985

Model answers

2.1 Parker—Balance sheets as at:

1 December 1986

	£		£
Equity	30 000	Bank	30 000

3 December 1986

Equity	30 000	Bank	50 000
Loan	20 000		
	50 000		50 000

5 December 1986

Equity	30 000	Premises	35 000
Loan	20 000	Bank	15 000
	50 000		50 000

7 December 1986

Equity	30 000	Premises	35 000
Loan	20 000	Stock	20 000
Creditor	20 000	Bank	15 000
	70 000		70 000

11 December 1986

Equity	31 000	Premises	35 000
Loan	20 000	Stock	15 000
Creditor	20 000	Bank	21 000
	71 000		71 000

20 December 1986

Equity	34 000	Premises	35 000
Loan	20 000	Stock	3 000
Creditor	20 000	Debtor	15 000
		Bank	21 000
	74 000		74 000

28 December 1986

Equity	34 000		Premises	35 000	
Loan	20 000		Stock	3 000	
			Debtor	15 000	
			Bank	1 000	
	54 000			54 000	

2.2

Equity

31 Dec 86 Bal c/d	34 000	(a)	1 Dec 86 Bank	30 000
			31 Dec 86 P & L	4 000
	34 000			34 000
			1 Jan 87 Bal b/d	34 000

Cranmer

31 Dec 86 Bal c/d	20 000	(b)	Bank	20 000
			1 Jan 87 Bal b/d	20 000

Ridley

28 Dec 86 Bank	20 000	(d)	7 Dec 86 Purchases	20 000

Sales

31 Dec 86 P & L	21 000	(e)	11 Dec 86 Bank	6 000
		(c)	20 Dec 86 Gardiner	15 000
	21 000			21 000

Profit and Loss

31 Dec 86 Purchases	20 000	31 Dec 86 Sales	21 000
31 Dec 86 Equity	4 000	31 Dec 86 Stock	3 000
	24 000		24 000

Bank

(a)	1 Dec 86 Equity	30 000	(c)	1 Dec 86 Premises	35 000
(b)	3 Dec 86 Cramner	20 000		28 Dec 86 Ridley	20 000
(e)	11 Dec 86 Sales	6 000		31 Dec 86 Bal c/d	1 000
		56 000			56 000
	1 Jan 87 Bal b/d	1 000			

Premises

(c)	5 Dec 86 Bank	35 000	31 Dec 86 Bal c/d	35 000
	1 Jan 87 Bal b/d	35 000		

Purchases

(d)	7 Dec 86 Ridley	20 000	31 Dec 86 P & L	20 000

Gardiner

(f)	20 Dec 86 Sales	15 000	31 Dec 86 Bal c/d	15 000
	1 Jan 87 Bal b/d	15 000		

Stock

31 Dec 86 P & L	3 000	31 Dec 86 Bal c/d	3 000
1 Jan 87 Bal b/d	3 000		

2.3 (a) *Definitions:*

(1) *Going concern.* Accounts are prepared on the assumption that the business will continue in operational existence for the foreseeable future.

(2) *Accruals.* Revenue and costs are shown in the accounts as they are earned or incurred, not when cash is received or paid, so that as far as possible expenditure is matched with related income.

(3) *Consistency.* There is consistent treatment of like items within each accounting period and from one accounting period to the next.

(4) *Prudence.* Income is only recognized in the accounts when earned and when it is the subject of a firm legal entitlement, while losses are provided for as soon as they appear likely to occur.

(b) *Alternative concepts:*

(1) *Break-up basis,* whereby assets are shown at the amount for which they could be sold on liquidation.

(2) *Cash basis,* whereby accounts report cash paid and received.

(3) *Flexibility,* whereby management choose the accounting treatment they regard as appropriate for each individual item.

(4) *Best estimate,* whereby the accountant tries to estimate the economic benefits arising from the activities of the business in the year.

(c) *Consequences of alternatives:*

(1) The break-up basis is not normally a realistic assumption, since an existing business will normally expect to continue operating. Many assets have a low resale value, particularly on a forced sale, leading to artificially low balance sheet figures.

(2) The cash basis focuses on only one resource of the business, cash, and fails to show the effects of expanding or contracting the investment in other resources.

(3)   Flexibility may result in a more economically realistic figure, but leads to a loss of comparability and objectivity in the accounts.

(4)   'Best estimate' involves the accountant in the opportunity to come closer to economic reality but at the price of a loss in objectivity. Prudence has the merit of pointing towards cautious decision making.

2.4   Answer would be based on last section of this chapter, expanded by examples drawn from future chapters.

3.1   Differences between internal and external auditors of limited companies can be summarized as:

	Internal	External
Appointed by	Management	Shareholders
Reports to	Management	Shareholders
Duties laid down by	Management	Statute
Legal status	At discretion of management	Required by law
Required qualifications	At discretion of management	Prescribed by law
Independence	Under control of directors	Protected by law and professional ethics

There is no legal 'necessity' to appoint internal auditors. However, they are generally regarded as a vital tool for pursuing management objectives in a large organization because they can cover a far wider range of financial and general management objectives than the external auditor.

3.2   (a)   The directors are responsible for managing the affairs of the company. One of their responsibilities is to ensure that each year the company presents a set of accounts that give a true and fair view and complies with the requirements of the Companies Act 1985. While in practice the directors will frequently employ others to perform this duty, they remain responsible for the performance. Their responsibility is indicated when two directors sign the balance sheet on behalf of the board. They also have a responsibility to ensure that the auditors receive all explanations they require.

(b)   The accountant is an employee of the organization and will be responsible to the directors for the duties they lay down. In practice, the directors would be expected to lay down as a responsibility the preparation of accounts that comply with the Companies Act 1985 and give a true and fair view. The accountant has a general duty not to connive at any breach of the law, and may have a more precise ethical code laid down by a professional body.

(c)   The auditor has, in the case of a limited company, a duty laid down by law to report whether the accounts give a true and fair view and whether they comply with company law. The auditor must also report if:

(1)   There has been any refusal to supply necessary information for the audit.
(2)   If the accounts do not accord with the books and records.
(3)   If proper books of accounts have not been kept.
(4)   If proper returns have not been received from branches.

In addition, the auditor who is a member of one of the major professional bodies must report non-compliance with SSAPs.

4.1 *Northeast Cape*

(a) Straight line:

$$(50\,000 - 5000) \times \frac{1}{5} \times \frac{9}{12} = £6750$$

(2) Service hours:

$$(50\,000 - 5000) \times \frac{6000}{30\,000} = £9000$$

(3) Productive output:

$$(50\,000 - 5000) \times \frac{120\,000}{500\,000} = £10\,800$$

(b)

	Straight line	Service hours	Productive output
Profit before depreciation	10 000	10 000	10 000
Less Depreciation	6 750	9 000	10 800
Profit/(loss)	3 250	1 000	(800)

These figures illustrate how three different accounting policies on depreciation can produce strikingly different profit figures.

Which figure is most meaningful depends on what causes are regarded as leading to the consumption or wearing out of the machine.

4.2 (a) *Larchmont Ltd*

(1) *Straight line*

	1983 £	1984 £	1985 £	1986 £
Profit before depreciation	200 000	200 000	200 000	200 000
Depreciation	87 000	87 000	87 000	87 000
Profit after depreciation	113 000	113 000	113 000	113 000
Net book value:				
B/fwd	400 000	313 000	226 000	139 000
Less Charge for year	87 000	87 000	87 000	87 000
C/fwd	313 000	226 000	139 000	52 000

(2) *Reducing balance*

	1983 £	1984 £	1985 £	1986 £
Profit before depreciation	200 000	200 000	200 000	200 000
Depreciation	160 000	96 000	57 600	34 560
Profit after depreciation	40 000	104 000	142 400	165 440
Net book value:				
B/fwd	400 000	240 000	144 000	86 400
Charge for year	160 000	96 000	57 600	34 560
C/fwd	240 000	144 000	86 400	51 840

(b) Both depreciation methods write off approximately the same total amount of depreciation over four years, and reduce the original cost of the machine to the same approximate amount.

The straight-line method gives an even depreciation charge and an even profit figure. The reducing balance method gives a heavier depreciation charge in the earlier years and a lighter charge in the later years, so that the trend in profit appears to be a steady increase over the years.

In view of the fact that, according to the question, the annual profits earned by the machine will be much the same in each year, the straight-line method would seem more appropriate.

4.3 (1)

	Smith		Jones	
	£000	£000	£000	£000
Sales		4500		4500
Opening stock	500		500	
Purchases	4100		4100	
	4600		4600	
Closing stock	1350		850	
Cost of sales		3250		3750
Gross profit		1250		750
Expenses		700		700
Net profit before tax		550		50
Taxation		330		330*
Net profit/(loss) after tax		220		(280)

*Since LIFO is not accepted by the UK Inland Revenue for tax purposes, a FIFO basis of stock valuation has been assumed in the tax computation.

(2) The economic reality of the business is the same in each case.

Smith's reported profit fails to match income with the most recent costs. Since stock sold will normally be replaced, it can be argued that Smith's accounts overstate the profit of the business because they fail to show as the cost of sales the full cost to be incurred as a result of sales. In this sense the LIFO method used by Jones gives a more economically realistic figure of profit.

Conversely the balance sheet stock figure for Jones is based on old cost figures, whereas the Smith FIFO stock figure is more economically realistic.

4.4 *Stoker and Coke Ltd*

(1)   Profit and Loss Account for the year ended 31 December 1981

	FIFO		LIFO	
	£000	£000	£000	£000
Sales (40 000 × 90 + 80 000 × 110)		12 400		12 400
Less Cost of sales:				
Opening stock	620		620	
Purchases (W1)	10 950		10 950	
	11 570		11 570	
Less Closing stock (W2)	1 900		1 370	

		9 670		10 200
Gross profit		2 730		2 200
Less Administration expenses	960		960	
Distribution expenses	744		744	
		1 704		1 704
Net profit		1 026		496

(2)   In times of rising prices, LIFO records a lower profit figure because the cost of sales figures is based on the most recent, and therefore highest, prices paid for purchases.

It can be argued that the 'real' expense incurred when stock is sold is the cost of a replacement item. On this basis the difference between selling price and replacement cost has been £15 per ton throughout the year, so that gross profit on this basis would be:

$$£000$$
$$120\ 000 \text{ tons sold} \times £15 = 1800$$

The LIFO gross profit can be regarded as coming closer to this figure than the FIFO gross profit, and is therefore more economically realistic.

In favour of FIFO, three points can be made:

(a)   FIFO best represents the normal order of consumption of stock and is therefore more realistic within the terms of the historical cost convention.

(b)   FIFO gives a more realistic balance sheet figure than LIFO.

(c)   Should stocks dip below 20 000 tons in the future, LIFO will result in the company including very old costs within the cost of sales figure.

In practice, LIFO is rarely used in the UK, because it is not allowed for tax purposes and is discouraged by SSAP 9.

Workings

(1)   *Purchases*

		Volume × *Price per unit* =	*Cost*
			£000
	pre-April	70 000 × £75	= 5 250
	post-April	60 000 × £95	= 5 700
			10 950

(2)   *Closing stock*

		Volume	
	B/forward	10 000	
	Purchased	130 000	
		140 000	
	Less Sold	120 000	
	C/forward	20 000	

Valued at:			£000
	FIFO	20 000 × 95	= 1 900
	LIFO	10 000 × 62	= 620
		10 000 × 75	= 750
			1 370

4.5 *Cavour Ltd*

(1) SSAP 9 provides that long-term contract work in progress should be shown at cost plus attributable profit, less foreseeable losses. 'Long term' is defined as the situation where a substantial part of the work extends over a period of more than one year. 'Attributable profit' should be computed on a prudent basis, and in particular should be taken as the appropriate proportion of total profit rather than comparing current value with costs to date. Applying these principles to our four contracts:

A.

$$\text{Total profit } 260\,000 - (159\,000 + 36\,000) = 65\,000$$

$$\therefore \text{Attributable profit} = \frac{200\,000}{260\,000} \times 65\,000 = 50\,000$$

So contract A is shown at:

	£
Cost	159 000
Attributable profit	50 000
Progress payments	(175 000)
	34 000

B.

$$\text{Foreseeable loss } 65\,000 - (57\,000 + 15\,000) = 7000$$

	£
Cost	57 000
Foreseeable loss	(7 000)
Progress payments	(40 000)
	10 000

C. This is not a long-term contract. Therefore the cost, £15 000, is shown as part of ordinary work in progress.

D. This contract is not sufficiently advanced for a 'prudent' estimate of profit to be made. Accordingly it will be shown at cost £4000.

2. Balance sheet will show:

Long-term contract QIP (A + B + D)	£48 000
Other WIP (C)	£15 000

4.6 *Conjuring Consultants*

The accounting policies used in preparing these accounts are inconsistent, in that overheads have been excluded from work in progress in 1979 and 1980 but included in 1981. To give a true and fair view, consistency of accounting policy is essential, since as the accounts stand both 1979 and 1980 carry the whole of the overheads incurred in those years while 1981 brings forward no overhead charge for 1980 and carries forward part of the year's overheads to 1982.

SSAP 9 requires inclusion of related overheads in stock and work in progress. Assuming that an overhead absorption rate of 50 per cent of direct cost is appropriate, then revised profits will be:

	1979	1980	1981
	£	£	£
Profit as reported	54 000	66 000	78 000

Less Overheads b/fwd	—	(30 000)	(42 000)
Add Overheads c/fwd	30 000	42 000	*
Revised profit	84 000	78 000	36 000

*Already allowed for in profit figure.

4.7   *Canvas Ltd—solution*

(a)   (1)   *FIFO*

	1976	1977	1978	1979	1980
	£000	£000	£000	£000	£000
Stock brought forward		8	18	30	44
Purchases	40	45	50	55	—
Stock carried forward	(8)	(18)	(30)	(44)	—
Cost of sales	32	35	38	41	44
Sales	40	44	48	52	56
Gross profit	8	9	10	11	12

(2)   *LIFO*

	1976	1977	1978	1979	1980
	£000	£000	£000	£000	£000
Stock brought forward	—	8	17	27	38
Purchases	40	45	50	55	—
Stock carried forward	(8)	(17)	(27)	(38)	—
Cost of sales	32	36	40	44	38
Sales	40	44	48	52	56
Gross profit	8	8	8	8	18

(b)   Comparing the results of these calculations, we can see that FIFO gives us a steadily increasing profit, while LIFO shows a constant profit figure for the first four years with a substantial increase in the final year. In the balance sheet, FIFO gives a larger stock figure than LIFO.

In times of inflation, provided that the specific costs of stock move in line with the general price level, LIFO will normally use more recent, and therefore higher, costs in the cost of sales figure than FIFO. Since the LIFO figure gives a closer approximation to replacement cost of stock consumed, it is widely regarded as giving a more realistic profit figure. However, if the stock volume falls, then LIFO will result in out-of-date cost figures from the past being introduced into the cost of sales figure producing a grossly unrealistic result, a danger illustrated by the 1980 figures for Canvas Ltd.

In the balance sheet, FIFO uses more recent cost figures and therefore is regarded as giving a more realistic picture than LIFO.

A problem in using LIFO is that to give an accurate stock figure it is necessary to keep detailed records of stock movements. For example, the information given in this question permits only an approximation of the LIFO figure to be given. FIFO is more in line with the principles of historical cost accounting than LIFO, while LIFO gives a picture which may, as in the 1980 figures for Canvas Ltd, not necessarily give a true current cost picture.

Workings
Stock units:

	B/fwd	Purchased	Sold	C/fwd
1976	—	100	80	20
1977	20	100	80	40
1978	40	100	80	60
1979	60	100	80	80
1980	80	—	80	—

Valuations:

			£
FIFO: 1976	20 @ 400 =	8 000	
1977	40 @ 450 =	18 000	
1978	60 @ 500 =	30 000	
1979	80 @ 550 =	44 000	

LIFO	1976	1977	1978	1979
	£	£	£	£
20 @ 400	8 000	8 000	8 000	8 000
20 @ 450	—	9 000	9 000	9 000
20 @ 500	—	—	10 000	10 000
20 @ 550	—	—	—	11 000
	8 000	17 000	27 000	38 000

5.1 The first three items each represents a kind of 'reserve', meaning that they record where a part of the shareholders' resources employed in the business has come from. Taking each in turn:

(a) A 'share premium account' records the amount subscribed for shares in the company in excess of their normal value. This constitutes part of the original investment in the company by shareholders, and company law specifically provides that dividends cannot be covered by this reserve.

(b) Unappropriated profits represent surpluses accumulated from the activities of the company which have not yet been paid out as dividends. Thus the company is legally permitted to set off dividends paid against these unappropriated profits.

(c) A 'reserve for general contingencies' represents a reserve to which the directors have decided to allocate part of the accumulated profits. There is no legal bar on the distribution of this amount as dividend, but in designating the reserve in this way the directors seem to be expressing an opinion that these profits should be retained in the business.

(d) The fourth item, 'provision for depreciation', represents the portion of fixed assets which has been consumed by the business. It should be regarded as a deduction from the original cost of fixed assets, the net amount representing the part of the fixed assets not yet consumed by the business. This has no relevance to the question of dividends payable.

We may observe that a large cash balance will not necessarily be available for distribution because:

(a)   The large cash balance may only be seasonal, being required for use in trading activities at other times in the year.

(b)   The cash may be held for some specific purpose, such as a new fixed asset purchase or a loan repayment.

In setting a dividend, the directors are constrained by two factors:

(a)   The need to obey legal requirements to limit dividends to the amount covered by distributable reserves.

(b)   The need to limit dividends to an amount that will not put an undue strain on the company's cash resources.

5.2   Bransford plc

(1)   Gearing can be measured by any ratio that expresses the relationship between equity and borrowed funds. One ratio that does this is that of borrowings as a proportion of total funds. This can be done by reference either to balance sheet amounts or market values as follows:

Balance sheet amounts:

$$\frac{800}{4700} = 17\%$$

Market values:

$$\frac{550}{5400} = 10.2\%$$

Market values can be regarded as more economically realistic in that they reflect the market's assessment of the economic value of equity and debt. They are also revised on each working day, compared to published accounts which may be presented some months after the balance sheet date. On the other hand, market values may be subject to short-term fluctuations and will not be comparable with companies which have some unlisted sources of finance.

(2)   A company can raise its gearing level either by increasing the borrowings or reducing the equity.

An increase in borrowing is likely to be planned by management on the basis that an increased level of risk is justified by the increased potential return to shareholders.

A deliberate reduction in equity is uncommon, although the Companies Acts do permit repayment of share capital under strictly controlled conditions. But if a high proportion of profits are paid out as dividends at a time when the business is expanding, then equity may diminish as a proportion of total resources as expansion will have to be financed by borrowing.

5.3 Waldron Superb Machines

Points to be made might include:

(a)   Bank overdraft finance might be negotiated. The bank may be prepared to agree a facility for a period of up to one year and, in practice, can often be pursued to renew the facility regularly. Interest rates will be relatively high, but only apply to the sums actually involved at any one time. In addition, a commitment fee may be charged on the unused portion of the facility.

(b)   Banks may also offer medium-term loans for specific purposes, such as those outlined here. Normally repayment will be by instalments, so that cash flow from the project must be sufficient in the early years to cover repayments.

(c)   Leasing or hire purchase of fixed assets. Hire purchase involves a rental agreement with an option to purchase at the end of the contract for a nominal sum, and has long been recognized as in effect amounting to an immediate purchase with borrowed funds. Leasing involves hiring an asset without an option to purchase at the end of the contract and may involve any length of time from a very short hire to effectively the whole asset life.

Each of the above is likely to involve the provider of any substantial sum of finance in scrutinizing the company's present financial structure, and it is likely that there will be a limit to the total amount of non-equity finance that can be raised in relation to the present equity. There are two other forms of short-term finance that may not involve the same type of scrutiny:

(a)   Extension of trade credit taken. Once cash discounts have been foregone, this source of finance does not normally involve any explicit additional cost. However, it may well involve loss of supplier goodwill and, if taken too far, may involve losing some sources of supply. Moreover, it is a high-risk source of finance which may be cut off at short notice.

(b)   Debt factoring. This involves a debt factor, normally a financial institution, advancing a proportion (up to, say, 80 per cent) of amounts due from debtors at the invoice date. Interest will be charged at a fairly high rate up to the point of payment.

5.4   *Mr Green*

Factors to take into account would include:

(a)   *Control of the business.* Mr White's offer (proposal (a)) appears to involve sharing control of the business, whereas the other options leave Mr Green with total control. It may be possible to come to an agreement with Mr White that gives him at least part of his share in non-voting shares, so that Mr White retains control.

(b)   *Costs.* The cost of each proposal can be regarded as:

Proposal (a)—half the profit to be earned.

Proposal (b)—interest charges of £5040 per year.

Proposal (c)—rent of £5000 per year, less interest which can be earned by surplus funds not employed in the business. In addition, there will be a loss of any prospective capital gain on the property.

(c)   *Risk.* Proposal (a) shares the risks of launching the business with Mr White.

Proposal (b) involves a gearing risk, in that cash flow from trading will need to be sufficient to cover interest and repayment.

Proposal (c) involves the risk that if, after two years, sufficient resources cannot be raised to buy the property, then the business will be involved in the disruption of finding new premises.

(d)   *Alternatives.* Each approach is capable of refinement. For example:

Proposal (a), to find finance from equity, might be more acceptable if the investment were shared among several investors so that Mr Green has the largest individual share-holding.

Proposal (b) might be more desirable if a longer term loan were agreed, with an interest rate tied to the bank's base rate so as to reflect any fall in interest rates.

Proposal (c) would be more attractive if rented premises with long-term security could be found, avoiding the risk of disruption.

6.1 (a) Extraordinary items are those items which derive from events or transactions outside the ordinary activities of the business and which are both material and expected not to recur frequently or regularly.

Examples might include a profit or loss from:

(1) The sale of an investment not acquired with the intention of resale.
(2) Expropriation of assets by a government.

Exceptional items are items of abnormal size or incidence which are *not* extraordinary items. Examples might include:

(1) Write off of a very large trading debt.
(2) Losses on a fixed asset written off in an early stage of its life because of obsolescence.

(b) Portland Ltd—Profit and Loss Account for the year ended 30 June 1983.

	£000	£000
Turnover		17 500
Cost of sales		10 585
Gross profit		6 915
Administration expenses	3 660	
Distribution costs	1 200	
		4 860
Net profit before taxation and extraordinary items		2 055
Taxation		805
Net profit after taxation and before extraordinary items		1 250
Extraordinary item		590
Net profit after taxation and extraordinary items		660
Dividend		100
Retained profit for the year		560

Statement of retained profits

Retained profit for the year		560
Retained profits brought forward:		
As previously reported	7 200	
Prior-year adjustment	425	
As restated		7 625
Retained profits at end of year		8 185

Note: The bad debt would be disclosed in the notes as an exceptional item.

6.2 *Barry plc*

(a) Current EPS $\dfrac{3.3m}{10m} = 33p$ per share

(b) *Earnings*

	Option (1)		Option (2)		Option (3)	
	£000	£000	£000	£000	£000	£000
Current earnings		3 300		3 300		3 300
New earnings:						
Additional income	2 000		2 000		2 000	
Interest	(1 920)		—		—	
	80		2 000		2 000	
Tax @ 40%	32		800		800	
	48		1 200		1 200	
Pref. dividend	—		1 440		—	
		48		(240)		1 200
		3 348		3 060		4 500
EPS		3 348		3 060		4 500
		10 000		10 000		12 000
		= 33.48p		= 30.6p		= 37.5p

(c) *Option (1)* Introduces long-term borrowing into the company. In the profit and loss account, interest cover will be:

$$\frac{3300 + 2000}{1920} = 2.8$$

In the balance sheet, the proportion of long-term funds derived from borrowing will be:

$$\frac{12\,000}{22\,000 + 12\,000} = 35\%$$

To move from a position of no gearing whatsoever to such a substantial level is a radical change in the company's financing policy, and one which hardly seems justified by the very small increase in earnings per share achieved.

Option (2) This option is more difficult to evaluate because of the peculiar status of preference shares. In law they constitute a form of share capital. Thus dividends can only be paid out of realized profits and in a liquidation all liabilities must be settled before any payment is made to the preference shareholders. However, from the point of view of equity shareholders they are interested in how far profits cover the preference dividend. Since this is paid out of post-tax profit, dividend cover will be:

$$\frac{3060}{1440} = 2.1$$

In the balance sheet, equity shareholders will observe that preference shareholders have contributed 35 per cent of the long-term resources of the business.

This option involves less risk than the debenture issue, but still involves a higher risk than the current financial structure. Since it involves an actual fall in earnings per share, it is distinctly unattractive.

Option (3) Involves no change in the gearing position. The apparent improvement in earnings per share from 33p to 37.5p will in practice be greater if the rights issue is at a discount, since we should apply to the 33p the factor:

$$\frac{\text{Theoretical ex rights price}}{\text{Actual cum rights price}}$$

However, we should consider whether shareholders will be happy to subscribe for the rights issue or sell their rights before choosing this option.

6.3 *Coningsby plc*

(a) EPS—as per accounts.

Weighted average ordinary shares 1986:

$$6/12 \times 12\,000\,000 = \underline{6\,000\,000}$$
$$6/12 \times 13\,500\,000 = \underline{6\,750\,000}$$
$$\underline{\underline{12\,750\,000}}$$

∴

1986	*1985*
$\dfrac{1210 - 200}{12\,750} = 7.9\text{p}$	$\dfrac{1100 - 200}{12\,000} = 7.5\text{p}$

Treating extraordinary items as exceptional:

$$\frac{1210 - 190 - 200}{12\,750} = 6.4\text{p}$$

(b) **Extraordinary items** are defined in SSAP 6 as 'those items which derive from events or transactions outside the ordinary activities of the business and which are both material and expected not to recur frequently or regularly'.

Extraordinary items should be shown, net of tax, separately in the profit and loss account, after the profit or loss on ordinary items and related taxation. The accounts should also include an explanation of each extraordinary item and related taxation.

Exceptional items were not specifically defined in SSAP 6, but a proposed update of SSAP 6, ED 36, offers the definition:

Exceptional items are those items which, whilst deriving from events or transactions that fall within the ordinary activities of the company, need to be disclosed separately by virtue of their size or incidence if the financial statements are to give a true and fair view.

Exceptional items must be included in arriving at the profit or loss on ordinary activities. SSAP 6 reinforces the Companies Act requirement to identify such items in the accounts, while ED 36 suggests that it may sometimes be necessary to identify an exceptional item on the face of the profit and loss account in order to give a true and fair view.

Prior-year adjustments are defined in SSAP 6 as 'those material adjustments applicable to prior years arising from changes in accounting policies and from the correction of fundamental errors. They do not include the normal recurring corrections and adjustments of accounting estimates made in prior years.

Prior-year adjustments must be accounted for by restating prior years, so that the opening balance of retained profits will be adjusted accordingly. The corresponding amounts will be similarly adjusted. Where there are prior-year adjustments, a statement of retained profits/reserves should be presented immediately after the profit and loss accounts.

In considering the treatment of closure costs in our example, the following points might be considered:

(a) In view of the impact on earnings per share, this item is clearly material. It will therefore require disclosure as either exceptional or extraordinary.

(b) Clearly a plant closure is likely to fall outside the scope of 'ordinary activities'. However, it may, in some circumstances, be a regular or recurrent item. A large business with a number of plants may regularly review plant performance, constantly closing some and commencing others. In such a case this would not be an extraordinary item.

(c) For some businesses, particularly with a small number of plants, a plant closure may not be a normal activity and might not be expected to recur regularly or frequently. In such a case the closure costs will properly be classified as extraordinary.

6.4 *Wildfell plc*

(a) 1985 as originally reported:

$$\text{Basic net EPS } \frac{2120}{12\,000} = 17.67\text{p}$$

$$\text{Basic nil EPS } \frac{2510}{12\,000} = 20.92\text{p}$$

$$\text{Diluted net EPS } \frac{2120 + 150}{12\,000 + 4000} = 14.19\text{p}$$

$$\text{Diluted nil EPS } \frac{2510 + 150}{12\,000 + 4000} = 16.62\text{p}$$

(b) 1986 disclosure:

	1986		*1985*
Basic net	$\dfrac{2610}{13\,800}$ = 18.91p		17.67 × 2/2.2 = 16.06p
Basic nil	$\dfrac{3020}{13\,800}$ = 21.88p		20.92 × 2/2.2 = 19.02p
Diluted net	$\dfrac{2610 + 150}{13\,800 + 4000}$ = 15.51p		14.19 × 2/2.2 = 12.9p
Diluted nil	$\dfrac{3020 + 150}{13\,800 + 4000}$ = 17.81p		16.62 × 2/2.2 = 15.11p

Workings

Earnings	*1986*	*1985*
	£000	£000
Profit after tax	2690	2200
Preference dividend	80	80
Net basis	2610	2120
Irrecoverable ACT	410	390
Nil basis	3020	2510

Income effect of dilution:	£000
Interest saving	250
Tax @ 40%	100
Additional earnings	150

Theoretical ex rights price

$$4 \times 2.20 = 8.80$$
$$1 \times 1.20 = 1.20$$
$$\underline{5} \qquad = \underline{10.00}$$

$$\therefore \qquad \frac{10.00}{5} = \underline{£2.00}$$

Number of ordinary shares

1985—original calculation	12 000 000
1986—12 000 000 × 8/12 × 2.20/2.00 =	8 800 000
15 000 000 × 4/12 =	5 000 000
	13 800 000

$$\text{Dilution effect } \frac{5\,000\,000}{1.25} = 4\,000\,000$$

6.5 *Brocmar plc*

(a) (1)
$$\frac{1.8m}{10m} = 18p$$

(2)
$$80\% \times £1.80 = £1.44$$

(3)
$$\frac{2.88m}{1.44} = 2 \text{ million}$$

(4)
$$\frac{1.8m + 0.4m}{12m} = 18.3p$$

(5)
$$5 \times 1.8 = 9$$
$$1 \times 1.44 = 1.44$$
$$\underline{6} \qquad \underline{10.44}$$

$$\frac{10.44}{6} = £1.74$$

(b) Other factors:

(1) In comparing EPS we should adjust EPS without share issue as follows:

$$18p \times \frac{1.74}{1.80} = 17.4p$$

This is to allow for bonus element in rights issue.

(2) Forecast only covers one year. Effect of project on future years also needs to be considered.

(3) Alternative sources of finance should be considered.

Note: In addition to these factors, other points required to appraise capital investment decisions are considered in Chapter 10.

6.6 *Ashcroft plc*

(a) *Debt−extra earnings:*

	£m
Increased income	0.6
Interest: 2.34m × 13%	0.304
Tax	0.296
Extra earnings	0.148
	0.148

EPS−debt alternative:

$$\frac{0.6m + 0.148m}{4m} = 18.7p$$

Share alternative−extra earnings:

	£m
Increased income	0.6
Tax	0.3
	0.3

EPS:
$$\frac{0.6m + 0.3m}{4m + 1.3m} = 17p$$

(b) Let profit = x million

∴
$$\frac{(x - 0.304) \times 0.5}{4} = \frac{x \times 0.5}{5.3}$$

∴
$$10.6x - 3.244 = 8x$$
$$2.6x = 3.224$$

∴
$$x = 1.239$$

∴
$$\text{Profit is } \underline{£1.239m}$$

(c) Factors to take into account will include:

(1) Availability of cash flow to meet the loan repayments.

(2) To what extent are the existing shareholders willing to accept a dilution of their equity in the business.

(3) Currently the company has no long-term borrowing. Are the directors and shareholders willing to accept a high gearing level.

(4) How subject to fluctuation are profits? The higher the level of fluctuation, the less acceptable is high gearing.

(5) The tax implications, in that loan interest is tax deductible.

(6) The length of time for which cash raised is needed and can be usefully employed.
(7) Legal restrictions. Does the proposed borrowing fall within the company's borrowing powers?

7.1 *Lancaster Ltd*

Profit and Loss Account for the year ended 31 December 1982

	£	£
Operating profit		315 000
Royalties		90 000
Dividends receivable (7000 × 10/7)		10 000
		415 000
Taxation:		
Corporation tax for the year	114 400	
Deferred tax	13 000	
ACT on dividend received	3 000	
		130 400
		284 600
Dividends paid	35 000	
proposed	140 000	
		175 000
Retained profit		109 600

Balance Sheet as at 31 December 1982

	£	£
Fixed assets—Cost		200 000
Less Depreciation		40 000
		160 000
Current assets:		
Stock, debtors and cash	1 469 500	
Deferred taxation (note 1)	47 000	
	1 516 500	
Less Current liabilities:		
Trade creditors	264 500	
Proposed dividend	140 000	
Corporation tax payable 30 Aug 83 (note 2)	102 400	
ACT payable	60 000	
	566 900	
		949 600
		1 109 600
Share capital		1 000 000
Retained profits		109 600
		1 109 600

Notes:

1. Deferred taxation:

	Provided	*Potential liability*
	£	£
Accelerated capital allowances	—	83 200
Short-term differences	13 000	13 000
	13 000	96 200
ACT recoverable	(60 000)	(60 000)
	(47 000)	36 200

2. Corporation tax:

Charge for year	114 400
Less ACT recoverable	12 000
	102 400

8.1 Ridd Ltd—Statement of Source and Application of Funds for the year ended 31 March 1986

	£000	£000
Sources of funds:		
Profit before tax		256
Adjustment for item not involving movement of funds:		
Depreciation		18
Total generated from operations		274
Other sources:		
Share issue		300
		574
Applications:		
Purchase of plant	27	
Taxation	145	
Dividend	66	
		238
		336
Increase/(decrease) in working capital:		
Decrease in stock	(63)	
Decrease in debtors	(117)	
Increase in creditors	(57)	
	(237)	
Increase in bank	573	
		336

Workings

Tax charge for year: $145 + 138 - 147 = 136$

$\therefore$ Profit before tax $= (150 + 573 - 663) + 136 + 60 = 256$

8.2   Doone Ltd—Statement of Source and Application of Funds for the year ended 31
December 1986

	£	£
Sources of funds:		
Profit before tax		101 700
Items not involving movement of funds:		
Depreciation		45 900
Loss on sale of equipment		1 000
		148 600
Other sources:		
Sale of equipment	500	
Loan stock	80 000	
		80 500
		229 100
Applications:		
Purchase of equipment	104 600	
Tax	19 500	
Dividend	31 800	
		155 900
		73 200
Increase/(decrease) in working capital:		
Increase in stock	19 200	
Increase in debtors	13 600	
Increase in creditors	(2 400)	
	30 400	
Increase in net liquid funds	42 800	
		73 200

Workings
Equipment

	B/f	Additions/charge	Disposals	C/f
Cost	394.8	104.6	(5)	494.4
Depreciation	78.4	45.9	(3.5)	120.8

Tax

C/f	42.8
Paid in year	19.5
Less b/f	(19.2)
Charge for year	43.1

Profit

Retained: 215.2 − 189.6 =	25.6
Plus Dividend: 3 + 30 =	33.0
Plus Tax: as above	43.1
	101.7

8.3 *Cohen Ltd*

Forecast Balance Sheet as at 31 December 1980

	£	£
Ordinary shares of £1		1 000 000
Share premium		40 000
Reserves		1 038 800
		2 078 800
Freehold property		660 000
Plant: Cost	1 628 100	
Depreciation	846 000	
		782 100
		1 442 100
Investments		90 000
		1 532 100
Current assets:		
Stock	1 167 200	
Debtors	742 000	
	1 909 200	
Current liabilities:		
Creditors	519 600	
Taxation	203 800	
Dividend	100 000	
Overdraft	39 100	
	862 500	
Net current assets		1 046 700
		2 578 800
Less 12% debentures		500 000
		2 078 800

Reserves

	£	£
B/fwd		625 000
Add Revaluation surplus	260 000	
Surplus on sale of investments	35 000	
Profit	437 100	
		732 100
		1 357 600
Less Taxation	203 800	
Dividend	115 000	318 800
		1 038 800

Workings

Plant	Cost	Depr.
B/fwd	1 446 600	617 900
Additions	206 500	—
Charge for year	—	247 600
Disposals	(25 000)	(19 500)
C/fwd	1 628 100	846 000

Note: The single figure of 'reserves' brought forward is not split into 'capital' and 'revenue' reserves, so no new split has been introduced in the answer. Note that within the reserves, the revaluation surplus would be capital, and a transfer to capital redemption reserve would have to be made for the preference share redemption.

8.4 *Penryn Ltd*

(a) Budgeted Statement of Source and Application of Funds for the year ended 31 May 1983

	1983 budgeted		1982 actual		
	£000	£000	£000	£000	Working
Source of funds:					
Profit for the year		80		50	(a)
Items not involving movement of funds:		26		24	(b)
Depreciation		—		—	
Generated from operations		106		74	
Applications:					
Dividends	32		20		
Fixed asset acquisitions	46		34		
Bank loan repayments	10		10		
		88		64	
		18		10	
Increase/(decrease) in working capital:					
Stocks	46		17		
Debtors	150		111		
Current liabilities	53		(103)		
		249		25	
Net decrease in cash		231		15	
		18		10	

(b) The funds statement shows sources of funds, divided between funds derived from operations and funds from other sources, and applications of funds. The term 'funds' can have many meanings, but in this context is normally taken to mean working capital. The statement also includes an analysis of changes in the component parts working capital, which identifies separately the movement of net liquid funds in the year.

   The statement for Penryn Ltd shows that, on the basis of the budgeted figures, there will be a substantial increase in funds generated from operations in the year 1982–3, and funds generated from operations will cover applications of funds in both years. In neither year are there any other sources of funds. However, in both years the increase in non-liquid working capital exceeds the net source of funds, resulting in a reduction of cash balances; this has particularly serious effects in 1982–3 when an opening cash balance of £15 000 will move to a closing cash deficit of £234 000.

The situation becomes clearer if we compute the cash flow from operations:

	1983 budgeted £000	1982 actual £000
Funds generated from operations	106	74
Funds absorbed by additional working capital requirements	249	25
Cash generated/(absorbed) by operations	(143)	49

The problem appears to be that in 1983 the sharp increase in working capital requirements will result in a large outflow of net liquid funds. It will be useful to compare the level of working capital requirements with the level of activity as follows:

	1980–1	1981–2	1982–3
Days debtors	$\dfrac{230}{1300} \times 365$ $= 65$ days	$\dfrac{341}{1587} \times 365$ $= 78$ days	$\dfrac{491}{1988} \times 365$ $= 90$ days
Stock turnover	$\dfrac{1300}{107} = 12.1$	$\dfrac{1587}{124} = 12.8$	$\dfrac{1988}{170} = 11.7$
Creditors' turnover	$\dfrac{1300}{100} = 13$	$\dfrac{1587}{203} = 7.8$	$\dfrac{1988}{150} = 13.3$

Thus it would appear that:

(1)   The period of credit allowed to debtors has increased, and is continuing to increase, substantially.

(2)   That in 1982 increased working capital requirements were financed by extending the amount of trade credit taken, but that this is not regarded as an appropriate policy for the future.

(c)   Two options available for improvement of cash flow are:

(1)   Reducing period of credit allowed to debtors. For example, if the average length of credit allowed were reduced to 1981 levels, debtors at 31 May 1983 would be reduced, with a corresponding improvement in cash flow, by (in £000):

$$491 - \left(1988 \times \frac{65}{365} \right) = 137$$

In considering the merits of this option it would be necessary to consider the extent to which it is expected that sales would be lost as a result of allowing less credit to customers. In order to justify the longer credit terms it would be necessary to show that the profit arising from additional sales secured is sufficient to compensate for the extra costs of financing an increased debtors figure. Debt factoring might be considered as a method of financing extended credit terms.

(2)   A rights issue of shares. If the company decides that, as a matter of policy, the period of credit allowed will be increased in order to encourage additional sales, and does not wish to factor the debts, then it will be necessary to find long-term finance to cover the additional working capital requirement. Since the company has decided against

increased long-term borrowing, such finance must come from shareholders. It does not appear that the amount of finance needed can be found by reducing dividends (to increase retained profit), so that a new issue of shares would seem to be the only acceptable source of long-term finance.

Workings

(a) The 1982 dividend and 1983 budgeted profit can both be computed by reference to the information that 40 per cent of profit is paid as dividend. Thus:

$$1982 \quad \text{Retained profit} = 158 - 128 = 30$$
$$\text{Dividend} = 30 \times \frac{0.4}{0.6} \quad = 20$$
$$\text{Profit for year} = 30 + 20 \quad = 50$$
$$1983 \quad \text{Dividend} \quad = 32$$
$$\text{Profit for year} = 32 \times \frac{1}{0.4} \quad = 80$$

(b) Computed as difference between fixed asset acquisitions and net balance sheet movement for year.

8.5 (a) The purpose of the value-added statement is to show the total wealth created by the business during an accounting period, i.e. the value added, and how that wealth has been shared among the wealth-producing team of employees, government and providers of capital, together with how much is retained in the business.

The advantage of such a statement from the viewpoint of shareholders is that it puts profit into perspective as a collective effort by employees, management and shareholders, thereby helping to create a more constructive attitude to financial performance by employees.

It also highlights the contribution made by the business to the well-being of employees and the community as a whole.

(b) The basic argument is whether depreciation should be regarded as a bought-in cost or as an allocation of gross value added under the heading of amounts retained in the business.

The arguments for excluding depreciation from bought-in costs are:

(1) Depreciation does not involve any cash outflows and therefore in substance represents an amount retained to maintain the business.
(2) The depreciation charge is subject to estimates of asset life and accounting policy chosen so that the figure lacks objectivity and may be viewed with suspicion by employee representatives.
(3) Most companies in practice follow this approach, so that gross value added will be more easily comparable with other companies.

On the other hand, it can be argued:

(1) Depreciation represents the allocation of the real bought-in cost of fixed assets and it is inconsistent to exclude it from other bought-in costs.
(2) Although depreciation is necessarily based on estimates, it is better to be approximately right than precisely wrong.

(c) A productivity scheme based on gross value added, as shown in the following declining trend in employee remuneration as a share of value added:

1979	1980	1981	1982	1983
$\frac{65}{125} = 52\%$	$\frac{65}{130} = 50\%$	$\frac{80}{185} = 43\%$	$\frac{80}{190} = 42\%$	$\frac{95}{245} = 39\%$

However, if we deduct depreciation we find that employee remuneration as a proportion of net value added is:

1979	1980	1981	1982	1983
$\frac{65}{115} = 56\%$	$\frac{65}{120} = 54\%$	$\frac{80}{135} = 59\%$	$\frac{80}{140} = 57\%$	$\frac{95}{175} = 54\%$

The more even trend reflects the fact that new fixed asset investment has produced extra production.

Thus 'net' value added is likely to prove a more suitable basis for a productivity scheme.

8.6   *Advanced Techniques plc value-added statement for the year ended 1 October 1981*

	£000	£000
Turnover		24 340
Asset produced for own use		1 023
		25 363
Bought-in costs		11 215
Value added by trading		14 148
Non-trading receipts:		
Royalty	49	
Investment	23	
		72
Total value added		14 220
Applied as follows:		
Employees:		
Wages and salaries		8 058
Government:		
Corporation tax		1 333
Providers of capital:		
Interest	1 106	
Dividends	980	
		2 086
Retained to maintain and expand the business:		
Depreciation	1 437	
Retained profit	1 306	
		2 743
		14 220

In preparing this statement, choices made include:

(a)   The new self-constructed asset has been shown as part of wealth created in the year. Alternatively it could have been excluded, in which case related bought-in costs and wages would be excluded.

(b) Depreciation has been treated as an application of value added rather than as a bought-in cost.

Other alternatives are shown in the workings.

Workings

Bought-in costs	£000	Alternative treatment
Material	5 110	
Power	1 321	
Other	2 431	
Rates	1 074	Treat as tax
Bank charges	6	
Administration	484	
R & D	140	
Plant materials	420	
Sub-contract labour	133	Treat as employees
Services	96	
	11 215	
Wages		
Manufacturing	4 574	
PAYE	1 115	Treat as tax
Other	1 435	
PAYE	560	Treat as tax
Plant labour	374	
	8 058	

8.7 Ec Ac Ltd—Value-added Statement

	(a) Union £000	£000	(b) Employer £000	£000
Turnover		4780		4780
Bought-in items		3870		4070
		910		710
Applied as follows:				
To employees:				
Wages and benefits		300		500
To providers of capital:				
Dividend	20		20	
Interest	110		110	
Rent	80		—	
		210		130
To government:				
PAYE	110		—	
Tax	50		50	
Rates	70	230	—	50

To provide for maintenance and expansion of assets:				
Depreciation	140			
Retained profit	30		30	
		170		30
		910		710
Employee share of value added		33%		70%

(c) Rent can be argued to involve buying in a service and therefore constitute a bought-in cost. Alternatively it can be argued that the business is paying for the use of a capital asset and, therefore, constitutes a payment to providers of capital.

Rates can be argued to constitute a levy paid to local government in the same way that tax is paid to central government. Alternatively it can be regarded as a form of payment for locally provided services.

Catering costs can be regarded as a bought-in item for business purposes. Alternatively they can be regarded as an employee benefit.

Depreciation can be regarded as an amount held back by the business for asset replacement. Alternatively it can be regarded, in line with the normal accounting conventions, as the allocation to the accounting period of the bought-in cost of fixed assets.

PAYE can be regarded as part of the contribution going to the government from the wealth-producing team. Alternatively, it can be seen as part of total wages, with the role of the business being purely as a collector.

Workings

Union objectives: first, to minimize amount allocated as employees; second, maximize value added by minimizing bought-in costs. Employer objectives are the converse.

Bought-in costs	Union	Employer
Purchases	3600	3600
Rent		80
Rates		70
Electric	120	120
Catering	90	
Depreciation		140
Sundry	60	60
	3870	4070
Employees		
Wages	300	410
Catering		90
	300	500
Providers of capital		
Rent	80	
Interest	110	110
Dividend	20	20
	210	130

Government		
PAYE	110	—
Rates	70	—
Tax	50	50
	230	50

8.8   Julius Limited—Statement of Source and Application of Funds for the year
ended 31 December 1988

	£000	£000
Source of funds:		
Profit for year		62
Adjustment for items not involving movement of funds:		
Depreciation		19
Loss on sale of fixed assets		1
		82
Total generated from operations		
Funds from other sources:		
Issue of shares	70	
Sale of plant	3	
Sale of fixtures	1	74
		156
Application of funds:		
Dividends paid	15	
Redemption of debentures	40	
Purchase of freehold	20	
Purchase of plant	39	
Purchase of fixtures	10	124
		32
Increase/(decrease) in working capital		
Increase in stock	15	
Increase in debtors	1	
Increase in creditors	(14)	
	2	
Movement in net liquid funds:		
Increase in cash at bank	30	32

9.1   Anglo Ltd—Consolidated Balance Sheet as at 31 December 1983

	£000	£000
Goodwill		
Freehold property		500
Plant		863
Investment in associate (note 1)		819
Current assets		872
		3054

Share capital		1000
Capital reserve on consolidation		118
Retained profit (note 2)		1256
		2374
Minority interest		62
Overdraft		374
Current liabilities		244
		3054

Note 1

	£	£
Associated company:		
Share of net tangible assets		565
Share of associate's goodwill	26	
Premium on acquisition	228	
		254
		819

Note 2

Retained profit:		
In accounts of holding company		1197
In associate		59
		1256

Workings

Bangle—Goodwill

Cost of investment		440
Less Revaluation surplus	108	
Share capital	180	
Retained profit	270	
		558
Capital reserve		(118)

Bangle—Minority

Revaluation surplus	12
Share capital	20
Retained profit	30
	62

Group retained profits

At 1 Jan 83	950
Anglo—For year	247
	1197
Share of Carmen	59
	1256

Investment in associate

Cost	760
Share of retained profit	59
	819

Made up of:	
Goodwill in books of associate (25% × 104)	26
Net tangible assets ((2364 − 104) × 25%)	565
	591
Premium on acquisition	228
	819

9.2 (a) Belmont plc—Consolidated Balance Sheet as at 31 December 1981

	£000	£000
Share capital—ordinary shares of £1		1200
Share premium		400
Group reserves		946
		2546
Minority		190
		2736
Plant and machinery—Cost (1420 + 500)		1920
—Depreciation (426 + 192)		618
		1302
Goodwill		60
		1362
Current assets:		
Stock	1381	
Debtors	730	
Bank	57	
	2168	
Trade creditors	651	
Overdraft	103	
	754	
Net current assets		1414
		2776
Less 12% debentures		40
		2736

Workings	£000	£000
Goodwill		
Shares issued		600
Less Share capital	300	
Reserves	90	
Revaluation	105	
Dividend	45	540
		60

Minority interest	£000	£000
Shares		100
Reserves		30
Revaluation		35
Profit for year		25
		190

Group revenue reserves	£000	£000
Per B/S		750
Profit for year B		121
T		75
		946

P & L for year	B	T
	£000	£000
Before depreciation	308	150
Depreciation	(142)	(50)
Dividend	(45)	
	121	100

(b) The dividend represents a transfer of pre-acquisition profits from Tredegar to Belmont. It is therefore necessary to exclude this amount from the group revenue reserves and show it as part of the net tangible assets of the subsidiary at the date of acquisition.

9.3   Tisch plc—Current Cost Profit and Loss Account for the year ended 31 December 1981

	£000	£000
Historical cost operating profit		355
Less Current cost operating adjustments:		
Depreciation	30	
Cost of sales adjustment	78	
		108
Current cost operating profit		247
Less Interest	60	
Gearing adjustment	(32)	
		28
Current cost profit before tax		219
Taxation		150
Current cost profit after tax		69
Retained profit 1 Jan 81		180
Retained profit 31 Dec 81		249

Tisch plc—Current Cost Balance Sheet as at 31 December 1981

	£000	£000
Fixed assets		825
Current assets:		
Stock	906	
Cash	50	
	956	
Less Corporation tax	150	806
		1631
15% debentures		400
		1231
Share capital		700
Current cost reserve		282
Other reserves		249
		1231

Workings

Depreciation adjustment

	HC £000	CCA factor	CCA £000
Fixed assets	125	$\dfrac{124}{100}$	155
			125
			30

COSA

	HC	CCA factor	CCA
Stock 1 Jan 81	600	$\dfrac{136}{130}$	628
Stock 31 Dec 81	900	$\dfrac{136}{144}$	850
Total increase	300		
Volume increase			222
			300
		COSA	78

Fixed asset revaluation

	HC	CCA factor	CCA
At 1 Jan 81	750	$\dfrac{120}{100}$	900
			750
Surplus			150
At 31 Dec 81	625	$\dfrac{132}{100}$	825
			625
			200

Stock revaluation	HC	CCA factor	CCA
At 1 Jan 87	600	$\dfrac{132}{130}$	609
			600
Surplus			9
At 31 Dec 81	900	$\dfrac{145}{144}$	906
			900
Surplus			6

Gearing proportion	1980		1981	
	£000	£000	£000	£000
Cash		(30)		(50)
Tax		100		150
Debenture		400		400
		470		500
Share capital	700		700	
Reserves	180		325	
Revaluation	159		206	
		1039		1231
		1509		1751

Average net borrowing $= (470 + 520) \div 2 = 495$
Average net operating assets $= (1509 + 1751) \div 2 = 1630$

$$\therefore \text{Proportion} = \frac{495}{1630}$$

$$\therefore \text{Gearing adjustment} = \frac{495}{1630} \times 108 = 32$$

Current cost reserve	£000	£000
Revaluations:		
Fixed assets		200
Stock		6
		206
Adjustment:		
Depreciation	30	
COSA	78	
Gearing	(32)	
		76
		282

9.4   Holford plc—Current Cost Profit and Loss Account for 1982

	£000	£000
Historical cost operating profit		29 000
Less Current cost operating adjustments:		
Depreciation	6 840	
Cost of sales	13 000	
		19 840
		9 160
Current cost operating profit:		
Interest payable	(5 000)	
Gearing adjustment	6 613	
		1 613
Current cost profit before tax		10 773
Taxation		10 000
Current cost profit attributable to shareholders		773
Dividends		7 000
Deficit transferred to retained profit reserve		6 227

Workings

COSA	HC	CCA factor	CCA
Opening stock	35 000	$\dfrac{135}{120}$	39 375
Closing stock	50 000	$\dfrac{135}{142}$	47 535
Monetary increase	(15 000)		
Volume increase			8 160
			15 000
COSA			6 840

       Depreciation adjustment

CCA depreciation 330 000 × 10% =	33 000
HC depreciation	20 000
Adjustment	13 000

       Gearing adjustment

⅓ × 19 840   = 6 613

9.5   *(a) and (b) Translation of the accounts of Acorn*

Balance sheet	Crowns	Crowns £		Closing rate	£	Temporal	£
Plant—Cost		604 800	$\dfrac{1}{15}$	40 320		$\dfrac{1}{20}$	30 240
—Depreciation		86 400	$\dfrac{1}{15}$	5 760		$\dfrac{1}{20}$	4 320
		518 400		34 560			25 920

	Crowns £	Crowns £	Closing rate £	£	Temporal £	£
Current assets						
Stock	129 600	$\frac{1}{15}$	8 640	$\frac{1}{16}$	8 100	
Cash	43 200	$\frac{1}{15}$	2 880	$\frac{1}{15}$	2 880	
		172 800		11 520		10 980
		691 200		46 080		36 900
Loan		(172 800) $\frac{1}{15}$		(11 520) $\frac{1}{15}$		(11 520)
		518 400		34 560		25 380
Ordinary share capital	345 600	$\frac{1}{20}$		17 280 $\frac{1}{20}$		17 280
Retained profit—1 Jan 85	129 600	$\frac{1}{20}$	6 480	$\frac{1}{20}$	6 480	
—For year	43 200	*	10 800	*	1 620	
		172 800		17 280		8 100
*Balancing figure		518 400		34 560		25 380

10.1   Any accounting system is designed to provide economic information that is useful for decision-making purposes. An external reporting system is normally concerned with the production of a single set of accounts which are prepared in accordance with externally imposed requirements and are published for the use of any interested party. Published accounts have a wide range of potential users, including shareholders, employees, trade contracts and government. They are normally subject to an external audit and must therefore be easily verifiable, as well as being designed to meet a wide range of user needs. An internal reporting system is concerned with the production of a range of accounting reports to managers inside the business, and can be designed to meet specific needs. Management can take whatever steps they choose to verify internal reports.

There are, therefore, a number of differences of emphasis between internal and external requirements, including:

(a)   External reporting will normally be based on historical cost, being an objective and verifiable basis of measurement. Internal reporting should be based on the economic value of resources involved in a decision.

(b)   External reporting presents a picture of what the business has done with the resources entrusted to it and therefore must fully account for all costs during the year; this is because one role of the accounts is to explain how the managers have conducted their 'stewardship' of the business. Internal reporting is designed to aid decisions on future actions and should therefore only take into account items having a relevance to the future: for example, 'abnormal' costs are excluded from most internal reports.

(c)   External financial reports are prepared in line with the 'prudence' convention to help ensure that excessive dividends are not paid. Internal financial reports should be prepared without bias.

(d)   There is often a conflict between precision and timeliness. External reports must have a greater need for precision and a lesser need for prompt presentation than internal reports.

10.2
(a) (1) *Variable costing*

	July £	£	*August* £	£	*September* £	£
Sales		18 000		30 000		42 000
Cost of sales		3 600		6 000		8 400
Gross profit		14 400		24 000		33 600
Distribution	720		1 200		1 680	
Advertising	3 600		6 000		8 400	
Production costs	8 000		8 000		8 000	
Administration	7 000		7 000		7 000	
		19 320		22 200		25 080
Net profit/(loss)		(4 920)		1 800		8 520

(2) *Absorption costing*

	July £	£	*August* £	£	*September* £	£
Sales		18 000		30 000		42 000
Cost of sales		8 400		14 000		19 600
Gross profit		9 600		16 000		22 400
Distribution	720		1 200		1 680	
Advertising	3 600		6 000		8 400	
Administration	7 000		7 000		7 000	
		11 320		14 200		17 080
Net profit/(loss)		(1 720)		1 800		5 320

(b) Stock valuatons end of July:

	£
Variable costing 2000×1.20	2400
Absorption costing $2000 \times \left(1.2 + \left(\dfrac{800}{5000}\right)\right)$	5600
Increased stock valuation	3200
Variable − loss	4920
Absorption − loss	1720
Reduction in reported loss	3200

(c) Which basis of accounting will be most useful depends on the type of decision to be taken.

For external financial reporting, the absorption basis gives the best view of what the business has achieved during the year; in line with the accruals concept it matches expenses with related income. SSAP 9 prescribes this approach.

For internal reporting there may be situations where variable costing may be more appropriate. This is because it is the difference between selling price and variable cost, known as 'contribution', which represents the true benefit to the business of additional sales, thus variable costing represents a more useful tool for management planning.

10.3   Deer Ltd

(a)   Revised Profit and Loss Account for 1981

		£	£
Sales			600 000
Less Prime cost of units		800 000	
Factory expenses		200 000	
		1 000 000	
Closing stock		600 000	
Cost of sales			400 000
Gross profit			200 000
General expenses			100 000
Net profit			100 000

(b)   Forecast Profit and Loss Account for 1982

	Prime cost		Total absorption	
	£	£	£	£
Sales		2 100 000		2 100 000
Less Prime cost	800 000		800 000	
Factor expenses	—		200 000	
	800 000		1 000 000	
Opening stock	480 000		600 000	
	1 280 000		1 600 000	
Less Closing stock	160 000		200 000	
		1 120 000		1 400 000
Gross profit		980 000		700 000
Factory expenses	200 000		—	
General expenses	160 000	360 000	100 000	100 000
Net profit		620 000		600 000

(c)   The accountant's suggestion would involve the company in coming into line with SSAP 9, which requires the cost of stock to be computed on a basis which includes all 'costs of conversion'.

The 'total absorption' basis of stock valuation is more realistic economically, since it recognizes that factory expenses relate to goods produced rather than to the level of sales.

The bank manager is likely to appreciate that the 'total absorption' figures are more meaningful. Note that whichever accounting policy is adopted, the underlying economic reality remains unchanged. Thus as long as the alternative presentation of the accounts is brought to the attention of the bank manager, it may not be necessary to revise the original accounts.

10.4 *Aluminex Ltd*

Summarized Profit and Loss Account for 1983

	(a) Evening Shift		(b) New plant	
	£	£	£	£
Turnover		750 000		750 000
Less				
Variable costs	525 000		450 000	
Depreciation	20 000		32 000	
Other fixed costs	122 000		160 000	
		667 000		642 000
		83 000		108 000

Balance Sheet 31 December 1983

Fixed assets—cost		200 000		320 000
Less Depreciation		100 000		112 000
		100 000		208 000
Working capital		300 000		300 000
Bank deposit*		28 000		—
		428 000		508 000
Financed by:				
Share capital		200 000		200 000
Retained profits		228 000		253 000
		428 000		453 000
Overdraft*				55 000
		428 000		508 000

*Balancing figure

(c) For option A (the evening shift), contribution per unit is:

	£	£
Selling price		5
Variable cost:		
Currently	3	
Increase	1.5	
		4.5
Contribution		0.5

Fixed costs increase by £2000 so the break-even point is:

$$\frac{200}{0.5} = 4000 \text{ units}$$

For option B (purchase of plant), contribution is:

	£
Selling price per unit	5
Variable cost	3
	2

Additional fixed costs are £40 000 + depreciation £12 000, so the break-even point will be:

$$\frac{52\,000}{2} = 26\,000 \text{ units}$$

Thus option A results in an increased profit if more than 4000 extra units are sold, while option B involves loss unless at least 26 000 extra units are produced.

At Ken Dowden's estimate of 30 000 units sold, extra profit will be:

	Option A £	Option B £
Contribution	15 000	60 000
Extra fixed costs	2 000	52 000
Extra profit	13 000	8 000

Thus we can see that if Ken Dowden is correct in his estimate, option A is preferable; but if his brothers are correct, option B is preferable.

In addition, option B requires extra finance to cover the new plant cost. Both options require an additional working capital investment, but apparently this will be covered by cash flow from operations over the year.

10.5   Carter

(a)

	Cash flows		Discount	Present value	
	Project I	Project II	factor 12%	Project I	Project II
Year 1	30 000	100 000	0.893	26 790	89 300
Year 2	60 000	90 000	0.797	47 820	71 730
Year 3	60 000	90 000	0.712	42 720	64 080
Year 4	60 000	90 000	0.636	38 160	57 240
Year 5	24 155	53 706	0.567	13 695	30 451
				169 185	312 801
Outlay	(140 000)	(280 000)	1	(140 000)	(280 000)
				29 185	32 801

(b) *DCF yield*
Project I—20%

	Cash flows	Discount factor	NPV
Year 1	30 000	0.833	24 990
Year 2	60 000	0.694	41 640
Year 3	60 000	0.579	34 470
Year 4	60 000	0.482	28 920
Year 5	24 155	0.402	9 710
			140 000
Outlay	(140 000)	1	(140 000)
			—

Project II—17%

Year 1	100 000	0.855	85 500
Year 2	90 000	0.731	65 790
Year 3	90 000	0.624	56 160
Year 4	90 000	0.534	48 060
Year 5	53 706	0.456	24 490
			280 000
Outlay	(280 000)		(280 000)
			—

(c)   *Conclusions*

Project II shows a higher net present value, while Project I shows a higher DCF yield.

The question informs us that the two projects are 'mutually exclusive', but does not explain why this is so. If the reasons are shortage of working capital, then Project I would seem more desirable because it has faster payback (2.8 compared to 3 years) and ties up only half the initial investment. If the reasons are not connected with availability of cash, then Project II, yielding a higher present value, may be more attractive, providing that we are confident that 12 per cent presents the desired return on capital. However, it is important to note that the validity of a decision based on the net present value depends on the reliability of the discount rate. At a discount rate of 13 per cent Project II is only marginally more attractive and at 14 per cent, Project I has a higher net present value.

10.6   *TVR Manufacturers Ltd*

(i)   Options available:

(1)   Sales of patent—present value: £50 000

(2)   Royalty—present value:

$$£15\,000 \times 4.868 = £73\,020$$

(3)   Sub-contracting—present value:

$$£13\,500 \times 5.335 = £72\,022$$

(4)   Manufacturing:

	£
Initial investment—	(80 000)
9 years' net receipt—£25 000 × 5.759 =	143 975
Working capital released—£30 000 × 0.424 =	12 720
	£76 695

(ii)   Other factors to be taken into account are:

(a)   *Risk*. The sale of the patent for cash is risk free, the receipt of the royalty is conditional on the ability of Contrast Ltd to pay and the binding nature of the contract, sub-contracting involves risk in terms of predicting the market and predicting the terms to be negotiated with sub-contractors, while manufacturing and marketing the product clearly involves the widest range of risk.

(b) *Management potential.* If the company's management is fully stretched by current activities, then there will be some reluctance to expand the manufacturing activity. Conversely, management may welcome the opportunity to expand the scope of their activities.

10.7 The Electrogram
(a) (1) *Computation of net present value*

Year	Cash flow £	Discount factor	Present value £
0	(240 000)	1	(240 000)
1	56 000	0.8772	49 123
2	64 000	0.7695	49 248
3	70 000	0.6750	47 250
4	100 000	0.5921	59 210
5	104 000*	0.5194	54 018
			18 849

*Includes scrap receipt £40 000

(2) *Payback period*

Cumulative
Cash flow to years:

1	56 000
2	120 000
3	190 000
4	290 000
5	394 000

Outlay is £240 000.
Therefore payback lays between years 3 and 4.

$$\text{Therefore} = 3 + \frac{(290\,000 - 240\,000)}{100\,000} = 3.5 \text{ years}$$

(b) Reasons for the popularity of payback include:

(1) Simple to apply and understand.
(2) Applied to earliest cash flow when predictions are most reliable.
(3) Minimizes time cash resources are tied up and therefore benefits liquidity.

10.8 Race Ltd
(a) Total future net cash flow:

	£000
Old machine	
Profit 5 × 10 000	50
Depreciation 5 × 6000	30
	80
Tax	40
Total net cash flow	40

Net machine	£000
Profit 5 × 18 000	90
Depreciation	40
	130
Cost of new machine	40
	90
Tax	45
Total net cash flow	45

(b)

Year	Future cash flows (per workings)		Discount factor @ 11%	Net present value	
	Old machine £000	New machine £000		Old machine £000	New machine £000
0	—	(40)	1	—	(40)
1	16	26	0.9009	14.414	23.423
2	8	26	0.8116	6.493	21.101
3	8	20	0.7312	5.850	14.624
4	8	13	0.6587	5.270	8.563
5	8	13	0.5935	4.748	7.715
6	(8)	(13)	0.5346	(4.277)	(6.950)
	40	45		32.498	28.476

(c) A calculation of total future cash flows show a net inflow for the new machine £5000 higher than for the old machine. However, if the time value of money is taken into account by discounting expected future cash flows to their present value, then the net inflow is some £4000 higher for the old machine. This is because the purchase of the new machine involves an immediate substantial cash outflow.

(d) Computation of the net present value points to the advantage of continuing to use the old machine. This option also involves less risk, e.g. the possibility of the new machine becoming obsolete. It should be noted that all calculations depend on the validity of assuming the cost of capital at 11 per cent, and the assumptions about the tax position.

Working

Future net cash flow

Old machine

Year	1 £000	2 £000	3 £000	4 £000	5 £000	6 £000
Profit	10	10	10	10	10	—
Depreciation	6	6	6	6	6	—
	16	16	16	16	16	—
Tax	—	(8)	(8)	(8)	(8)	—
Net flow	16	8	8	8	8	(8)

New machine

Year	1	2	3	4	5	6
	£000	£000	£000	£000	£000	£000
Capital investment	(40)	—	—	—	—	—
Profit	—	18	18	18	18	—
Depreciation	—	8	8	8	8	—
	(40)	26	26	26	26	—
Tax	—	—	(6)	(13)	(13)	(13)
Net flow	(40)	26	26	20	13	(13)

10.9 *Striker Light Engineering Company*
(a) *Cash budget for the six months ending 30 September 1979*

	April	May	June	July	August	September
	£000	£000	£000	£000	£000	£000
Inflows						
Sales—cash	10	12	10	14	12	14
—credit	40	40	48	40	56	48
—special order						20
	50	52	58	54	68	82
Outflows						
Purchases—cash	11.76	17.64	17.64	14.7	14.7	11.76
—credit	21	28	28	42	42	35
Overheads	7.5	7.5	8	7.5	8.5	8
Wages	13	14	14	12.5	12	12
Commission				1	1	1
Van				5.5		
	53.26	67.14	67.64	83.2	78.2	67.76
Bal b/f	150	146.74	131.6	121.96	92.76	82.56
Net movement	(3.26)	(15.14)	(9.64)	(29.2)	(10.2)	14.24
Bal c/f	146.74	131.6	121.96	92.76	82.56	96.8

(b) Although the cash budget shows a substantial cash surplus, if customers were to take an extra two months' credit this would result in cash deficits in August and September of:

	August	September
Balance as projected	82.56	96.8
2 months' debtors payments postponed	96	104
Deficit	13.44	7.2

If these demands cannot be resisted, then it will be necessary to consider ways of financing this deficit.

Workings

Wages	April	May	June	July	August	September
From previous month	2.5	3.5	3.5	3.5	3	3
For present month	14	14	14	12	12	12
Less Paid next month	(3.5)	(3.5)	(3.5)	(3)	(3)	(3)
Cash	13	14	14	12.5	12	12

10.10 *Popplewell Ltd*

(a) *Cash budget*

Cash in	March £000	April £000	May £000	June £000	July £000	Aug £000	Sept £000	Oct £000	Nov £000	Dec £000
Debtors				13	13	13	13	3	13	13
Cash out										
Plant	80									
Purchases		7.5	5	5	5	5	5	5	5	5
Wages		3	3	3	3	3	3	3	3	3
Overheads	1.9	1.9	1.9	1.9	1.9	1.9	1.9	1.9	1.9	1.9
	81.9	12.4	9.9	9.9	9.9	9.9	9.9	9.9	9.9	9.9
B/f		(81.9)	(94.3)	(104.2)	(101.1)	(98)	(94.9)	(91.8)	(88.7)	(85.6)
Movement	(81.9)	(12.4)	(9.9)	3.1	3.1	3.1	3.1	3.1	3.1	3.1
C/f	(81.9)	(94.3)	(104.2)	(101.1)	(98)	(94.9)	(91.8)	(88.7)	(85.6)	(82.5)

(b) *Forecast profit and loss*

	£000	£000
Sales (8 × 100 × £130)		104
Cost of sales (8 × 100 × (50 + 30))		64
		40
Overheads	19	
Depreciation (£80 000 × 1/5 × 3/4)	12	
		31
Net Profit		9

(c) *Bank balance at 31 December 1981*

	£000
Cash flow from existing operation:	
Profit	93
Depreciation	37
	130
Outflow from new operation	(82.5)
Net inflow in year	47.5
Balance b/fwd	24
Balance c/fwd	71.5

(d)   The cash requirements for the new project can be comfortably covered by the cash inflow from existing operations, so that it would appear that the overdraft facilities will only be required briefly.

The forecast profit to 31 December 1981 covers only eight months' sales but includes 10 months' expenses. Thus future years can be expected to improve substantially.

Similarly, the project generates monthly cash flow of £3100 per month, or £37 200 per year.

Thus from the bank's point of view, this appears a very acceptable proposition.

10.11   Connecticut plc
(a)   *Earnings yield basis*

	1980	1981	1982
	£000	£000	£000
Profit per the accounts	126	210	240
Additional depreciation	(16)	(16)	(16)
Stock write-off:			
Exceptional item	56		(14)
Adjusted earnings	166	194	210

$$\text{Average } \frac{166 + 194 + 210}{3} = 190$$

Less Preference
dividend $\underline{\quad 20 \quad}$
                170

$$\text{Value } 170\,000 \times \frac{100}{20} = \underline{£850\,000}$$

Liquidation basis

	£000	£000
Equipment		240
Stock		600
Debtors		580
		1420
Less		
Liabilities	340	
Costs	52	
Preference shares and dividends	220	
		612
		808

Dividend yield basis

$$80\,000 \times \frac{100}{12} = \underline{£666\,667}$$

(b)   All three valuation figures are well below the 'book value' of the shareholders' equity, but nevertheless leave ample cover for the overdraft.

Earnings yield is based on historical earnings, which are only significant insofar as they indicate potential future earnings.

The liquidation basis indicates a minimum value for the business. However, it would be hoped that the business is sufficiently profitable to continue.

The dividend yield basis, valuing on the basis of the return actually received by shareholders, is only meaningful insofar as it is expected that the stream of dividends can be maintained.

The overdraft facility is amply covered by the realizable value of assets, and cash flow from the current level of earnings appears ample to cover orderly repayment. However, no mention has been made as to how the company plans to finance the substantial investment in new fixed assets which is apparently necessary, and discussion on this potentially difficult point might well be deemed desirable pending any firm overdraft arrangement.

10.12 *Allerton Ltd*

(a) *Proposal 1*

	£000	£000
Unpledged assets:		
Plant		20
Stock		290
Debtors		250
		560
Pledged assets:		
Building	70	
Overdraft	195	
Deficiency	125	
Liquidation costs		10
		550
Preferential creditors		30
		520
Floating charge		400
		120
Unsecured creditors:		
Bank	125	
Others	175	300
Deficiency		(180)

Unsecured creditors receive $\dfrac{120}{300} = 40\text{p}$ in £

	£000
Thus bank received:	
Secured	70
Unsecured 125×0.4	50
	120

Proposal 2

		£000
Received immediately 20% × 195		39
After one year 75% × 156		117
		156

(b) To compare the two proposals, both must be shown at present value. Thus proposal 1, involving immediate payment, has a present value of £120 000. Proposal 2 has a present value:

	£000	Discount factor	£000
Received immediately	39	1	39
After 1 year	117	1/1.12	104
			143

Proposal 2 therefore has a substantially higher present value, but is subject to the degree of confidence the bank has in the ability of Shipley plc to meet its commitments. Project 2 is also more attractive from a public relations point of view, in protecting the bank's good name for supporting the continuance of the business.

10.13 *Arches (1980) Ltd*

Balance Sheet as at reconstruction date

	£	£
Fixed assets		156 000
Current assets:		
Stock	90 000	
Debtors	64 000	
Cash	13 000	
	167 000	
Current liabilities:		
Creditors	93 000	
		74 000
		230 000
15% debentures		50 000
		£180 000
Ordinary shares of 20p:		£
Issued to debenture holders		45 000
Issued to existing shares		55 000
Issued for cash		80 000
		£180 000

Workings
(1) Debentures to be issued:

$$£100\,000 \times 10/20 \qquad = £50\,000$$

(2)   Debenture interest:

$$£50\,000 \times 15\% \qquad = \quad £7\,500$$
$$\text{Previously } £100\,000 \times 12\% = £12\,000$$
$$\text{So shortfall } 12\,000 - 7500 \quad = \quad £4\,500$$

(3)   New appropriation account to show:

Profit	43 500
Interest	7 500
	36 000
Dividend (50%)	18 000
	18 000

$$\therefore \text{ Dividend per share } \frac{£18\,000}{900\,000} = 2p$$

(4)   Required shares for debenture holders:

$$£4500 \times 1/0.02 = 225\,000$$

10.14   *Lowdown Ltd*
(a)   *Proposal A*

	£000	£000
Unpledged assets:		
Equipment		12
Stock		18
Debtors		65
Cash		5
		100
Pledged assets:		
Property	20	
Loan	(30)	
Deficit—ranks as unsecured	10	
Liquidation costs	16	
Preferential creditors	12	
Debenture	32	
		60
Available for unsecured creditors		40
Less:		
Residue of loan	10	
Creditors	37	
Libel action	53	
		100
Deficiency		(60)

$$\text{Unsecured creditors receive } \frac{40\,000}{100\,000} = 40p \text{ in } £$$

Thus bank receives	£
Secured	20 000
Residue £10 000 × 0.4	4 000
	£24 000

Proposal B
Bank to receive:

$$£30\,000 \times 0.85 = £25\,500$$

(b)   In comparing the two proposals it is necessary to discount the amount receivable under proposal B to present value in order to make a fair comparison with the amount currently receivable under proposal A. At 12 per cent interest, the present value of proposal B is:

$$25\,500 \times 1/1.12 = £22\,768$$

Thus proposal A is financially more attractive.

On the other hand, unsecured creditors received 85p in the £ under proposal B compared with 40p in the £ under proposal A. From a public relations point of view the bank might prefer to be seen to support proposal B, cultivating the goodwill both of other creditors and employees.

10.15   *Eastgate Ltd*

	£	£
Assets not specifically pledged:		
Plant		10 000
Investments		16 000
Stock		47 000
Debtors		160 000
		233 000
Pledged assets:		
Property	60 000	
Secured loan	68 000	
Deficiency carried to unsecured creditors	8 000	
Liquidation costs		6000
		227 000
Preferential creditors		57 000
		170 000
Debenture		50 000
		120 000
Unsecured creditors:		
Creditors (209—57)	152 000	
Balance of overdraft	8 000	
		60 000
Deficiency		(40 000)

Creditors to receive $\dfrac{120\,000}{160\,000} = 75\text{p in } £$

Ordinary shares will be valueless.

(b)   If the minority are correct, then the sale of the property will produce a surplus of:

	£
Proceeds	150 000
Secured loan	68 000
	82 000

The liquidation will then proceeds:

	£
Available to unsecured creditors	202 000
Less Creditors	152 000
Available to members	50 000

$$\text{Members will receive } \frac{50\,000}{100\,000} = 50\text{p per share}$$

The bank holds 6000 shares @ 50p = £3000
This comfortably covers the overdraft.

10.6   *Kester & Co*
(a)   (1)   *Kester—balance sheet value:*

	£000
Fixed assets	350
Stock	210
Debtors	145
Creditors	(105)
	600

(2)   *Wang—replacement cost*

	£000
Fixed assets	490
Stock	250
Debtors	145
Creditors	(105)
	780

(3)   *Pollins—earnings*

	£000
$\dfrac{(125 + 150 + 145)}{3} - 100 \quad \times 8 =$	320

(4)   *Fraser—realizable value*

	£000
Fixed assets	295
Stock	220
Debtors	145
Creditors	(105)
	555

(b)   Kester's book value approach fails to take into account the nature of published accounts, which do not claim to take into account fluctuations in the value of individual assets, and totally ignore the 'goodwill' generated by the business.

Wang's replacement cost approach is more realistic in taking 'value' rather than the cost of assets into account. However, the business only has this value to a purchaser who would otherwise need to purchase similar assets. This approach fails to reflect what could be earned by using or disposing of the assets.

Pollins has correctly observed that the value of a business is linked to the earnings it can produce. However, this valuation is based on past rather than expected earnings. It may be argued that the P/E ratio of listed companies reflect their marketability, and a lower P/E ratio is appropriate for a small business. Finally, drawings reflect both partners' remuneration and return on capital, so that a more precise measure of the cost of the partners' own services is desirable.

Fraser's realizable value approach is only meaningful if the business is to be discontinued. It might be regarded as indicating a minimum value for a business, since the proprietors have the option of selling off the individual assets rather than selling the business as a whole.

(c) *Earnings yield valuation*

	1982 £000	1983 £000	1984 £000
Profit per the accounts	125	150	145
Bank interest	4	8	10
Additional depreciation	(20)	(20)	(20)
Stock	32		
Salaries	(20)	(60)	(60)
	81	78	75

$$\text{Average is } \frac{81 + 78 + 75}{3} = 78$$

$$\therefore \text{Value} = 78 \times 8 = \underline{\underline{£624\,000}}$$

10.7 (a)

(1) *Dividend yield*

$$\frac{0.7}{4} \times \frac{10}{7} \times \frac{100}{7} = £3.57 \text{ per share}$$

(2) *P/E ratio*

$$\text{EPS} = \frac{1.2}{4} = 30\text{p}$$

$$\therefore \text{Value is } 30\text{p} \times 8 = £2.40 \text{ per share}$$

(3) *Net assets*

$$\frac{6.4}{4} = £1.60 \text{ per share}$$

(b) The dividend yield basis is only meaningful if the company can be expected to generate future dividends in line with current expectations for the industrial average. It is more commonly used for valuing a small shareholding, where the owner has no control over the management of the business and is dependent on the stream of dividends paid by the company to derive any benefit from the shareholding.

The P/E ratio basis depends on the extent to which current earnings are maintainable. Thus a computation based on some estimate of future earnings might be more useful. It may also be appropriate to reduce this value to some extent in order to reflect the fact that shares in an unlisted company are less marketable.

The net assets basis suffers from two major drawbacks:

(1) The amount at which assets are shown in the accounts does not necessarily bear any relationship to their value.
(2) The accounts fail to identify the value of the goodwill of the business. However, some awareness of the real value of the business assets will be useful in estimating the share value.

11.1 (a) (1) *Net profit %*

$$A \qquad\qquad B \qquad\qquad C$$

$$\frac{45}{3029} = 1.5\% \qquad \frac{67}{1556} = 4.3\% \qquad \frac{43}{206} = 20.9\%$$

(2) *Total asset turnover:*

$$\frac{3029}{568} = 5.3 \qquad \frac{1556}{1822} = 0.9 \qquad \frac{206}{1766} = 0.1$$

(3) *Return on gross assets**

$$\frac{45}{568} = 7.9\% \qquad \frac{67}{1822} = 3.7\% \qquad \frac{43}{1766} = 2.4\%$$

(4)

$$\frac{9}{184} = 0.05 \qquad \frac{201}{301} = 0.67 \qquad \frac{1347}{778} = 1.73$$

*If figures were available, interest would be added back to profit.

(b) Company A is the grocery store chain. Indications include:

(1) High asset turnover and low net profit percentage, it being normal in this business to turn over stock rapidly at low margins.
(2) Virtually no debtors, most sales being for cash.
(3) Safe operation on a low liquidity ratio.

Company B is the steel manufacturer. Indications include high fixed assets, as required for a manufacturing process.

Company C is the finance company. Indications include:

(1) Few fixed assets and no stock, as is normal in this kind of business.
(2) High net profit percentage and low asset turnover.
(3) High debtors and high creditors, again to be expected in financial dealings.

11.2 *Ratios*

	The company		Industrial average	
	1982	*1983*	*1982*	*1983*
Return on total assets	$\frac{92}{924} = 10\%$	$\frac{147}{1153} = 12.7\%$	12%	14%
Return on equity	$\frac{70}{546} = 12.8\%$	$\frac{129}{775} = 16.6\%$	15%	16%
Return on long-term funds	$\frac{90}{746} = 12\%$	$\frac{144}{925} = 15.6\%$	14%	15%
Profit margin*	$\frac{90}{826} = 10.9\%$	$\frac{144}{1043} = 13.8\%$	9%	10%
Sales turnover ratio*	$\frac{826}{746} = 1.1$	$\frac{1043}{925} = 1.1$	1.5	1.5
Fixed assets ratio*	$\frac{420}{924} = 45\%$	$\frac{492}{1153} = 43\%$	30%	40%
Debt equity ratio	378:546 = 0.69:1	378:775 = 0.49:1	0.4:1	0.45:1
Current ratio	$\frac{504}{178} = 2.8$	$\frac{661}{228} = 2.9$	2	2.1
Liquid ratio	$\frac{204}{178} = 1.1$	$\frac{305}{228} = 1.3$	0.9	1.1
Days debtors	$\frac{200}{826} \times 365 = 88$	$\frac{300}{1043} \times 365 = 105$	70	75

Note: Although the question only requires computation of the 1983 ratios, 1982 has also been computed for comparison purposes.

*Based on return on long-term funds—this best fits multiple of industrial average ratios to give primary ratio.

(b)   Management have improved their return on capital employed substantially during the year. In particular, return on long-term funds has improved from below to above the industrial average. The improvement has been achieved by a substantial increase in the profit margin from 10.9 per cent to 13.8 per cent—well ahead of the industrial average in both years.

By contrast, asset turnover, at 1.1, lags well behind the industrial average of 1.5, in both years. This may well be attributable to a relaxed control of working capital, suggested both by the high, and increasing, days debtors, and also by the high current ratio compared on the liquid ratio, an indicator of relatively high stock holdings.

Shareholders will note the substantially improved return on equity, now above the industrial average. £200 000 has been raised by a share issue, yet dividends have been doubled from £35 000 to £70 000. Assuming the shares were issued by a rights issue, this is not a very tax-efficient exchange from the shareholders' point of view.

Debenture holders will note the redemption of debentures ahead of time, and the fall in the debt:equity ratio to a figure close to the industrial average. Thus the debentures now look substantially more secure.

Trade creditors will note the strong liquidity position compared to the industrial average. They may, nevertheless, feel some concern at the relaxed working capital control shown both by the ratios and the funds statement, and be looking carefully at the next year's account to see how this trend develops.

11.3 (a) Return on total assets:

Greywell	Kendall
$\dfrac{4000}{30\,000} = 13.3\%$	$\dfrac{5000}{25\,000} = 20\%$

(b) Net profit %

$\dfrac{4000}{40\,000} = 10\%$	$\dfrac{5000}{60\,000} = 8.3\%$

Asset turnover:

$\dfrac{40\,000}{30\,000} = 1.33$	$\dfrac{60\,000}{25\,000} = 2.4\%$

Proof: $10\% \times 1.33 = 13.3\%$ $\qquad 8.3\% \times 2.4 = 20\%$

(c) Greywell's performance appears inferior to that of Kendall, in that Kendall's return on total funds employed is half as high again as Greywell's. When this ratio is analysed into the secondary ratios we find that Greywell manages to earn a somewhat higher rate of profit on sales than Kendall, but that Kendall generates a far higher level of turnover in relation to assets employed.

Potential shareholders will be interested in the impact of gearing on earnings available for equity shareholders, in information on dividend policy, and for information on the share price in order to gain a view of how the market esteems the quality of earnings for each company.

Potential loan creditors will also be interested in the gearing position, insofar as it affects risk. They will also wish to examine the liquidity position, particularly wishing to see if Kendall's high asset turnover is achieved at the risk of dangerously low working capital.

An important point is to establish whether the two companies have a similar asset structure. For example, if Greywell owns property while Kendall operates from rented premises, then this might explain the difference in asset turnover between the two companies.

11.4 *Rufus Ltd*
(a)

		Industrial average
Current ratio	$\dfrac{325}{95} = 3.4$	5.7
Acid test	$\dfrac{125}{95} = 1.3$	2.3
Total borrowing as a proportion of total funds	$\dfrac{175}{475} = 37\%$	25%
Interest cover	$\dfrac{45}{8.8} = 5.1$	6.5
Stock turnover	$\dfrac{505}{200} = 2.5$	4.5

Days debtors	$\dfrac{70}{690} \times 365 = 37$	40
Return on total assets	$\dfrac{45}{475} = 9.5\%$	10%
Related secondary ratios:		
Asset turnover	$\dfrac{690}{475} = 1.5$	2
Net profit %	$\dfrac{45}{690} = 6.5\%$	5%
Pre-tax return on equity	$\dfrac{36\,200}{300\,000} = 12.1\%$	11.3%

(b) The current ratio and acid test suggest lower liquidity than the industrial average, though the size of the cash balance indicates that there is no immediate cause for concern.

Return on total assets indicates a slightly weaker performance than the industrial average. The company earns a higher profit on sales than average, but this is outweighed by generating less sales from assets than the average. A substantial part of the reason for this is the low rate of stock turnover, and it would seem sensible for management to consider whether a tighter stock control policy might release funds for more profitable use in the business.

Gearing is above the industrial average and interest cover, though ample, is below average. The higher gearing at Rufus Ltd explains why, despite a below average rate of return on total assets, return on equity is above average.

11.5 Goodtrade plc

(a)   Statement of Sources and Applications of Funds for the year ended
31 March 1983

	£000	£000
Sources from operations:		
Profit before taxation		3520
Items not involving movement of funds:		
Depreciation		1960
Generated from operations		5480
Other sources:		
Sale of shares		3750
		9230
Less Applications:		
Taxation	770	
Dividends	665	
Loan repayment	2050	
Purchase of plant	3100	
Purchase of investments	740	
		7325
		1905

Increase/(decrease) in working capital:

Increase in stock	8695
Increase in debtors	8360
Increase in trade creditors	(8420)
Increase in accrued expenses	(1300)
	7335

Movement in net liquid funds:

Decrease in cash	(890)	
Increase in overdraft	(4540)	(5430)
		1905

The statement shows how it is possible to have a sharp reduction in net liquid funds despite an increase in profit. Although the profit, together with the sale of shares, resulted in a cash inflow of £9 300 000, a large part of this was absorbed by applications of funds, in particular the loan repayment and the plant purchase. The net inflow of funds, £1 905 000, was not sufficient to cover increased working capital requirement; this is not surprising in view of the 56 per cent increase in turnover.

(b)   This analysis of Goodtrade's performance in 1983 is based on the following list of ratios and funds statement.

Return on equity has increased substantially. This is attributable to an increase in the return on long-term funds, magnified by the effect of gearing. If we look more closely at the secondary ratios we find that the company's success has risen from a substantial increase in asset turnover, reflecting a higher level of sales in relation to the assets employed. The profit earned on sales has not changed.

The increased level of turnover has created an increased need for working capital; moreover, both stock control and credit control appear to have been relaxed. The funds statement shows how this has absorbed the resources of the business. The fall in creditors' turnover suggests that the company is failing to pay suppliers promptly, a policy that carries some risk to the good name of the business.

The use of short-term borrowing to cover working capital needs has resulted in total borrowings remaining over 70 per cent of total funds employed, despite the company's obvious wish to reduce gearing as evidenced by the share issue and loan redemption during the year.

The company, therefore, faces severe liquidity problems. Recommended action might include:

(1)   A limit on further expansion, with any effort to improve profit concentrated on obtaining improved profit margins on sales.
(2)   Tighter working capital control.
(3)   Any expansion to be financed by new equity rather than borrowing.

	1982	1983
After tax return on equity	$\dfrac{970}{12\,350} = 7.9\%$	$\dfrac{1900}{18\,335} = 10.4\%$
Pre-tax return on equity	$\dfrac{1740}{12\,350} = 14.1\%$	$\dfrac{3520}{18\,335} = 19.2\%$

Return on long-term funds	$\dfrac{1740 + 1310}{12\,350 + 15\,450} = 11\%$	$\dfrac{3520 + 1230}{18\,335 + 13\,400} = 15\%$
Return on trading assets (excluding investment)	$\dfrac{1395 + 1310}{15\,625 + 8395} = 11.3\%$	$\dfrac{2960 + 1230}{17\,765 + 9450} = 15.4\%$

Secondary ratios based on trading assets:

Asset turnover	$\dfrac{62\,410}{15\,625 + 8395} = 2.6$	$\dfrac{97\,340}{17\,765 + 9450} = 3.6$
Net profit %	$\dfrac{1395 + 1310}{62\,410} = 4.3\%$	$\dfrac{2960 + 1230}{97\,340} = 4.3\%$
Gearing (long term)	$\dfrac{15\,450}{12\,350 + 15\,450} = 55.6\%$	$\dfrac{13\,400}{18\,335 + 13\,400} = 42.2\%$
Gearing (total)	$\dfrac{15\,450 + 17\,110}{12\,350 + 15\,450 + 17\,110} = 72.5\%$	$\dfrac{13\,400 + 32\,220}{18\,335 + 13\,400 + 32\,220} = 71.3\%$
Current ratio	$\dfrac{25\,505}{17\,110} = 1.5$	$\dfrac{41\,670}{32\,220} = 1.3$
Acid test	$\dfrac{11\,240 + 920}{17\,1210} = 0.7$	$\dfrac{19\,600 + 30}{32\,220} = 0.6$
Days stock	$\dfrac{365 \times 13\,345}{52\,310} = 93$	$\dfrac{365 \times 22\,040}{81\,100} = 99$
Days debtors	$\dfrac{365 \times 11\,240}{62\,410} = 66$	$\dfrac{365 \times 19\,600}{97\,340} = 73$
Creditors' turnover	$\dfrac{62\,410}{9840} = 6.3$	$\dfrac{97\,340}{18\,260} = 5.3$

11.6   Gamma and Delta

(a)   (1)   Profit before interest and tax:

$$= 11.6\% \times 18\,000\,000 = \text{£}2\,088\,000$$

(2)   Sales turnover:

$$= \frac{2\,088\,000}{0.16} = \text{£}13\,050\,000$$

(3)   Profit after interest and tax:

$$5\% \times 9\,720\,000 = \text{£}486\,000$$

(4)   Total shareholders' funds:

$$54\% \times 18\,000\,000 = \text{£}9\,720\,000$$

(5) Issued shares:

$$\frac{486\,000}{0.6} = £810\,000$$

(6) $\qquad 9\,720\,000 - 810\,000 = £8\,910\,000$

(b) Ratio B shows us what management have achieved in terms of profit they have earned in relation to the assets at their disposal. This can be regarded as a multiple of two ratios:

(1) The net profit percentage, presented here as ratio A, showing what profit mangement have achieved in relation to the level of sales.
(2) The asset turnover ratio, showing what level of turnover the management have achieved in relation to the resources at their disposal. Although not given to us in the question, we can work out asset turnover as the balancing figure in the equation:

	ROCE =	Net profit %	×	Asset turnover
Gamma	11.6% =	16%	×	0.725
Delta	14.5% =	5.9%	×	2.46

Thus we can see that each company has a different strategy.
   Gamma achieves high profit margins on a low level of sales.
   Delta achieves low profit margins on a high level of sales.

(c) Delta's relative performance measured by ratio D is even stronger than shown by ratio B. The difference between the two ratios is explained by three factors:

(1) Delta is more highly geared than Gamma, meaning that a higher proportion of Delta's capital employed is represented by borrowing rather than equity.
(2) The two companies may well be paying different rates of interest on their borrowings.
(3) Because of differences between accounting conventions and the way in which taxable profits are computed, tax as a percentage of profit may be substantially different between the two companies.

(d) The earnings per share figure in no way reflects efficiency, because the ratio excludes the reserves owned by shareholders. We would expect Gamma to have a high earnings per share because of the high ratio of reserves to share capital.
(e) Ratio B, in that it measures what management have achieved with the funds at their disposal, is a significant measure of achievement. However, it is subject to a number of limitations, including:

(1) Published accounts do not, and cannot, give a complete picture of the economic reality of the company's income and capital.
(2) Management have to manage the company's solvency, as well as performance. High profits can sometimes be achieved in the short term at the expense of liquidity, with the problem of having a potential liquidity crisis.
(3) Management can boost this ratio by disposing of those parts of the business which generate a lower ROCE, despite the fact that these parts of the business might nevertheless be beneficial to the shareholders.

11.7 (a) *Profit statement*

	£	£
Turnover		80 000
Cost of sales		32 000
Gross profit		48 000
Selling expenses	12 000	
Fixed costs	12 000	
		24 000
Net profit before interest and tax		24 000
Interest		4 000
Net profit before tax		20 000
Taxation		8 000
Net profit after tax		12 000
Dividend		3 000
Retained profit		9 000

(b) Capital employed:

$$£24\,000 \times \frac{100}{20} = £120\,000$$

∴ Long-term debt:

$$£120\,000 \times \frac{1}{1+2} = \underline{£40\,000}$$

Fixed assets + Current assets − Current liabilties = £120 000

let current liabilities = X

$$2X + 3X - X = 120\,000$$

$$\text{Current liabilities} = X = \underline{£30\,000}$$

Assumptions to be made in answering question:

(1) 'Pre-tax return' is also 'pre-interest' and capital employed = long-term funds employed.
(2) Debt = long-term borrowings.
(3) Divi payment % = % profit.

(c) A financial model is used to express the relationship between interdependent variables. Thus in this example the interdependent variables are sales, various expenses, capital employed, and the different forms in which the net assets of the business are held. To verify the validity of the model for purposes of prediction, we would:

(1) Consider the validity of the relationships expressed in the model, e.g. the gross profit percentage. Comparison with past performance would be useful for this purpose.
(2) Consider the validity of the figures on which the predictions are based. Thus in this example the model depends entirely on the predicted sales figures.

11.8 Points to be made in reply to question on Sentinel Ltd:

(a) A good answer would include the computation of certain accounting ratios, and possibly a funds statement. It is good practice to include such information as an appendix to the answer, and that is done in this case.

(b) The funds statement shows that funds generated from operations are not adequate to cover increased working capital requirements; combined with the application of funds on fixed asset acquisitions during the year, this has resulted in a substantial cash outflow.

(c) The increase in return on shareholder's equity is largely attributable to an increased asset turnover ratio. The asset turnover ratio based on total funds has changed very little, and the explanation lies in the substantial increase in gearing in 1980. Thus the trading profitability of the firm has changed very little, and the increased return on shareholders' funds is attributable to the change in financial structure.

(d) Although the net profit percentage shows only a slight increase, there has been a substantial change in the operating structure of the company. The gross profit percentage has dropped by a third, while other expenses have barely increased in real terms and have dropped substantially in relation to turnover.

(e) Both the current ratio and the acid test, show a substantial fall. The ratios for stock turnover, creditors' turnover and number of days debtors, all show an increase in the component parts of working capital relative to the company's activity level. This is in line with point (b) above. There must be some concern as to whether the level of trade creditors can be maintained without damaging the company's standing with suppliers.

(f) The detailed information given relating to sales and debtors is worrying in two respects:

(1) The substantial debt due from Norton is more than four months old. It is necessary to consider why this amount has been outstanding for so long and to decide whether provision should be made against this debt; such a provision would clearly have a considerable effect on the company's accounts.

(2) Norton Ltd accounts for 48 per cent of turnover in 1980, and the loss of this customer would make it difficult to achieve the 'further growth' which Mitchell believes 'is possible'.

(g) Shareholders' equity might be regarded as:

		£000
		1980
Per the accounts		
Less Goodwill	260	
Doubtful debt	620	880
		1100
Add Excess of freehold value over cost		180
		1280

(h) On the basis of the information given, Mitchell's plan to expand the business is wildly optimistic. Attempts to expand in the past year have resulted in weak working capital control, leading to a serious bad debt risk. However, if a plan to control the working capital requirements of the company can be agreed, it may be appropriate to offer overdraft facilities to help the company overcome its immediate financial difficulties.

Appendix 1

Some key ratios:	1979	1980
Return on shareholders' equity	$\dfrac{200}{1600} = 12.5\%$	$\dfrac{380}{1980} = 19.2\%$
Net profit percentage	$\dfrac{200}{4640} = 4.3\%$	$\dfrac{380}{7740} = 4.9\%$
Asset turnover	$\dfrac{4640}{1600} = 2.9$	$\dfrac{7740}{1980} = 3.9$
Return on total funds:	$\dfrac{200^*}{1880} = 10.6\%$	$\dfrac{380^*}{3000} = 12.7\%$
Asset turnover	$\dfrac{4640}{1880} = 2.5$	$\dfrac{7740}{3000} = 2.6$
Net profit percentage	$\dfrac{200^*}{4640} = 4.3\%$	$\dfrac{380^*}{7740} = 4.9\%$
Gross profit percentage	$\dfrac{2240}{4640} = 4.8\%$	$\dfrac{2540}{7740} = 32.9\%$
Expenses as percentage sales	$\dfrac{2040}{4640} = 44\%$	$\dfrac{2160}{7740} = 27.9\%$
Current ratio	$\dfrac{1140}{280} = 4.1$	$\dfrac{2180}{1020} = 2.1$
Acid test	$\dfrac{420}{280} = 1.5$	$\dfrac{780}{1020} = 0.8$
Stock turnover	$\dfrac{4640}{720} = 6.4$	$\dfrac{7740}{1400} = 5.5$
Days debtors	$\dfrac{300}{4640} \times 365 = 24$ days	$\dfrac{760^{**}}{7740} \times 365 = 36$ days
Creditors' turnover	$\dfrac{4640}{280} = 16.6$	$\dfrac{7740}{840} = 9.2$
Gearing (based on total funds)	$\dfrac{280}{1880} = 14.9\%$	$\dfrac{1020}{3000} = 34\%$

*If the information were available we would add back bank interest to profit
**Excludes non-trade debtor

Appendix 2

Sentinel Ltd—Statement of Source and Application of Funds for the year ended
31 December 1980

Sources:	£000	£000
Profit		380
Add back Items not involving movement of funds:		
Depreciation		60
Total generated from applications		440

Applications:

Purchase of motor vehicles	140	
Deposit on property	20	160
		280

Increase/(decrease) in working capital:

Stock	680	
Debtors	460	
Creditors	(560)	
	580	
Decrease in net liquid funds	(300)	280

11.9   *Fast Developments Ltd*

Over the past three years return on equity has risen dramatically, from 22.9 to 56.7 per cent. This has been partly attributable to high and increasing gearing, but return on long-term funds has also increased from 14.5 to 27.4%. However, the growth in return on long-term funds in 1983 has only been from 25.9 to 27.4 per cent.

Computation of the secondary ratios shows that during 1983 a sharp drop in profitability on sales was more than compensated for by an increase in the amount of sales generated from each £1 of assets. Further analysis of the asset turnover position shows a dramatic increase in the rate of turnover of both fixed assets and working capital.

Despite the substantial increases in asset turnover, the increase in sales, at 170 per cent in 1983, has been so great that substantial new long-term loans have been raised, raising borrowing as a proportion of long-term funds from 37 per cent in 1981 to 52 per cent in 1983.

Thus although the company's strategy so far has produced a substantial improvement in performance, there is considerable reason to doubt whether this can continue and to worry about the future. Causes for concern are:

(a)   The gross profit percentage has fallen by one-third over two years, and the net profit percentage has fallen and is still falling. It seems unlikely that asset turnover ratios can be boosted to compensate, particularly as the growth in the overdraft and the level of the current and liquid ratios indicates the current strain on working capital management.

(b)   To achieve a doubling of turnover requires substantial new finance for fixed assets and working capital.

(c)   Reduced profit margins will cut the cash flow from operations.

Suggestions to cope with these problems might include:

(a)   Seeking new equity finance for expansion.

(b)   A reduction in dividend levels, which over two years have grown substantially.

(c)   A scaling down of expansion plans, with an attempt to restore gross and net profit margins.

(d)   Forward planning should include detailed cash budgets.

Appendix

	1981	1982	1983
Return on equity	$\frac{6.4}{28} = 22.9\%$	$\frac{17.5}{36.5} = 47.9\%$	$\frac{28.1}{49.6} = 56.7\%$
Return of long-term fund	$\frac{6.4}{44.2} = 14.5\%$	$\frac{17.5}{67.6} = 25.9\%$	$\frac{28.1}{102.6} = 27.4\%$
Net profit %	$\frac{6.4}{90} = 7.1\%$	$\frac{17.5}{170} = 10.3\%$	$\frac{28.1}{460} = 6.1\%$
Long-term asset	$\frac{90}{44.2} = 2$	$\frac{170}{67.6} = 2.5$	$\frac{460}{102.6} = 4.5$
Gross profit %	$\frac{19.8}{90} = 22\%$	$\frac{34.4}{170} = 20.2\%$	$\frac{69.2}{460} = 15\%$
Fixed asset turnover	$\frac{90}{30} = 3$	$\frac{170}{42.3} = 4$	$\frac{460}{64.7} = 7.1$
Working capital turnover	$\frac{90}{14.2} = 6.3$	$\frac{170}{25.3} = 6.7$	$\frac{460}{37.9} = 12$
Long-term gearing %	$\frac{16.2}{44.2} = 37\%$	$\frac{31.1}{67.6} = 46\%$	$\frac{53}{102.6} = 52\%$
Sales increase		$\frac{170-90}{90} = 89\%$	$\frac{460-170}{170} = 170\%$
Current ratio	2.7	2.6	1.6
Liquid ratio	1.5	1.6	0.8

Notes on computation of ratios:
(a) Interest figure is not available to add back to profit for return on long-term funds.
(b) Working capital is computed as:

$$\text{Long-term funds} - \text{Fixed assets}$$

11.10 *Schwarz, Weiss and Blau*
(a) (1) Return on capital employed:

$$\frac{1.1}{43} = 25.6\%$$

(based on *total* funds)

(1) Current ratio

$$\frac{1.4}{2} = 0.7$$

(3) Debt equity ratio (based on total funds):

$$2:2.3 = 0.87:1$$

(4) Debtor turnover:

$$\frac{5}{0.8} = 6.25$$

(b) (1) The ratio of return on capital employed is designed to show what profit the business has achieved with its resources. The ratio can be computed in a number of ways, the view taken here being that return on total assets is most useful; however, if short-term liabilities are subject to fluctuation or manipulation, return on long-term assets might be a better measure of management performance.

(2) The current ratio indicates the relationship between short-term assets and liabilities, giving an indication of liquidity. A major problem here is whether the ratio should include the bank overdraft as a current liability, since this may in practice be a long-term source of finance for the business.

(3) The debt equity ratio expresses the relationship between the part of the total resources of the business derived from borrowings and the part provided by the proprietors. The higher the portion provided by borrowing, the higher 'geared' the business. High gearing involves higher risks but offers shareholders a larger share from any increase in trading profit. Computational problems arise in relation to 'off-balance sheet finance', where some forms of funding may effectively be concealed in the accounts.

(4) Debtor turnover gives some indication of how tightly credit control is managed, with important implications both for liquidity and asset turnover. The problem with this ratio is that it can be misleading if there is not an even pattern of sales throughout the year.

(c) Limitations include:

(1) Blau is a subsidiary of another company, so that debtors and creditors may include inter-company items. This may, for example, explain the relatively high creditors' figure.

(2) Blau's profit may be disturbed by artificial transfer pricing arrangements or by the syphoning off of profits by artificially high transfer prices.

(3) Since all the accounts are prepared on a current cost basis, the asset valuations are reasonably comparable, but each company may have very different inherent goodwill.

(4) The example illustrates the problem of whether to measure gearing and return on capital by reference to total funds or long-term funds. Comparing on a long term fund basis, Schwarz would seem to have no gearing compared to a highly geared Weiss, yet on a total funds basis Schwarz's gearing may be subject to short-term fluctuation on manipulation.

(5) Weiss's substantial preference shares present a technical problem of defining gearing, having the same impact on equity income fluctuations as borrowing but from the lender's point of view carrying the same rights as equity.

11.11 The return on capital employed ratio compares the profit shown in the accounts with the resources employed by the business as shown in the accounts. This is generally a useful tool for considering how much the management of a business have managed to achieve with the resources entrusted to them. However, where the accounts fail to reflect the true resources of the business, then the ratio ceases to be of any value.

In the case of the two kinds of enterprise quoted in the question, the major asset of the business is likely to be the 'inherent goodwill' attributable to trading connections, and the skills and reputations of those involved in the business. This inherent goodwill is not normally reflected in the accounts, and even where goodwill is shown it rarely reflects a meaningful figure. Thus for an advertising agency or professional partnership the return on capital employed ratio has little significance.

11.12   *Inter-firm comparison*
The following points might be included in an answer:

Advantages
(a)   Makes available comparative data for the industry in far more detail than can be obtained from published sources.
(b)   Enables management to identify key areas for improvement. For example, if net profit percentage is below average we can identify which types of expenditure require control.
(c)   Makes available data which can be used as the basis for setting achievable targets.
(d)   Enables participants to pool their experience, hopefully resulting in mutual benefit.
(e)   May be useful in disputes with Inland Revenue over the credibility of the accounts.

Problems
(a)   To preserve confidentiality, the survey coordinator must be independent and trustworthy. Data must be presented in a way that does not permit identification of participants.
(b)   Participants must be comparable in the nature of their operations. This may involve, in our example, not only retailing similar types of goods but also serving a similar type of market and, perhaps, operating in a similar region.
(c)   It may be necessary to adjust the data submitted by participants to reflect common accounting policies.
(d)   Arrangement of an inter-firm comparison is a highly skilled job that commands an appropriate fee. Participants must be prepared to share this cost, as well as incurring costs in the submission of data for consideration.
(e)   In the use of inter-firm comparison data, as in all ratio analysis, it is important to be aware of how material each ratio is. For example, a small variation in the gross profit percentage may be more important than a substantial variation in cleaning costs as a percentage of sales.

**AQ.1   (a)   Milford Ltd—Profit and Loss Account for the year ended
31 December 1982**

	£	£
Turnover		862 150
Less Cost of sales (484 500 − 23 300 + 4900)		466 100
Gross profit		396 050
Less		
Distribution costs	25 000	
Administration (185 700 + 15 000 + 6600 + 15500)	208 000	
		233 800
Operating profit		162 250
Less Interest payable		12 000
Profit on ordinary activities before taxation		150 250
Taxation		77 000
Retained profit for year		73 250

Statement of retained profits

Retained profit for year:		
Retained profit at 1 Jan 82		73 250
As previously reported	96 800	
Prior-year adjustment	23 300	
		73 500
Retained profit 31 Dec 82		146 750

Milford Ltd—Balance Sheet as at 31 December 1982

	£	£
Fixed assets:		
Intangible assets: development costs	9 100	
goodwill	26 400	35 500
Tangible assets: land and buildings	116 500	
plant	126 600	243 100
		278 600
Current assets:		
Stock	139 400	
Debtors	91 200	
Cash at bank and in hand	14 000	
	244 660	
Creditors: amounts falling due within one year:		
Trade creditors	62 000	
Current corporation tax	77 000	
	139 000	
Net current assets		105 600
Total assets less current liabilities		384 200
Creditors: amounts falling due after more than one year:		
12% debenture		100 000
		284 200
Capital and reserves:		
Called-up share capital		100 000
Share premium account		4 450
Revaluation reserve		33 000
Profit and loss account		146 750
		284 200
(b) Retained profits		146 750
Depreciation on revaluation surplus		1 500
Distributable profits		148 250

Workings

Adjustment to retained profit for year:	£	£
Per question		77 950
Add Uplift of 1981 stock		23 300
Less		
Research costs	15 000	
Goodwill write off	6 600	
Creditor	4 900	
Additional depreciation	1 500	
		28 000
		73 250
Profit b/fwd	96 800	
Prior-year adjustment	23 300	
		73 500
		146 750

AQ.2 *Accounting policies*

(a) LIFO is likely to produce the more conservative profit figure because the most recent (and therefore higher) costs of stock are matched with sales.

(b) Marginal cost produces the more conservative profit figure because with a rising stock figure an increasing proportion of fixed costs would be absorbed in 'total cost', and therefore not charged in the year.

(c) Marginal cost produces the more conservative profit because it results in all fixed costs in year 1 being charged against profit.

(d) Application of the rule to separate items of stock and WIP produces the more conservative figure. Application to groups of items means that within each group a loss on some items may be offset against an unrealized gain on others.

(e) Reducing balance produces the more conservative figure because a higher proportion of the asset costs is written off in the early years.

(f) Current cost gives the more conservative figure because revaluation surpluses are taken direct to reserves rather than through the profit and loss account, and the depreciation charge will be based on the increased revalued amount.

AQ.3 *Wiley Ltd*

Course of action	Net profit £	Bank overdraft £	Working capital £	Liquidity ratio
(1)	50 000	60 000	550 000	$\frac{160}{200} = 0.8$
(27	40 000	60 000	550 000	0.8
(3)	50 000	Nil (bank balance 40 000)	650 000	$\frac{200}{140} = 1.4$
(4)	70 000	60 000	640 000	0.8
(5)	47 000	23 000	547 000	$\frac{120}{163} = 0.7$

QQ.4 *Hatfield Ltd*

A. In compliance with SSAP 9, stock should be shown at the lower of cost and net realizable value (NRV), cost being computed on a total cost basis and the lower of cost and NRV being taken by each group of items. Thus there will be shown under the heading 'current assets' stock of £151 000.

B. Work in progress is also shown as a current asset in the balance sheet, as:

	£
Cost	51 000
Attributable profit 60% × 30 000	18 000
	69 000

C. (1) At 1 January 1984 property was shown as:

	£
Cost	380 000
Less Depreciation 40% × 300 000	120 000
	260 000

Revaluation surplus of £540 000 is credited to revaluation reserve. Depreciation for year, shown as an expense in the profit and loss account, is:

$$(600\,000 - 100\,000) \times \frac{1}{20} = £25\,000$$

Property is shown in the balance sheet as a tangible fixed asset:

	£
As valued 1 July 83	800 000
Accumulated depreciation	25 000
NBV	775 000

(2) SSAP 12 states that on a change in depreciation method the new method should be applied to the written-down value of the asset. Thus the depreciation expense in the profit and loss account will be:

$$£70\,000 \times 30\% = £21\,000$$

And the tangible fixed asset in the balance sheet will be:

	£
Cost	100 000
Less Depreciation	51 000
	£49 000

D. The strict conditions laid down in SSAP 13 for capitalization of development expenditure are clearly not met here. Thus the entire £6500 should be written off as an expense in the profit and loss account.

AQ.5   Malham Ltd—Balance Sheet as at 31 March 1984

	£000	£000
Fixed assets:		
Intangible assets (note 1)		48
Tangible assets (note 2)		1191
		1239
Current assets:		
Stocks	436	
Trade debtors	391	
Prepaid expenses	13	
Cash at bank	75	
Cash in hand	24	
	939	
Current liabilities:		
Bank loan (note 3)	20	
Creditors	191	
Deferred income	15	
Proposed dividend	64	
	290	
Net current assets		649
		1888
Bank loan (note 3)		120
		1768
Share capital—ordinary shares of £1		800
Revaluation reserve		270
Retained profit		698
		1768

Notes to the acounts
1. *Intangible assets*
   Goodwill:

	£000
Cost:	
Acquired in year	60
At 31 Mar 84	60
Depreciation	
Charge for year	12
At 31 Mar 84	12
Net book value 31 Mar 84	48

2. *Tangible assets*

	Property	*F & F*	*Total*
Cost:	£000	£000	£000
At 1 Mar 84	780	150	930
Additions	—	67	67
Revaluation	270	—	270
At 31 Mar 84	1050	217	1267

At 1 Apr 83	—	54	54
Charge for year	—	22	22
At 31 Mar 84	—	76	76
Net book value 1 Apr 83	780	96	876
Net book value 31 Mar 84	1050	141	1191

Workings

	£000	£000
Profit per TB		229
Stock—at cost	464	
—at lower of cost NRV	436	
	28	
Goodwill depreciation	12	
Dividend	64	104
		125

Further reading

Chapter 1
Carsberg B. and Hope A., *Current Issues in Accounting*, Philip Allan.
Blake J., 'Accountants and the Finance Function' in Elliott K. and Lawrence P. *Introducing Management*, Penguin.

Chapter 2
A wide range of textbooks introduce the accounting system, including:
Blake J., *Financial Accounting—An Introduction*, Hutchinson.
Glautier M. W. E. and Underdown B., *Accounting Theory and Practice*, 3rd edn, Pitman.
Pizzey A., *Accounting and Finance—A Firm Foundation*, Holt.
Wood F., *Business Accounting I*, Longman.

Chapter 3
Blake J., *Accounting Standards*, Longman.
Underdown B. and Taylor P., *Accounting Theory and Policy Making*, Heinemann.

Chapter 4
Blake J., *Accounting Standards*, Longman, Chapters 9, 12, 13.
Also—detailed reading as for Chapter 2.

Chapter 5
Parish F. and Briston R., *Business Finance*, Pitman.
Samuels and Wikes, *Management of Company Finance*, Nelson.

Chapter 6
Blake J., *Accounting Standards*, Longman, Chapter 4.
Lee G. A., *Modern Financial Accounting*, Nelson.

Chapter 7
James S. and Nobes C., *The Economics of Taxation*, Philip Allan.
Kay J. A. and King M. A., *The British Tax System*, Oxford University Press.

Chapter 8
Blake J., *Accounting Standards*, Longman, Chapter 10.
Knox R. W., *Statements of Source and Application of Funds*, ICAEW.
Morley M., *The Value Added Statement*, Gee & Co.

Chapter 9
Accounting Standards Committee *SSAP 20 Foreign Currency Translation*.
Clayton P. and Blake J., *Inflation Accounting*, Longman.
Jaeger H. K., *The Structure of Consolidated Accounting*, Macmillan.

Chapter 10
Brealey R. and Myers S., *Principles of Corporate Finance*, McCraw Hill.
Sizer J., *Insight into Management Accounting*, Penguin.

Chapter 11
Blake J., *Interpreting Accounts*, Van Nostrand.
Reid W. and Myddelton D. R., *The Meaning of Company Accounts*, Gower.

Index